Freeman's
Animals

Previous Issues

Freeman's
Animals

Est. 2015

Edited by

John Freeman

Grove Press UK

First published in the United States of America in 2022 by Grove Atlantic
First published in Great Britain in 2022 by Grove Press UK, an imprint of
Grove Atlantic

Managing Editor: Julia Berner-Tobin
Assistant Editor: Emily Burns
Copy Editor: Kirsten Giebutowski

"The Cat Thief" by Son Bo-mi was originally published in Korean in
Maenhaeteunui Banditburi (*The Fireflies of Manhattan*) by Maum Sanchaek in
2019.

"IV - VII" from *Aednan* by Linnea Axelsson and translated into English by Saskia
Vogel. Available in August 2023 from Alfred A. Knopf.

"The Masks of Animals" by Olga Tokarczuk was published in Polish in *Krytyka
Polityczna*, nr 15, 2008.

1 3 5 7 9 8 6 4 2

A CIP record for this book is available from the British Library.

Grove Press UK
Ormond House
26–27 Boswell Street
London
WC1N 3JZ

www.groveatlantic.com

Trade paperback ISBN 978 1 61185 424 4
Ebook ISBN 978 1 61185 871 6

Printed in Great Britain by Bell and Bain Ltd, Glasgow

MIX
Paper from
responsible sources
FSC® C007785

Contents

Introduction

JOHN FREEMAN

Like almost everyone I've come to love, she turned up as if from nowhere. A door in the maze of fate flapped open and through it Martha materialized. 105 pounds of silver-haired, cheese-eating, grumpy perfection—a Weimaraner, mostly, but probably part pit bull too. She looked like a museum gargoyle or a ghost on the lam. Her past was a swirling pot of Dickensian vapors. Someone left her in the rain. A warring couple came to blows, and she escaped. She'd been starved. Cruel men trained their dogs on her to fight. None of this was apparent upon meeting her. Martha simply showed up on my mother-in-law's couch, a new adoptee in a home fond of hard-luck cases, sporting that ducking self-consciousness all dogs wear when they've been hit before and are unsure whether this new life is real or a dream.

She adapted quickly. Soon enough the couch was hers, and the spot next to it, where she'd curl up when she wanted to be close, but not bothered. Within months, she tithed all meals, especially toast, and a failure to acknowledge her rights was often remarked upon. I've known many dogs and all of them have communicated, but Martha came closest to speaking. I don't mean her barking sounded like words, but she could pattern out a very clear message, as if her foot-tap (*hello*) and blink rate (*excuse me, excuse me, ready for toast now)* and eye contact and eyebrow movement (*seriously? you're not going to share that with me?*) and bark (*I'm standing right here!*) was the clearest iteration of messaging I've ever received from an animal. *Give that to me, now, please, put it where toast belongs in my face, thank you Jesus, faster next time is there more?*

She was impatient, tetchy, like the house was a train station and she was both its clock and its conductor, trying to keep everything running on time. For almost five years, most of my mornings started around 7:30 or 8. We'd bang into my mother-in-law's tall London house. At the sound of the door, a drumbeat of dog-feet would begin at the top of the house and cascade downward. Have I said she was a bit chunky? Down the thumping rolled, growing louder and more raucous, until it was like a rock and roll drummer on an overlong solo. Just when you began to expect not one dog but ten, she'd hustle round the corner at the foot of the stairs, just her, grey ears flapping, flashing her tiny, lethally sharp teeth, head turning left, right, left.

She actually smiled. She began each day with a big, frankly very odd cockeyed grin. I think she was mimicking what she saw us do when we were happy, flashing her teeth, saying hello, hello. If you didn't know her you'd think she was snarling. Then she'd hustle us into the car, circling our legs to herd us, observing our route to the common as we drove off, barking if we stopped in traffic or took a wrong turn, positively squealing if the ride took more than five minutes. Upon arrival she'd explode out the back gate of our wagon, and I'd load up the thrower and she'd sprint after the flung ball like a racehorse, actually chewing up bits of turf with the force of her propulsion, a softer drum-beat now as her feet traveled across grass. Her face upon return an expression of unmitigated triumph.

* * *

L
ike so many of us, I spent the past three years in the pandemic
with an animal. With several, in fact, but in Martha's case,
developing a relationship I think it's absurd to call by any name
but love. What do you call a being whose body gives you comfort?
Who doesn't need words to communicate? Who delivers and
receives with acute awareness of these acts? Who has a person-
ality? Who counts? Who makes judgments about people? Who
wears coats? Who has moments of vanity? Who dreams? Who is
frightened? Who comforts others when they're frightened? Who
mourns? Who feels jealousy? Who feels pain? Who worries about
the future? Who enjoys pasta? Who likes the rain? Who tries to
get you to look at beautiful things? Yes, Martha often did this:
she'd come get me and take me outside to smell something. Or,
given my imperfect understanding of her mind and heart, that's
what I think was happening.

As with any compact, be it with a friend or a lover or with
God, not knowing made the relationship more powerful. You
know nothing really important, if there's no risk to the heart. If
you glean without risk, what you've gained is merely information.
Maybe this is why, as a species, humans have done so little to
stop destroying the planet we share with millions of other living
beings, only a small portion of whom are dogs or cats or other
domesticated animals. Perhaps it's simply information to us—the
absolutely clear, undeniable lesson that we've pumped far too
much carbon into the atmosphere and have jeopardized not just
our own future on earth, but that of millions of others species
too—because we have lost the ability to conceive of our not
knowing as crucial a form of intra-species knowledge. It's as if
we need animals to go on strike, to send letters to the editor, to
turn up on CNN. Meanwhile, watch the world leaders at global

climate crisis conferences. They don't know when, or exactly how, the models can't be trusted, proof there's more time. As if our bodies aren't also all vibrating with an epidemic of anxiety.

Animals have never been so meaningful—so freighted with meaning—as they are now, as humans face but don't face our extinction. And yet, because they are so often glimpsed through the keyhole of our greed, our guilt, our passive-aggressive morbid doom-scrolling curiosity, animals remain simultaneously unseen. Show me yourself suffering, now appease my guilt with your cuteness. What is adorableness in the animal kingdom when it is the thing standing between us and the apocalypse? We can marvel at the long songs of deep sea whales, at feather-light octopi and their seemingly intimate behavior, at birds and their patterns of migration, adapting to dried-up water sources and greater predator threats, but unless you have the luxury of being an extremely well-informed consumer, the very next day, due to the structures of the world's food supply, it's quite possible to eat the meat of an animal which has been tortured and either not care, or, just as likely, be too exhausted to do anything about it.

The stakes of this moment in time, our contradictory attitudes about its moral dilemmas, and our always-intense curiosity about the lives of animals have made it an important period to re-narrate our relationship to the animal world. To strip this interaction from the fantasy of purity—as if it's ever possible to truly know a wild living thing, or to observe it without altering its life—and to accept the messy, imperfect not-knowledge of at least some form of creative regard. Of acknowledgment by virtue of symbolic or actual engagement of shared stakes.

This issue of *Freeman's* is dedicated to opening the rich space that exists between us and the earth itself, the place that animals inhabit, where they are at once symbolic and actual, part of culture and part of the food supply, a world in which they inform our everyday lexicons, but remain as far away as a howl in the night. This is not a zoo, but a highly subjective and accidental bestiary filled with animals who come from the imagination and the world itself—passenger pigeons, jaguars, ultra-black Dobermans, just-born lambs, rabbits. Bears. Stray dogs. Giraffes. Reindeer. Sloth. Boars who rustle in the wilderness behind a Roman couple's disquieted home.

We learn to read by imagining the lives of animals. At some point, around ages ten or eleven, they retreat from the center of our reading life, especially in fiction. What would life feel like if that weren't the case? Would we have more stories like Cynan Jones's riveting account of four Welsh farmers struggling to survive a brutal lambing season while one of their cows gives birth? Or maybe animals would feel more like trusted guides or protectors, as in Kali Fajardo-Anstine's short story about a young woman on the precarious edge of ruin in the pandemic, who needs the strength to make a hard decision. She finds it in the form of a radically unashamed stripper and her Doberman. Or maybe there'd be more exquisitely ironic stories about mascots with racialized characters, like Shanteka Sigers's "Lucky Land," in which a man has a shocking face-to-face encounter with a human-sized lemur behind the scenes at a popular amusement park.

Where do the animals we meet go, the ones of our childhood, in the afterlife of memory or culture? In Lily Tuck's story, a girl's encounter with a bear spins inside her like a top, a dynamo of portent which is forever turning as her life itself evolves and she ages. Elsewhere, in a moving essay, "First Salmon Ceremony," Sasha taqʷšəblu LaPointe describes her decades-long arc away from the fish she ate heartily in her youth, into veganism, and then back toward salmon in adulthood: a journey which charts her own feelings of shame, curiosity, and finally pride about her native identity.

It takes a force as strong as hate to prize such bonds apart, those between us and animals. A violence of policy, of laws. Linnea Axelsson's breathtaking novel-in-verse is set in Lapland in the early years of the twentieth century and revolves around a world on the cusp of that rupture, wherein a Sami family migrates its reindeer across tundra, up against barriers only nations could erect. In a world now run by these failing but enshrined idealized identities, what nation do animals belong to, what rights do they have, Olga Tokarczuk asks in her stunning essay. What role do our stories play in adjudicating this complex zone? What other function do these stories serve?

Maybe to help us remember, maybe to not forget? They're different things. Several pieces in this issue function like eulogies to past times—except, as always, humans are there too, behaving in familiar ways. Matthew Gavin Frank recreates an era when passenger pigeons covered the skies thick as storm clouds, inspiring a frenzy of anxiety and then a mass killing. A. Kendra Greene's tale sardonically invites us to imagine the life of a sloth frozen still as taxidermy. Wherever animals are held in captivity there's disquiet, like in Mieko Kawakami's tale of a girl and a boy meeting in a zoo, the speaker quietly, effectively negged by the boy before the gaze of a lugubrious giraffe.

As always, Kawakami finds a way to turn this passive interaction inside out, the speaker's stoppered tongue turning giraffe-like in the story's second half. Ultimately, it sets her free. Perhaps Darwin had it wrong, Rick Bass reminds in his essay, it's not survival of the fittest, it's the lucky who adapt and survive. What does luck mean though if it's not chance, but sometimes a bit stranger? Maybe luck is a question of conception, not simply a happening: as in, if you can imagine the impossible, you can speak your way out of silence. If you can add functions to your very body, you can swim out of danger. If this is the case, and we as a species are even going to try to fathom a way out of the current catastrophe, we'll have to embrace better models of survival, Samiya Bashir suggests in her exquisitely burning poem "Here's the Thing:", which draws the speaker close to the rat. We're also going to have to envision deeper ways to conceive what is happening, Debra Gwartney writes in "Blue Dot," because the fires that have come to our very doorstep once were impossible and now they're here. She knows this because she's standing in the cindery rubble of a plot of Oregon woods she shared with her late husband Barry Lopez, contemplating how little the forestry service knows of the world around their destroyed cabin. The birds and beasts which called that parcel of forest their home are equally bereft.

Perhaps in a thousand years, as Camonghne Felix writes in her peacefully bleak poem, the world will recover, and we will be the slip of memory. The scar in the earth of a time weathered, and born. In this sense, to deal with life in a time of terror one needs to practice picturing a world without us, something extremely possible during the pandemic, as Anuradha Roy points out in the opening essay. It's an essay that tests the morality of this exercise, however, for a world without us is not a fate that affects only humans. One of the first casualties of the pandemic in her part of the Himalayas were stray dogs, no longer fed by humans in parks because the residents of her town couldn't go out.

Animals, in spite of the stories we are told as children, are not here to rescue us or be rescued by us. That is simply one narrative about them. Perhaps one reason we don't see animals so much in adult life is because the reality of our dominion is simply too bleak. Animals are stolen like objects, as in Son Bo-mi's story about a cat, or they're treated casually like trophies, as in Tess Gunty's dazzling story set in a twenty-first-century house party that overflows with luxury, and rabbits. Or they're brutally killed in surrogate ways, as in Chiara Barzini's terrifying tale about two Roman couples and the sexual games they play to rejuvenate their marriages during midlife doldrums.

What's scary about these stories is not so much what animals may do to us, but what we do to them. Maybe we'd be kinder were we more in touch with the bird inside us, as Martín Espada is in his poem, or if we listened more acutely, as Arthur Sze does in his, stepping outside into a multitude of song, of living-ness, or if we could imagine what abilities can still be activated within us, as Stuart Dybek does in his searching, watery poem-fable that begins: "A theory on the descent of Man has it / that humankind evolved not from bands of monkeys / in the trees, but from a lost race of aquatic apes."

Humans have got so much wrong over the years about our fellow travelers on this planet, even on the level of language. Diego Báez writes in a poem that while his family comes from Paraguay, there are no longer jaguars there, as popular myth has it, so life, for him, involves daily sapping of such undetonated falsehoods. In the occupied territories of Palestine, Ameer Hamad sets a tale about what happens when such fantasies of otherness come home to roost. A young boy makes his visiting cousin from America an unwitting accomplice in his mission to bring home a rabbit from the pet store.

An animal is not a toy any more than you and I are, something Martha so often made clear to me when I spoke to her like one. She simply refused to listen. She walked away. And I'd be ashamed that some atavistic part of me had reared up and addressed her in the manner I may have once spoken to a Lego, a stuffed animal, a part of the world that seemed animate to me as a child, but wasn't. Martha may not have spoken English, but she had the dignity of all living beings, from trees to bees to bears and yes, twelve-year-old Weimaraners. She had her own sense of the world, a powerful juxtaposition, a series of instincts as deep in her as mine were in me.

I wish I had known what she wanted us to do when she got sick. Did she want our medicine? Did she want to die? On this question she was mute, or we couldn't read the signals. We did in the end what we would have wanted, which was to secure more time, and thanks to a very good vet, she got it. Two months. In a dog's life, it was a year. A whole cycle of the inner planet, falling in the dark through dreams, night storms, toast crusts. I had never seen her run so fast the day she returned home from the vet and we removed the cone around her neck. She bounded back onto the common and beat lurchers, vizslas, even a fleet-footed dalmatian to her ball. She sniffed the flowers, she visited her two favorite trees, which she seemed to greet by running up to them and stopping abruptly, then standing at attention as all hunting dogs do when they've found something important. She stood there those last few days, beneath the trees, like there was a field of impossible beauty all around her. And she was right, there was. There still is.

Freeman's
Animals

Six Shorts

ABOUT THE DOGS

Some years ago, when I walked through a stretch of unkempt parkland that connected one down-at-heel part of Delhi to another, I would often encounter a woman feeding a pack of dogs. As soon as she appeared, these residents of the park would race in from nowhere and prance around her, a blur of wagging tails and pink tongues, before settling in an orderly circle, patiently awaiting their turn. The food she brought for them was all that this ragged crew survived on, apart from garbage scraps. We chatted often because, apart from the dogs, the hills united us. She was a native of the town where I had moved to and she asked for things from there that nobody else would bring her: local sweets, seasonal fruit. The woman lived in a two-room tenement nearby, and she confessed her family thought her certifiable for sharing what little they had with strays in a park. And yet she never missed a day.

During the two long covid lockdowns across India, parks were shut. The dogs waited but nobody came, and not merely to the parks. No humans were to be seen anywhere, and this meant no kitchen scraps, no fallen food. Within days it became clear that starving strays were one of the least anticipated crises of the lockdown.

1

I live in a forested hamlet in the Indian Himalaya called Rani-khet. Here, as elsewhere, the market emptied out, street-food shacks closed, and people imprisoned themselves *en masse*. Around the shuttered tea shops the benign old mastiff everyone called Tommy, the two black pups, both called Kali, and the mangy lame fellow with no name, all began to starve. Those who normally fed them pleaded for curfew passes and funds even as unfed dogs wandered haplessly through the urban desolation vacuuming the roads for anything with a promising smell. It took days for authoritarian bureaucrats preoccupied with the finer points of lockdown discipline to register anything as inconsequential as starving dogs.

As the streets emptied, forested towns like mine began to go through a slow process of wilding. Jackals and leopards began roaming roads, verges, parking lots. They had sensed the retreat of the humans. In the way hill roads disintegrate into earth and weeds after monsoon torrents, our town reverted to forest once people left the streets and locked themselves indoors. It was like the slow blooming of a long-awaited transformation, a thing we didn't quite understand, not as yet, because it was so new for humans to feel helpless before nature, to which it now appeared we no longer belonged. During the bird flus and the swine flus we had slaughtered millions of birds and pigs to keep ourselves safe. But this new superbug was killing only humans. Thus far, animals and plants seemed immune to it, and they were reclaiming the world.

Lonely afternoon walks began to spring scary surprises: villagers out foraging for wood in the forest came back shaken; cows grazing far from home did not return; pet dogs disappeared. The proximity of our cottage to the forest means we have always had to be careful. More so now because leopards, usually nocturnal patrollers within dog-sniffing distance from our home, were being sighted in the day. We have four dogs. They often raced off deep into ravines and valleys after deer and pheasants. It meant nothing. We were vicariously happy watching their wild abandon, their domesticity so suddenly shaken off and thrown to the winds, because they had always come back. But now, in these strange times, if they did not come back within minutes, a blazing afternoon grew as menacing as night. An innocuous straw-colored stand of grass could be camouflage for a waiting leopard, a wild creature who, like us, had lost his sense of day and night and time and place.

We had never planned to be the keepers of four dogs. They found us. Our town has one main street, and the few stray British who once passed through named it Mall Road. It has five shops, a low parapet for tea drinkers to perch on, and eight or ten resident dogs. The number of dogs is forever indeterminate because, even as puppies are born, death and disease take away the adults.

Some years ago one such dog, maybe two years old, appeared on our doorstep and sat there with an air of finality. His legs said he had come home, his eyes asked if he had. By dusk his legs had won the day. We sheltered him indoors to keep him from becoming leopard-food. That was nine years ago and he now owns the house. He has allowed in three other strays, who have joined him in allowing us a small corner of their home. For our rural, working-class neighbors, our dogs are often the topic for rueful reflections on destiny.

In a country of overwhelming inequality, human-animal conflict brings out almost as much animus as race and religion elsewhere. Hostility to dogs can run deep. The boundaries of compassion are seen as transgressions when they seem to encompass creatures who ought really to find their own sustenance in the wilderness. Sparing morsels for dogs can be seen as the profligacy of the affluent. Through the months of lockdown, and its deep, disastrous consequences for the poor, what used to be a stray accusation, often unspoken, was articulated loud and clear: *people have nothing to eat and they're feeding dogs.*

Culling strays, as in the West, is illegal in India. There is, instead, a well-meaning government policy to sterilize them. Like virtually everything done by the state here, this has become one more route to corruption. Bills are fudged, accounts cooked up, and the numbers of dogs sterilized vastly inflated because they are impossible to track. On the ground, the effort to contain dog populations is largely left to charities or individuals—who are demoralized and exhausted by the Sisyphean futility of it. As a result the stray population keeps rising, as do cases of rabies. Every incident of a stray attacking a human becomes reason for another uproar against what is seen as lordly affectation, a species betrayal. People who feed strays, sterilize them, and treat their wounds have been physically attacked. Feeding cows and feral bulls, on the other hand, is celebrated, since they are thought sacred. If animals were slotted into castes, as humans are in India, dogs would be the untouchables, the outcaste, the forever suffering.

Yet stray dogs, as much as wandering cows and fakirs, have long been an archetype of Indian street life. In the nineteenth century, Shirdi Sai Baba, an Indian holy man revered equally by Hindus, Muslims, and Zoroastrians, was said to appear to his followers as a dog. His teachings included exhortations—perhaps apocryphal—to feed strays because you might be feeding god himself. Iconography shows him hand-feeding dogs or surrounded by animals. The dogs with him are never purebreds. They are "Road-Asians," as lovable and lovely to look at as the dogs by Gauguin, roaming their localities and befriending the odd human who appears a soft touch. They move effortlessly between classes, know nothing of religion or its close companion, human warfare.

The dogs with the saint of Shirdi are the humble Indian strays of indeterminate parentage, curly tails, and lopsided ears without whom our streets would be empty and unrecognizable.

Last year cities were filled with the dead and dying, all over India, rivers were choked with corpses. Every single one of us lost friends and relatives. In Delhi, cremation grounds ran out of space. What happened to the woman in the park? Her phone number doesn't connect anymore. What happened to the dogs?

I like to think of them resurrected, bounding out again from nowhere to her, and sitting in a ring around her as she feeds them. *In my head I will her on.* I will her on eternally, because one corner of this park, to which I haven't been able to return for two years, always has the same woman in it, with the same dogs, and I blind myself to what I have seen and read and been through by saying she will go on forever, talking to her strays in the same affectionately admonishing way as she feeds them one by one.

—Anuradha Roy

BLUE DOT

And then there was the March day I pulled into our driveway to find our remaining trees, many of them, painted with a single blue dot. Like the blue dots marked on Douglas fir, cedar, hemlock, maple, alder, up and down the McKenzie River. Meaning these trees had been given a death sentence.

I got out of the car to walk the edge of our fire-scarred woods, making my way through the cluster of blue-dotted trees to our gray house on a hill. If I was in a charitable frame of mind that morning, I might have remembered how my husband and I often spotted the curved backs of Roosevelt elk through misty rain in this same spot, their white breath steaming in the winter air; or I might have recalled the many bears Barry had chased from the recycling bin over five decades of living on this land. I could have worried about the young fox that had lately, before the outbreak of fire, sauntered to the house on given mornings, weaving through our cars and pooping on the stone path while pretending he didn't see us watching from a window. But I crunched over the fire's detritus consumed only by my own loss, rage already balled up in me over this new layer of damage upon damage.

Who had painted on the dots? Oregon's department of transportation, or the subcontractor hired by the department of transportation, or the subcontractor hired by the subcontractor: I'd soon be on a convoluted path seeking someone with enough authority to explain what was happening here. I'd also soon start counting the logging trucks leaving the McKenzie River Valley with full loads, one every forty-five seconds, every thirty seconds, some trucks packed with a single tree sawed into multiple pieces, a two- or three-hundred-year-old fir, unburned, not a lick of flame on it, cut from the forest for reasons I couldn't decipher. Now I've been counting trucks for fourteen months, which means I alone have witnessed tens of thousands of trees heading out of our valley to local sawmills. What do I know about forest management? Not much, but I can say with some certainty that the trees would have preferred to stay home.

The dots painted on the trees on our property were sky blue, dainty blue, a mark the size of a dessert plate, the shade of a first blanket they might wrap your infant in at the hospital. It was Temple Grandin, wasn't it, who wrote about the necessity of calm around a cow before the whack, and maybe this is what the state arborists had in mind, too—cradling the trees into a fugue of distraction before the saw bit the bark. Almost a cheery decoration until you noticed the bar code stapled into the bottom of each trunk like a death tag tied on a toe.

Between the day of the September fire that consumed a twenty-mile stretch of our Oregon temperate rainforest valley—173,000 acres burned and about 700 structures destroyed—and his death a few swift months later, my husband arranged for a logger to take the dead and dying trees from our property. Danger trees that might hit the house (one of the few houses saved by firefighters); trees that had been burned through the bark and into the cambium layer, beyond rescue; and others whose crowns had been engulfed, halting photosynthesis. Trees left in place were preserved for a reason—the longtime logger and my husband both were certain they'd live on. Some of the oldest, strongest firs and cedars would survive. They would support the trees we'd plant over the next few years, as well as seedlings that would root in this soil on their own until, after a few human lifetimes, the forest might flourish again.

Barry was the one who'd always tended to the timber around our house, and though he'd report in about this plan and that, I didn't involve myself more than standing on the porch to watch a tree come down, waiting for the *whoosh* through brush and the thud as it landed and bounced once off the ground. The boom vibrated the bottoms of my feet and up my neck into my tingling hair. I wish I'd asked more questions. I wish I'd learned the language of tree care, the tools and the logic of the forest, whatever my husband might have imparted to me before he was gone. I let myself believe he'd always be there to take care of it. During our twenty-plus years together, he cut only the standing dead trees, ones that posed a threat, and then he split the wood into logs for our fires or left rounds on the forest floor to degrade into soft duff that became the ideal bed for Doug fir and cedar seedlings. Before we built our guest cottage a few hundred feet from the house, Barry commissioned a map of every tree on the site, snugging the small building in so that only two trees had to be felled. He asked us all, me, our friends, our four daughters and their spouses and children, to stay away from the steep and shaded forest patches. For the half century he lived on this property, he made sure this land was set aside for animals to remain undisturbed by humans.

The logger brought in his skidder and his backhoe and took out eight truckloads, hundreds of trees that assured Barry and me that we had done what was right for the forest, for ourselves, for our neighbors, though my husband drooped each time a tree was loaded on the truck. *Goodbye, old friend.* He and I talked often about how we'd care for the rest. We would turn down offers to salvage log our land in return for obscene amounts of money. We would reason with neighbors who might accuse us of promoting tree-munching beetles and deadly fungus. How could we live with ourselves if we allowed the trees to go?

After phone calls, emails, texts about the blue-dotted trees, I was granted a meeting with a logging supervisor. He didn't wear a mask when he emerged from his truck. He touched my shoulder and said he was sorry my husband had died, even while pronouncing me one of the nuisance homeowners. One of those pains-in-the-ass, ha ha, he'd have to soothe through what he called *the process.* We walked through our small forest so he could explain eminent domain, how matters of public safety allowed him to cut any conifer or deciduous tree his company's arborist deemed dangerous, as in any tree, burned or not, that might fall and tumble to the highway and possibly, at some point, cause harm to a human being. That was the one and only criteria for painting the blue dot on a tree: a person might, in some future moment, suffer. The arborist was sanctioned to mark trees as far as two hundred feet from the road, up the hillside of our property where the largest and tallest trees lived, and there was nothing I could do about it. Or so I told myself. Maybe I simply had no more strength or will to fight the inevitable. In the weeks to come I'd stand alone to watch cranes move into the swale in front of our home so men could climb and limb branches, their saws roaring while the whomp of ancient trees resounded in my bones. One after another the trees were felled, until swaths of our land were laid bare.

*

A few weeks after the fire, when we were allowed in only if accompanied by a pilot car, Barry and I drove to the house from the apartment we'd rented in Eugene. Our second trip up since the night we were evacuated, and this time we were by ourselves. We stomped through the ash and the crumpled brush. In later weeks, we'd rake through burned debris from the lumber shed, the tool shed, paying careful attention to any remnants of the archive building where Barry had meticulously stored materials from his writing life. But now, too soon after, we could do little more than stand and stare. We poked at his burned-to-cinders truck. We sat on our charred deck, seeking a patch of shade in the 90-degree heat, and ate tomato sandwiches while we watched the goopy brown river through a scrim of ash, the river vacant of waterfowl, vacant of osprey, absent of eagle. After a few hours, we realized we had nothing to do here. No power, no water, a refrigerator and freezer full of stinking, rotten food, and gritty air almost impossible to breathe. I asked my husband if we could drive a couple miles upriver to see if spring chinook salmon had made it back to a spawning channel we often went to, though this late-September day was a beat past prime spawning time. The visit to the creek would either add to our despair or lighten it. I was willing to take the risk. When we arrived, we were both word-lessly joyous to find it was the latter. Shiny chinook as long as my thigh, torn and bruised from the long return from the ocean, dozens of them, had somehow barreled through smoldering trees in the river and swum far enough into the shallows to sweep out their redds. They'd returned despite the now-burned cotton-woods that had forever kept this cool water in shade, despite the fried grass and blackberry bushes turned brown and crisp, their berries cast on the meadow like beads from a broken necklace. Barry and I sat on our haunches to watch the splashing in the creek, reaching out to touch each other, to lay a palm on each other's taut thighs, a quick rub of the back or shoulder. We held each other's hands on our way back to the car.

Within minutes, an overly officious sheriff's deputy stopped us and refused to allow us to pass without a pilot car in the lead. We couldn't convince him to let us return to our own house a mile downriver. It was nearly two p.m., and the next pilot car was scheduled for five. The deputy insisted we must wait at the side of the road behind a line of idling refrigerated trucks for our eventual release.

Oh that long afternoon. The broiling, sticky, smoke-choked afternoon. A hideous stench in the air. The miserable hours that ticked by like a slow metronome, the sweat pouring off our faces and down our armpits, the swarms of flies that crawled across our eyes and noses. I would give about anything to return to it. Barry and I were fresh from the swelling hope of the salmon—there's no way to be in the presence of those last-gasp fish without a renewed sense of possibility. I remember how those salmon lifted us from our gloom. On that day, we believed our community would forge on (and they have). We still believed public officials would stand with us to restore the corridor, to plant new trees and to allow the forest to recover as it knows best. The trees that could live on would be allowed to live on. We'd care for the survivors on our property. Barry had hatched a plan with his friend Dave, a California nurseryman, to replant burned parts of our woods with incense cedar and fir. We'd already seen shoots popping from scorched sword fern stumps—surely other ground cover would eke its way back, too, after a few weeks of rain.

This was the shape of our hope.

Inside our car that grueling afternoon, it was sweltering and, good god, those flies. I swatted one off Barry's sweaty forehead and he grumbled at me for waking him—sleep was his respite. We didn't dare roll down our windows. Outside was worse than in. The fry-an-egg heat of the road. The denuded hillside with its last scarred trees. The thick air that nearly crunched with particulates and banked like sand in our lungs. Mostly we avoided the wafting odor of seared flesh spoiling in the sun, the smell of dead bear and mountain lion, fox and vole and bushy-tailed woodrat and river otter. Deer and elk and short-tailed weasel, dog and domestic cat. The animals that died when a wild wind toppled a tree that hit a transformer that in turn sparked one of the worst wildfires in Oregon's history. The two of us stayed put in the car, parceling our water, avoiding talk and seeking sleep. There was nothing to do but wait for our pilot, the one who would lead us out. The one, I could pretend then, who'd take us to safety, to a place of grace and healing, where we could breathe the fresh, clean air of our home and the sparkling river with its scent of trout and sun-baked boulder. Where my husband and I could sit under our towering trees and learn to begin again, holding tight to each other.

—Debra Gwartney

THE TONGUE

*D*id you gain a little weight? he asked, looking into my face. We were at the zoo on a Sunday afternoon, sitting on a wooden bench just in front of the giraffe enclosure, each trying to bite into an ice cream cone that was rock-hard from being left in the freezer box for at least half a year. *Do I look like I did?* I asked back. *No, maybe that's not it. Your face looks different from last week. Your chin looks rounder somehow . . . but that's a good thing*, he replied. *Hmmm*, I murmured, putting my teeth against the cliff-like surface of the ice cream, wondering what it meant that it was "a good thing" that my chin looked a bit rounder. Being round is good? Was it the same as liking? What did that have to do with my chin? Noticing my silence, he tried to change the subject and began to ramble about a pair of giraffes inside the fence. Why their necks were so long, where their color and patterns came from . . . little bits of information that seem amusing on the spot, but that you soon forget about. *Did I say something wrong?* he asked later with an apologetic look on his face, but by then I had already forgotten what he had said. *You're so quiet, I thought maybe you were angry*, he said. *No, it's not like that . . . sorry.* Both feeling awkward, we decided to skip the tropical birds and go home. *See you in school tomorrow.* We waved goodbye. My head and temples ached.

When I came home and looked in the mirror, the shape of my face did seem changed somehow. There was an odd swelling below my cheeks. I held my face in my hands and wondered if I had the mumps. But could you get the mumps at seventeen? Wasn't that for kids? What were the symptoms anyway? I had no fever, but I couldn't shake off my headache and the pain around my temples.

During supper, my older sister sat across from me and stared into my face. *Did your face get bigger?* she asked. Mother and Father ate their chicken in silence. I, too, continued to chew on a piece of chicken in silence. Perhaps because of all the chewing, the pain slowly moved to my jaw and, by the time supper was finished, my entire face was hurting. I kept on chewing until I couldn't bear it any longer, and as I got up to go to my room, I blurted out to no one in particular, *My whole face hurts.* Mother and Father remained silent. My sister laughed. *That's what happens to petty people . . . they're scared and cowardly, but hate to lose and always try to look good. It makes their faces all tensed up. Isn't that right?* she said as she retreated to her room. Between the clanking of plates, I heard my father's voice, so unfamiliar these days—*Why don't you go see the doctor tomorrow?*

The pain in my face kept getting worse as the night grew deeper. Why didn't I go see the doctor earlier? I regretted but climbed into bed telling myself that everything would be okay tomorrow. In the hazy darkness, the animals I saw during the day appeared one by one, then disappeared. They were all different types, but their bodies were covered in brown or white fur and seemed extremely heavy. How did I end up at the zoo? I didn't want to go; I was asked to. Deep in the smell mixed with grass and manure and dirt, I could see the clear eyes of sheep and elephants, crouched in a hole-like place that was narrow and dark. I could have said no. I felt somewhat guilty for meeting a boy I didn't particularly like on a weekend. It wasn't fun. Even among friends, it was difficult to express myself when I wanted to say no, and using that as an excuse, I'd run away. Maybe I will always be like this, so ambivalent, and my eyes grew hot. But if I cried, some irreversible kind of fear might come crawling up from under the blanket, so I held my breath. Then, feeling something strange, I stuck my head out and looked over to the window. There she was as usual, beyond the glass—my sister, staring at me from between the curtains with her back to the night.

I woke up feeling short of breath. It must have been in the middle of the night, since the sky was still dark with not the faintest sound of morning approaching. Putting my hand to my face, I felt it bounce off something large and elastic that seemed to be coming out of my mouth. It was a tongue. The tongue grew bigger and bigger until it no longer fit inside my mouth, and when I looked down, I saw the tongue curled up on top of my chest. So that explains the pain, I thought to myself—the tongue was trying to escape.

The tongue overflowed like fluffy foam, without pause, and soon it was as big as my body. It got bigger and bigger until it spilled over the edge of the bed and slithered across the floor. There was no longer any pain in my mouth or chin or face or head, and as I turned over, the left side of my body landed on the soft tongue. It was a sensation I had never known before, different from any bed or grass or earth that I had lain down on. As I looked on, I noticed something that resembled a meadow unfolding before me. I climbed down into it and looked up at the blue sky that opened in an oval shape. At my feet were the animals I had seen during the day. With nothing to constrain them, they seemed lost, not knowing how to behave in their newly obtained freedom. As I walked in the direction that smelled like south, a warm, giant wind blew again and again and shadows ran and cut across the grass. I could see, among a herd of mountain goats, Father and Mother seated across from each other and eating chicken at their usual dining table. They were in tears as they chewed the chicken. *Hey, you don't have to keep eating*, I wanted to tell them, but because of the condition my tongue was in, I could not utter a sound. The chicken grew cold on their plates, and Father and Mother kept moving their icy fingers as they chewed in tears. It's always like this, I can never speak up when it's really important, all I can do is watch. It makes me sad, it makes me want to do something. That's not a lie. So how come I always pretend like nothing is wrong? Why do I forget so quickly?

With the banging of the door, the meadow shook and low dark clouds quickly covered the sky. My sister is here, I thought. Or was it the boy I went to the zoo with today, the boy I barely know? Perhaps they are standing there together. The banging of the door didn't stop, it only got louder. Hearing a sound of wind I'd never heard before, I looked up to see a giant rock floating in the sky. The sound became more and more unbearable. The rock will come crashing down soon, I thought. It will crush the animals on the grass and the dining table of Father and Mother, and create a hole in the exact shape of itself. And so before they arrived—my sister, the boy—I rolled up my tongue using all my strength, and swallowed up all there was that lay before me.

—Mieko Kawakami
Translated from the Japanese by Hitomi Yoshio

USELESS TO SPEAK:
ON THE EXTINCTION OF THE PASSENGER PIGEON

In 2020, the scientific and conservation communities declared 168 species extinct, and that doesn't include the more than 8,300 species of mites (more than 15 percent of the world's mite species) that disappeared this past year. Though seemingly insignificant to us, conservationists stress that when the mites go, entire ecosystems—dependent on the mites' machinations—will soon follow. In 2020, we lost 22 species of frogs, including the iridescent maroon and blue-gray speckled Chiriqui harlequin frog that once dominated the stream margins of Central American rainforests. We lost the Deppea splendens tree and its ribbed emerald leaves and pink-and-gold flowers (once known as the "holy grail" among botanists and gardeners). We lost 32 species of orchid, 65 North American plants, 17 freshwater fish. We lost palm trees and cacti and praying mantises. We lost herbs and spices. We lost lichen. We lost a gazelle.

On a grand scale, we can't seem to adequately adjust our habits that have led to such extinctions, continuing to spread as we do into the deserts and mountains, savannahs and forests; continuing to warm the oceans with our industries. It's easy to forget how easily we can kill things off—whether absentmindedly or intentionally. The fate of the passenger pigeon may serve as cautionary tale, or frightening testament to the range, effects, and consequences of our power begotten of self-interest.

Until about 1870, the skies over North America were dominated neither by clouds nor stars, but by the now-extinct passenger pigeon. The species was so abundant that the size of her sky-blotting flocks often comprised in excess of 3.5 billion birds, and were over a mile-and-a-half wide and 350 miles long. Such sizable flocks took, to the aghast human observer, over fourteen hours to pass overhead, the sound of the wingbeats reminiscent of a hurricane. In number, the species was second only to the Rocky Mountain locust, that plague of the prairies. Once, to the indigenous peoples of North America, the passenger pigeon was holy; the birds were believed to have the power to carry the souls of deceased ancestors, inspiring the sacred pigeon dance.

The bird's blood healed our eyes, and its stomach lining, when dried and powdered, cured our dysentery. Even its dung alleviated our headaches, and our lethargy. The passenger pigeon made us briefly pain-free, and a little happier. Simon Pokagon, a Potawatomi tribal leader in the nineteenth century, referred to such flocks as "meteors from heaven."

The trees of their nesting grounds—concentrated around the Great Lakes—once collapsed under the weight of their flocks as if the land had been clear-cut, the poor squabs taking their first meals on the ground often crushed, or drowned in a pool of dung several feet deep. In the autumn of 1813, John James Audubon stood on the banks of the Ohio River and watched such a flock. "The air," he wrote, "[so] filled with pigeons the light of noonday was obscured as by an eclipse, the dung fell . . . not unlike melting flakes of snow, and the continued buzz of wings . . . lull[ed] my senses to repose." When they landed, they filled their crops to the size of a grapefruit, with up to a quarter of a pint of food. At once, they could accommodate 19 acorns or 30 beechnuts, or 101 maple seeds, fist-sized amounts of snails and earthworms, caterpillars, buckwheat, pokeberries, and grapes. The fruit of the dogwoods. The saltiest of the soil. If they found a new foodstuff they liked better, they could vomit up the old at will. Each squab had, according to an 1880 article in the *Detroit Post and Tribune*, "the digestive capacity of half a dozen 14-year-old boys." When they landed in lakes and ponds to drink, "the birds that landed first would drown under the weight of newcomers." Those who survived would make their way to land, flop onto their sides in the mud, and raise their wings into the wind to dry them before, once again, taking off.

This particular flock of passenger pigeons continued to pass for three days, and the boys and men of Kentucky lined up beneath them with their guns. Into bird-darkened skies, they fired and fired. "For a week or more," Audubon writes, "the population fed on no other flesh than that of pigeons, and talked of nothing but pigeons." Families assigned roles to their individual members—shooting the birds down, clubbing the squabs from their branches with bats made of hickory, setting fire to nests and controlling the burn, scrambling after the unfledged would-be escapees with nets, collecting the dead in buckets and baskets, pickling them, salting them, boiling them, baking . . .

Observers, gobsmacked and grounded, claimed that this particular flock contained 2,230,272,000 passenger pigeons, but, given that it would take a single human observer 25,814 days, or about 71 (sleepless) years to count up to 2,230,272,000, and given that the average human life expectancy in Kentucky at the time was 37 years, it's likely that this number bears only the illusion of precision. Besides, observers were too busy working themselves into a panic worthy of the apocalypse to accurately count each individual bird navigating the thermals above them. "The hum increased to a mighty throbbing," one witness reported. "Now everyone was out of the houses and stores, looking apprehensively at the growing cloud, which was blotting out the rays of the sun. Children screamed and ran for home. Women gathered their long skirts and hurried for the shelter of stores. Horses bolted. A few people mumbled frightened words . . . several dropped on their knees and prayed."

Once, the passenger pigeon was a stitch in this quasi-Biblical tapestry, the thing that people conversed about, even as they chewed its meat. They couldn't stop. They feared them, and their bellies were full of them, and, after a week's worth of pigeon omelets, pies, roasts and fricassees, even when they tired of the taste of the birds, they still couldn't stop being afraid. In eating these pigeons, they took such multitudes into their bodies. As such, the great flocks were thinned, and the skies therefore brightened over the people's homes. Still, they compared the flocks to waterfalls and curtains, threshing machines and giant steamboats, scriptural storms and prophetic plagues. In 1857, America's first symphonic composer, Anthony Philip Heinrich (called by one critic the Beethoven of America), who was to die neglected and in poverty, penned a nine-movement opus titled *The Columbiad* in response to passenger pigeon migrations, in which the choral section bellowed:

In darkening clouds the wandering flock unnumbered fills the heavens.

The winged thunder shakes the sky and echoes in the winds . . .

The forest trembles crouching low . . .

The waves roar on the shore . . .

And Earth herself gives back the song of the legions of the air.

After the flock finally passed over, the towns, and the Earth herself, "looked ghostly in the now-bright sunlight that illuminated a world plated with pigeon ejecta," according to an Ohioan observer at the time.

Though passenger pigeons were hailed by Audubon as "evolutionary geniuses," they couldn't keep up with human ingenuity and the attendant rapaciousness, and—most rapidly between 1870 and 1890—they dwindled, giving in to mass deforestation, and to the revolutionizing of human communication over distances via railroad expansion and telegraph services. In this way, the birds' once secret roosting sites were made public, and along came angry mobs of farmers whose crops the pigeons destroyed, and market hunters, armed with guns, batons, nets and fire, rakes, rocks, pitchforks and potatoes, bent on selling pigeon meat and pigeon feathers. They trapped them and named them, *stool pigeon,* gluing their feet to round, stool-like surfaces set atop tiny, makeshift teeter-totters, and, with ropes and pulleys, compelled the birds to teeter and totter in a way that resembled, to the flock passing overhead, a safe feeding. And when their duped companions descended, the men and the women and the children raised their guns, swung their bats.

They set pots of burning sulfur beneath the birds' roosting trees, and the fumes elicited vertigo so fierce, they tumbled from their nests and their branches like so much confetti. The juveniles, upon hitting the ground, were still so fragile, their bodies burst open. One observer described this as resembling countless "golden red apples" falling from the tree. In certain nesting sites, it was reported that over 80,000 passenger pigeons were killed per day (per site!) over the course of about six months. Those who escaped and forged new, clandestine nesting sites were hunted down by private passenger pigeon bounty hunters hired by state legislatures.

By 1890, so many passenger pigeons were dead but—in spite of the advent of refrigerated train cars and fancy restaurants like New York's Delmonico's, which included the passenger pigeon on its menu as Ballotine of Squab à la Madison (stuffed with truffles, pork, liver, ham, and pistachios, coated with madeira, and garnished with jellied tongue and veal fat molded into the shapes of shells and griffons)—we couldn't eat all of them, and so they became feed for our hogs, and slave-owners adopted them as the chief and cheapest food source for those they enslaved. The meat of some hogs who fed on the pigeons was later ground in Delmonico's kitchen, and stuffed inside the bodies of other pigeons, morbidly returning bird to bird, as part of some serpentine and doubling-back-on-itself network of consumption.

Their eggs were smashed for sport and, unlike the rock dove who lays an average of 12 to 18 eggs per year, the passenger pigeon often laid only one. The great flocks disappeared, and yet people still claimed to see them, concocted ridiculous hypotheses in a meager attempt to solve no real mystery. Rumors were spread, saying that the flocks were simply convalescing and regrouping in the otherwise uninhabitable deserts of the world; or that they were taking refuge at the tops of unscalable mountains, or beneath the matted tufts of long prairie grass in places like Independence, Kansas, the childhood home of Laura Ingalls Wilder. "The flocks," writes Jonathan Rosen in the *New Yorker*, "were like phantom limbs that the country kept on feeling. Or perhaps the birds' disappearance, and the human role in it, was simply too much to bear."

Perhaps, in beholding another species that seemingly wanted to consume everything, wanted to dominate both earth and sky, we felt also a sense of communion we couldn't quite bear, a plurality that unnerved us. And so, communion begat competition, ever that sweaty, explosive pathway toward the singular victor—in this case, us, as chief destructor. "If you're unfortunate enough to be a species that concentrates in time and space," says Stanley Temple, Professor Emeritus in Conservation at the University of Wisconsin-Madison, eulogizing the passenger pigeon, "you make yourself very, very vulnerable," and it seems he's speaking of, and to, all of us. The birds simply couldn't keep up with the carnage, and eventually the species succumbed to what Audubon called the sort of "uproar and confusion" into which he "found it quite useless to speak." So quickly, the passenger pigeon—once the topic of incessant conversation—became the totem of such gaping silence.

Martha, the world's last passenger pigeon, died in captivity at the Cincinnati Zoo, at age twenty-nine, on Tuesday, September 1, 1914, at approximately one p.m. The weather was unseasonably cool. The circumstances of Martha's death are leashed to the word of the head zookeeper, Salvator "Sol" Stephans, a former circus-elephant handler with a boorish reputation. According to Stephans, the zoo held a funeral ceremony of sorts for Martha, her cage surrounded by grieving zookeepers and dancers from the nearby Empress Burlesque theater, where Stephans was a regular patron.

In one account, Stephans and his son, Joseph, led the crowd in a choral humming of the hymn "Nearer, My God, to Thee," then mistakenly believed to be the last song played (a scant two years prior) by the RMS *Titanic* orchestra as the ship sank into the North Atlantic. In another version, Stephans claimed that it was only he and his son who hummed Martha and, in turn, her species into the great avian beyond. More likely, she was found by William Bruntz, the evening shift keeper in charge of cleaning the cages, who scraped up her carcass with a shovel. Soon, Stephans, having negotiated for himself a price that would allow him to be the man of many hours over at the Empress, commanded that Martha's body be encased in a 300-pound ice block, which he shipped on a three-day train passage to the Smithsonian.

"There will be no funeral for Martha," reported the *Cincinnati Enquirer*. "Instead, her remains, along with the feathers she has shed . . . will be shipped to Washington [to] be shown to posterity, not as an old bird with most of her plumage gone, as she is now, but as the queenly young passenger pigeon that delighted thousands . . ."

Today, in the Smithsonian National Museum of Natural History, beyond the rotunda and two-ton Fénykövi elephant, the Ocean Hall and Hall of Human Origins, the escalators and the gift shop, a taxidermied Martha is displayed, twisted into a perch position on a branch in her cage of glass. Her body has traveled throughout the United States for display at festivals named "Jubilee" and "Birds of the World," conferences with "Memorial" in their titles, and finally back to the Smithsonian, where she headlined the museum's short-lived "Once There Were Billions" exhibit. She always flies first class, in a fifteen-pound box amid packing peanuts, ever perched on her little branch, on the laps of the airline companies' flight attendants. Sometimes, the flight crew announces Martha's presence to the other passengers, and sometimes these passengers whisper excitedly among themselves, but mostly they remain silent and unimpressed. Martha returns every so often to Cincinnati, where new generations of zookeepers refer to her as their "feathered conscience," and where they put her on display from nine a.m. to six p.m., wherever they have the space for her—usually in the Reptile House. The Smithsonian offers a 360-degree view of her on their website, and her image, bearing all of the static and pixilation of the afterlife, spins and spins according to some new code.

Martha became a focal point of the de-extinction debate, wherein conservationists, naturalists, futurists, and molecular biologists, backed by corporate offshoots with names like "Revive & Restore," "The Whole Earth Catalog," and "The Long Now Foundation," banter about the pros and cons of bringing her species back (along with others, like the woolly mammoth) via the re-engineering of her genome from the toe pads of pickled museum specimens and the band-tailed pigeon, a closely related extant species. They consider "whether a de-extinction project holds real environmental promise or is only an ancient longing for resurrection disguised as bioengineering" (Jonathan Rosen, *New Yorker*). They have not come to any consensus, and the heat has recently leaked from the debate.

Martha inspired the hashtag #RememberMartha, which is used less frequently as the years pass. Installation artists have worked their hands toward cramping while folding thousands upon thousands of Marthas out of paper, these origami flocks flimsy and immobile symbolic recreations of her species' great historic peregrinations. Bronze statues have been commissioned and erected and commemorated and forgotten.

Every September 1st, on the anniversary of her death, hundreds of afternoon boozers flock to the Cincinnati Zoo for the "Martinis with Martha" commemoration. They meander, intoxicated, through the zoo's renovated pagoda-like aviaries, gawking at the passenger pigeons that bird trainer Gary Denzler carved out of wood. To the sufficiently drunk, the carvings appear to move, come to life. *Roadside America* rates this attraction with three (out of five) smiley-face water towers (their version of stars), which means: "Worth a detour—A solid attraction with extra payoff or unintentional comedy."

Historians and authors, artists and naturalists continue to make their own pilgrimages to see Martha in her stuffed incarnation—not quite sure what they're searching for, not sure if her corpse, secured to a small branch and mounted on a Styrofoam cube, is everything they thought it would be. They leave disappointed, underwhelmed, retaining the problems they thought the sight of her, in death, could somehow impossibly solve; also a little agitated at the time and expense tallied by their futile crusades. They, too, continue to ask easy questions that they deem unanswerable—as if mystery really had anything to do with mass extinction.

We can't seem to stop ourselves. In 2020, we lost songbirds and salamanders, bats with cat-faces and lovely long ears, and mynas whose calls have been described as the most human-like of all birds. We lost a shark called the lost shark. And we lost the smooth handfish, which had the most beautiful leopard spots, and strolled along the seafloor using its pectoral and pelvic fins like we use our legs, and sported on its head a stunning fin that bore an uncanny resemblance to the human hand. In old video footage, when that fin was aroused by the water, it looked as if that hand was waving goodbye.

—Matthew Gavin Frank

MEGALONYX JEFFERSONII

I know. You want to talk about the giant sloth. You want to know why this particular giant sloth in this particular museum is wearing a hula skirt. That's fine. We'll get to that. But it will be easier if we start with the right terms. If you don't mind, then, first a few words on gender identity and the giant ground sloth, this giant ground sloth. Then we'll proceed.

By convention, Rusty is a him. Visitors encountering Rusty for the first time use the masculine pronoun instinctively, without even meaning to sex the sloth. I'm not reprimanding you. Staff often make the same mistake. I myself still slip into saying "him," and I know better. I suspect that him happens because Rusty has so much character. Did you notice, for instance, his tongue wrapping around the reproduction oak leaves? His little tail curled in a half-wag on the facsimile prairie floor? Anyway, my hunch is that we take a liking to the sloth and that inspires a kind of friendly familiarity, which leads to the possibly benign if thoroughly unscientific personification of him. It's all very natural to say him. But it's wrong.

Rusty is a model. A fiberglass form covered over with wiry hair clipped from thousands of modern-day cows' tails. The bristly faux fur was all dyed to the same muddy red—browsers tend to be monochromatic, after all—the hue itself suggested by the auburn fur of a related sloth find excavated in South America. You're right: South America is a long way from Iowa. It was a little closer in the Late Pleistocene. But no, not a lot closer.

I was saying: Rusty is a model. An object. Hence, sexless; ergo an "it." It has no visible mammary glands, no sex organs of any kind. Its eyelashes have mostly broken off. Even if the model makers had been less prudish, had possessed enough information to fashion detectable primary or secondary sex characteristics, those features still wouldn't be particularly meaningful, not in the way of the specimen skins: the fading foxes and cracking zebras and hundred-year sparrows postured throughout Mammal Hall and the Hageboeck Hall of Birds upstairs. And this difference in the origins of models and specimens, the difference between what never was and what no longer is, is why we can dress up Rusty. Models are governed by a different code of ethics than specimens. We wouldn't put so much as a paper crown on a specimen.

A lot of people fail to notice that Rusty is not, in fact, a specimen. I understand. It's a dark room. The wall text is unobtrusive and dimly lit. The informational paragraph is intentionally kept brief enough that you'll bother to read through to the part about this being an extinct species from the Ice Age, but it's posted at adult eye level, and children rush beneath it, crowd along the guardrail and call out to their parents and guides and chaperones to see what they see, to bear witness to this enormous and unbelievable creature parked on its haunches and forever drawing down a leafy branch with four eight-inch claws. It could distract you from ever reading anything.

And clearly extinction alone is not enough to rule out Rusty being a specimen. We have specimens of extinct species on view throughout the museum. None quite so old as *Megalonyx jeffersonii*, perhaps, but natural history is nothing if not a sequence of unlikely and unexpected events—that we are standing here upright with the language to have this conversation perhaps the most unlikely one of all. If you believe in the feathered reptiles and the egg-laying mammals and the fossil ferns and the Devonian ocean, why shouldn't we have the original hide of a 10,000-year-old ground sloth taxidermied and on display? Isn't that exactly what we would do if we had one? How could you be expected to know that Rusty is only speculation, the painstaking and flawed interpretation of a thing we know only from fragment?

26

The first thing Rusty ever wore was a tie. Two ties, actually, purchased one at a time from the university bookstore across the street, the second tie after it became very apparent that the first would scarcely encircle the giant sloth's throat. Dr. David Brenzel refers to this observation as Sloth Dressing Lesson #1: Scale.

Dr. Brenzel pioneered sloth dressing. In 1999, the Faculty Senate was scheduled to hold a reception in the University of Iowa Museum of Natural History's galleries. The president of the Faculty Senate, looking around, asked the director of the museum, Dr. George Schrimper, if something could be done to "make the place less stuffy." Shortly thereafter, against Dr. Schrimper's better judgment, Dr. Brenzel's curatorial authority expanded to include spiffing up the sloth. You can imagine: a necktie-wearing sloth the size of a small elephant was rather droll and very well received by the assorted academics and administrators milling through Iowa Hall with drinks in their hands. Dr. Schrimper said nothing. Dr. Brenzel started thinking about Halloween.

Halloween is the core of sloth dressing. It's the only consistently recognized holiday on the sloth calendar, and every year Rusty wears something new. The first costume, the one that founded this tradition, was Zorro. Specifically, the 1981 George Hamilton *Zorro, the Gay Blade* Zorro, with black eye-mask and teeth-clenched rose and ball-fringed Spanish gaucho hat and everything.

With the exception of Halloween, the official sloth calendar remains in flux, observing a motley and intermittent combination of holidays and cultural events. You may see Rusty with wings and bow and heart-tipped arrows on Valentine's Day. It's a top hat and dark beard for Lincoln's birthday—or white beard and HMS *Beagle* seasickness bag on Darwin Day. Then there's Pilgrim sloth. Olympic athlete. Santa. Rudolph. King Tut, complete with pipe-cleaner eyeliner. Curiously, Rusty has yet to honor

Thomas Jefferson, though the former president's 1797 paper on *Megalonyx* is arguably the founding American publication in vertebrate paleontology, and it's the man himself honored by a French scientist in the species name, *jeffersonii*. Perhaps we'll get to that next year. We've been busy. Sure, the butterfly net was on hand, but it takes a while to find a pith helmet big enough for Explorer sloth. And I think we all know leprechaun costumes don't make themselves.

Rusty was always meant to catch your attention, to be what they called an "Oh, wow!" moment when the museum was redesigned in 1984. At the time there were plenty of mammoths and mastodons in other museums; so this museum (the second oldest museum west of the Mississippi River) commissioned the first life-size model of an Ice Age sloth and strategically stationed it here near the south entrance where any of three main paths will deliver you. It may be the most important exhibition decision here since the 1914 unveiling of Dr. Homer Dill's cyclorama of Laysan Island revolutionized, no circular pun intended, the art of dioramic presentation.

When we first met, Rusty was sporting white bunny ears and a powder-puff tail, a larger-than-life carrot dangling from the half-open maw where usually there's a mouthful of leaves. Outside, the wind was chill and biting and March. Inside, there was Easter sloth. It was all very incongruous. And it was precisely the moment when I realized that Iowa and I would get along just fine, that it was perhaps the very sort of place I would have been searching for if I'd had any idea it could exist.

And that was months before Sarah Horgen granted me sloth dressing privileges. Before I moved here and she let me design new costumes and suggest new holidays the sloth might observe. It was certainly before I knew that to reach around Rusty's neck, to drape a toga or adjust a cape or straighten a collar, my cheek would have to brush the sloth's and the fingertips of my left hand would only just touch the fingertips of my right.

Ms. Horgen, the museum's education and outreach coordinator, was thinking about Sloth Dressing Lesson #1 at the fabric store this October as she charged to a museum account five yards of red felt and a slightly smaller amount of red silk lining. The clerk ringing her up asked in a chummy kind of way if she was working on a Halloween costume.

"Little Red Riding Hood," Ms. Horgen replied. Ms. Horgen wavers on whether it's worth going into detail while on these errands.

The clerk squinted. "That's a big trick-or-treater," she said. Little Red Riding Hood was not Ms. Horgen's first choice. Ms. Horgen had been hoping for Marilyn Monroe, but for logistical reasons was suggesting a vampire or mad scientist or some such thing when she entrusted me with designing and constructing Rusty's costume this year. Ms. Horgen is one of the people who doesn't say "him" when she talks about Rusty. Nor does she say "it." Ms. Horgen is part of a growing contingent that says "her."

Rusty, as I have explained, is, emphatically, an it. But the specimen Rusty is based on, the American Falls discovery, well that's another story. Rusty is intended to represent Iowa's Ice Age megafauna, but it's the rare Iowa sloth that's found even thirty bones complete, which leaves a lot to be inferred. So, because a sloth skull collected in Turin, Iowa, is almost identical to one found at American Falls, Idaho, Rusty's proportions are borrowed from the more complete specimen. *More* complete is an understatement. The American Falls discovery is indeed the *most* complete giant sloth specimen ever found: not a bone missing from the waist up.

It's what's missing from the waist down, however, that leaves Rusty's gender identification up for debate. That debate got a lot livelier when Dr. H. Gregory McDonald suggested in a 2005 paper that, based on comparative analysis of the diastema of the jaw, the American Falls specimen was, in fact, female.

It's gotten a bit heated. Dr. Holmes Semken, leader of the Tarkio Valley Sloth Project, discounts the available sample set as inadequate to prove that the smaller specimens are the females—the reverse is certainly true for some mammals. Dr. Brenzel stresses that it may not be sexual dimorphism at all, but merely individual variation. Both Dr. Semken and Dr. Brenzel are at pains to underscore that a mistake is entirely possible in the McDonald conjecture. Heck, the smaller specimens could be juveniles! There's just not enough information to reach a consensus. Which, conversely, also means there's not enough data to discount this surprisingly inflammatory thesis: Rusty was a girl.

You'd never guess it from the costumes. Not until recently, anyway. In the last six months Rusty has evoked Little Red Riding Hood, the Statue of Liberty, and Rosie the Riveter—in honor of Halloween, Election Day, and Women's History Month, respectively. But before that, in a decade of sloth dressing and some twenty-two documented costumes, there was maybe one even arguably hinting at a female icon or traditionally feminine attire or anything not obviously masculine or patently ambiguous. Yes, exactly. The Hula sloth.

You wanted to know about the hula skirt, why Rusty is wearing one? Why indeed. Because the Hawaii-based animated film *Lilo and Stitch* opened in 2002 and Rusty has a thing for movie premieres. Because outside it is warm after so long being frozen. Because I asked for the ring of small brass keys and opened every storage panel in Iowa Hall until I found the grass skirts and the leis knotted together and long enough to span, respectively, a twelve-foot waist and a fifty-inch neck. The efficient cause, the final cause, it's all the same thing. We dress the sloth because it amuses us. Because it's strangely compelling. Because we are drawn to it for what it is, even as we want to make it something else. Because, how else to say this, it needs to be done.

Dr. Schrimper was always a little worried about Rusty, you know. George was a stickler for proper procedure and best practice, and he sensed the power of Rusty to eclipse everything else he loved about the museum. It doesn't, I don't think, but he worried. And he's right: a big thing can obstruct the big picture. One can introduce a single element and have it overwhelm or belittle or change everything else. He didn't want this to be a museum of the sloth—he said that a lot. But he never said anything about his staff dressing up Rusty. He understood that, I think. He didn't need to ask why.

—A. Kendra Greene

THE CAT THIEF

"I was away from Korea for a long time," he said.

We were having tea at a downtown café. I tried to recall the last time I'd seen him, but couldn't. When I made some offhand comment about the tea timer on top of our table and how pretty it was, he reached for it at once and stuck it deep inside my purse. Shaped like an hourglass, the timer contained blue ink that flowed in reverse from bottom to top.

"This is stealing," I whispered, glancing around the café.

"I'm good at it. On my travels in the past few years, I've stolen many things."

31

He kept the things he'd taken in a glass cabinet in his living room. A silver fork from a Paris café, a teacup saucer from a London restaurant, a bamboo basket that had held orchids from a New Delhi bed-and-breakfast, and a pen belonging to a worker at a museum information desk in Berlin. There had also been an ashtray from an Osaka hotel (though he was caught red-handed and had no choice but to return it), as well as a cat from New York.

"Wait, you stole a cat?"

"Actually, that was the first thing I ever stole."

He began to talk about the New York apartment he'd lived in after his divorce.

"It was a run-down building, but clean. Across the hall from me lived a man in his early sixties named Emerson. He lived alone. Well, not exactly alone. He lived with his cat Debbie. He was an old, overweight man living alone with his cat."

Because of his weight, Emerson tottered comically when he walked. Surprisingly, he had an extremely soft voice. They talked in the hallway now and then, and each time he had to strain his ears in order to understand what Emerson was saying. Emerson had never been married. They even joked about their marital status, calling themselves "the divorcé and the bachelor." Perhaps because of all the joking, they became quite comfortable with one another.

One weekend, Emerson invited him over to his place for a few beers. "And there she was—Debbie. She was all black, except for her white belly and paws. Until then, I hadn't known he owned a cat. When we'd been smoking and chatting for a while, I noticed she was watching us from under the couch, with just her head poking out. I'd never seen a cat so close up before. I tried to pet her, but as soon as I raised my hand, she dashed under the couch.

It was only then that I realized all the framed photos on the walls were of her. In other words, Debbie was Emerson's only family."

After that, he and Emerson got together every so often. They joked, drank, and smoked together, and Debbie would stare at them for a while and disappear under the couch. He found his life satisfactory in its own way. Objectively speaking, though, it would have been a stretch to call his life satisfying.

He had followed his American girlfriend to the States, despite not knowing a single soul in the country, but after being married for less than three years, she had left him. Then due to various overlapping circumstances, he was forced to quit his job.

"Because of her, I had my life stolen from me. Don't you think?"

Still, he didn't think his situation was all bad. Happiness and boredom, abundance and loneliness filled his life with order, as if these emotions had been woven together in a plaid pattern, and as a result, his life felt strangely balanced. To top everything off, he'd made a friend named Emerson. However, while he was intoxicated by this sense of equilibrium, his bank balance lost its equilibrium, which then unraveled the woven balance of his life.

"Luckily my old company called me. They said if I wanted to keep working for them, they could transfer me to their Philadelphia branch. I no longer had any reason to stay in New York, so I decided to leave. But first, I wanted to say goodbye to Emerson. The night before I left, we got sloshed at his place. I may have cried. He may have patted me on the back, who knows. Then I passed out on his couch."

In the middle of the night, he felt a stare and snapped awake. Something in the dark was watching him. It was Debbie. She was sitting elegantly before him and Emerson, who had also fallen asleep on the couch. He got up, carefully moving Emerson's arm that was splayed across his feet. The entire time, Debbie kept her

33

eyes on him. When he stepped into the hallway and was about to close the front door, he realized Debbie was still watching. She walked slowly toward him. She then sat on her haunches and gazed up, stretching her front paws up toward him.

"It was as if she was saying, 'I want to leave, I want to leave this place. Please take me with you.' All of a sudden, it seemed wrong to leave her behind. I don't know why I thought that."

Debbie's eyes glittered in the dark. He picked her up. He walked out of the building and left New York.

"That was a very bad thing you did," I said.

"About two weeks later, I went back to New York with Debbie. I had to. Since I didn't have the courage to explain my actions to Emerson, I planned to secretly drop her off at his apartment. But his place was completely empty. When I asked the property manager what had happened, he said that Emerson had committed suicide."

"Suicide?"

"They found him a week after I'd left. He'd hanged himself."

"Where's Debbie now?"

"She's home, back at my place. Why? Do you want to meet her?"

I hesitated for a moment. "No," I said at last.

He nodded.

We talked about other things after that and had many good laughs. Yet, the whole time, I was thinking, *Murderer!* When a little more time passed, that thought faded from my mind, and instead I was picturing myself back in my own home, peering at the tea timer and the blue ink making its way to the top.

—Son Bo-mi
Translated from the Korean by Janet Hong

CYNAN JONES is an acclaimed fiction writer from Wales. His work has appeared in over twenty countries, and in journals and magazines including *Granta* and the *New Yorker*.

Cow

CYNAN JONES

- Clear.
- Clear?
- Negative.
- Well. Then we can go, then.
- Yes.
- It was better to check.
- Yes.
- And it's not raining.
- Miracle.
- I thought. Really. The way I felt.

The degradable jacket hung opaque and torn in the branches. Struggled, flicked in the light wind that set across the top of the farmland.

- Every time, I think it's a lamb in a tree.

The top of the ash was bare with dieback.

He was trying to picture it. A lamb gently lifted up by a breeze and blown into a tree, or slipped from a bird.

   –   Mm.

He drove the lane more carefully than usual, to avoid the deeper pits that had been eaten down by the rain.

The earlies were out in the field. Some still had their jackets. The polythene had gone clouded, like plastic drinks bottles left to the weather, and stood off in ripped angles from the lambs.

He tried to imagine the old farmers he grew up around putting rain jackets on a lamb.

Dark ribbons decorated the field where the quad bike and trailer had tracked up the ground. The thorn was just beginning to green; here and there bursts of bright yellow gorse.

On the turn of the lane there was strewn dead bracken, shallow runs up the banks to either side. The bracken was crisp and dry and everything else was wet.

   –   They go backwards you know.

The car bounced.

   –   What?

He imagined her middle bounce.

   –   They go backwards. When they carry the bracken, the bedding.
   –   Shut up.

38

– Yes. Badgers. They shuffle backwards with it.
– Shut up.

He slowed into the yard, sensed her soften, minutely let go.

When he braked, the wheels crunched briefly on the stones that had washed down the lane. The smaller the stones, the farther they ran. They went in a diminishing moraine across the yard.

With the clap of the car doors, a cloud of starlings lifted off the adjacent pasture. After they had gone, the ground, with all the wet going through it, seemed to still flitter with the sound of their wings.

There were bleats from the shed. A restful bovine low from the cattle barn. The big dun backs of the cows over the stalls.

He saw her reflect in the tight black plastic of the haystack as she went ahead, a presence in the broad round bale, then disappear into bright sheen.

Where the wrap had failed, the stack was studded with embryonic wraiths of white fungus.

When they looked over the galvanized sheet gate into the shed they saw just her father's bent back, the flank of the ewe, the pens portioned by bars of low February sunlight through the slatted timber wall.

– Ah! Her father seemed to halt a dry cough. Still bent in the stall, called, ready for some work? He let the cough

39

happen. Bloody thing. Could have meant the cough or the lamb he was trying to make drink.

A racing pigeon pecked at the dropped chaff on the walkway in front of the stall. Pecked flecks of straw into the air. One of its feet was only a stump. A grainy pink line.

- Where's Mam?
- She's on a sleep. Long night. Three twins and a triplet. Not problems. She just didn't get in.

Then he did something funny with his throat, as if he tried to clear it discreetly.

- Calver at it, too. Big old girl.
- Well. What can we do? Do you want a break?
- No. No. I want to get some turned out. While we've got the weather.
- It's going to rain more.
- They'll have their jackets.

The shed was full. Three solid weeks of rain, disorder had developed. There were too many lambs. They clattered up and down the wooden feed troughs that ran between the pens.

- Well. Okay. Are you tarring them?
- It seems to work.

He watched her eyes as she daubed the strong, creosotey tar on the lamb's hind with the old woolbag peg, then did its neck. Watched how she was.

Her eyes looked like she fiddled with small buttons.

When he lifted the lamb away from himself, the warmth stayed for a moment.

She manhandled the lamb into the jacket, legs through the holes, talked to it quietly.

With the sticky tar then the jacket on he had a thought of the lamb like one of the wrapped sweets she always had in her pockets. A cartoon fox. Delicious. The tar doing the opposite job to the one they put it on for.

Even though he knew it wasn't actual lambs you eat, it was sheep, he always had this thing, of dotted lines, as in cookery books, describing how they'd portion up into butchery cuts. This time it made him feel a little odd.

- That one was big.
- That was a heavy one.

On the ground, the heavy lamb clopped its feet one then the next, then the next, then the next, as if it counted its legs after the procedure. It did two jumps on the spot, perhaps to assess the effect of the thin coat, then nuzzled the bars of the hurdle they'd penned the corner off with.

As he held the next single, he passively read the copy on the box of lamb jackets. *Mis-mothering is not a problem.*

He wanted to go back and check the test. Distrusted it to change the moment he'd set the thing down.

The ruminant crunch, patient groans when the prone ewes shifted. Utter maternality. Inflated bags, some so huge you could think it was where the unborn lamb was carried.

He watched her. *Is she okay? Is she okay with all this? If she really thought it? How could a test be more right than her body?*

The *crack* of the quad bike, *rattle* trailer, *thrum* then and the sounds seemed to regroup as it came across the field.

He waited with the gate while Da backed the trailer in so that one side more or less met the warming box and when Da got off the bike and went past, he walked the gate against the other side of the trailer. With the hatch in its back open, the trailer was the only place to go.

Thin cough.

– Who have we got?

Da looked tired of the cough. He looked tired but pent-up, to get himself over the tiredness.

– Here. Have a sweet. Fished from her pocket a handful.

Da picked one. Incongruous bits of colored beach glass.

– That one's quite strong. Eucalyptusy.

– Good. Maybe I'll actually taste it. I had a mint earlier. Crap. Barely had any taste.

A sheep gave a cough, as if it would get a sweet of its own.

– Mam's probably right. Kicked a discarded pad of rotted grass part-stuck to the floor. It's probably this bloody hay. But. We might as well get it used.

Da lifted a lamb from the makeshift keep, hung it floorwards from its front legs so the backs of its back legs dragged the ground, twisted it to see its number.

– Thirty-nine.

– The blackface. Over by the far wall.

The pigeon had come up to Da and stood by his feet, examined his wellingtons. When Da took the lamb into the pen, dangled so it kicked its trailed legs at the straw, looked tottered on tiptoe, the pigeon clobbered after him.

The blackface looked for a while from the wall, then came up, nosed the lamb. She gave an affirmative huff and when Da carried the lamb out of the pen she followed and the pigeon came with them. They'd lost the old terrier before Christmas, and lambing was no time to get a new dog. It was not possible to see the pigeon without the thought there'd been some swap.

Da swung the big lamb without ceremony into the wired-off section at the front of the trailer and as it scrabbled to its feet the mother went cooperatively in through the door.

– It's enough, Da.
There was not feasibly any further room.

– We can get. Or. Well. Maybe with the ground wet, then.

Good.

His knee barked. He was short of breath. His fingernails burned from dragging the ewes that wouldn't go into the trailer. Stubborn-headed, stiff-legged refusal to step up, faces hefted in then front feet, all their bulk slumped so he had to shunt bodily. The first one had been a fluke.

– You two want to take them? Da asked.

But he was hesitant. He didn't want responsibility for the trailer on the wet fields. He was off-sided by the thump of his pulse. Unfit. *Seven weeks since I've kicked a ball.*

– I'll come, bright.

She liked to see the lambs go onto the grass for the first time. He wanted to say be careful, be careful on the bike.

– You go. I'll do the water.
– Maybe do the milk. It's about right for it.

Sun lit the dust motes that passed in front of the clock. The clock was on an angle and made him turn his head to read the time.

They'll be kicking off. They'll be kicking off about now.

He watched her get onto the bike behind Da and hold on to him. *Cough.* Then the quad *crackracked* again, and he swung the gate shut as they rattled off.

He went to the first stall and picked out the bucket. It was misshaped with use. There was a hank of wet straw, a pinecone of dung that stained the water.

He swirled the water and sluiced it under the gate where years of the same process had eaten a shallow into the shed floor. Then he took the bucket to the standpipe, swilled it clean, and hung it on the tap.

While it filled, he half-heartedly checked the back ends, *don't lamb, none of you lamb*, for glistening strips, for lips that seemed to mutter, teeth being ground, ropes of slime. Blatant vulvas, swollen, candy pink; felt the same protective sensation as when he found pinprick sprays of blood on the underside of the toilet seat. *Dignity.*

Collect, sluice, swill, fill. *Click* the kettle on to boil.

It could happen. It could have, and then like that we'd be in it.

Squeezy bottles of gloop, and iodine. Sprays. Rubber O-rings and the tailing pliers *so the tail rots, falls away*. Antiseptic wipes. A Stanley knife. Strips of variously colored ear tags, the tagging gun *that punches through their ear*. Syringes. Needles. Little packets. A brief wave through him. Made his balance travel. Thought of his knee, opened, the physio saying, You wouldn't need a general. Then, of her, a canula in the back of her hand. *But it isn't happening. It's not what's happening.*

Thought horribly of the ochre stain spreading in the water bucket.

Nude flesh bulged around a prolapse spoon.

The *pat pat* of the quad, coming down from the top land, the sound through the shed then puttering onto the saturated fields at the bottom of the farm.

When they'd loaded the trailer again and gone off with the next batch he got on with the milk. The incongruous ice cream smell. Two amounts into the measure cup. Added the powder to the water, swirled the jug, thought of snow, flour, cake, a child in an apron. Upended the open bottle to the inside of his wrist.

Beside him, the overflowing bin, the rolled latex of the condomy gloves, cutaway scraps of bale wrap compacted into balls. The pitch-black plastic, with the light flashed off it, one of the brightest things in the shed. Flashes of light.

    – *Can you get on the floor, please, get on the floor.*

Grey when the physio lifted the injection.

    – *I don't want to have to catch you.*

I won't faint. I've never fainted. Not a spin, but a sickishness, emptying. Why? I don't know why I've got it.

    – *Bigger boys than you have, and me five foot and a fart.*

Focus. Don't faint. Just accept it.

    – *"Mummy," you hear that, then they go.*

Mummy?

    – *A lot of them. Just before they fall.*

As he fed the molly lambs, the pigeon lumbered over to the shallow under the gate and drank from the dirty puddle. He *sissed* but it ignored him.

Every time the bird dipped, its rainbowy neck feathers caught the light.

He didn't feel he could get up from the lambs, tried to scuff-kick loose pebbles at the pigeon. The pink line of its leg. Saw the lambs' middles swell and tighten. Their tails fluttered. Their nostrils flared with little pumps.

The *pat* of the quad on its way back again. The hushed shed, the hospital sense of compromised bodies. Resting, recovering, waiting. Relegated to a purpose.

It's better. It's better we're not.

When they'd had enough, the lambs unlatched themselves, which sent little sprays of milk up his hands. Then they shook their heads, to flick the milk drops from their muzzle, quivered, stepped back in some sort of happy shock. They looked like they'd swallowed a ball, then bounced off as if they had.

He refilled the bottles, got the next orphan pair. Lifted them from their stall.

Then he had the idea of the stain again spreading out in the water and couldn't watch the pigeon anymore, so he went over with the lambs infantly furious about him and footed the bird, which bobbed under the gate. It didn't fly. It didn't take off. Maybe it didn't think it was a pigeon. Or else it thought, flying got me into trouble.

She brought the bike in onto the hard area in front of the shed and parked it out of the way by the old dip.

Sitting on the bike had pushed her coat and the bodywarmer up so when she dismounted it looked like she had a belly.

She came in and set the gate open. More watery light came into the shed.

- Where's your dad?
- Checking the cow and getting a bale.

The bike had disturbed the sparrows and they were loud now in the scrub holly that flanked the far side of the shed.

- Aren't we doing another load?
- He wants to get a bale in.

He raked gouts of bad hay to the side of the floor. Grunged pads, white with mycorrhizal net. When a tine caught a raised stone in a particular way the pitchfork sang out.

- Did you feed?
- Mm. Toed a flat pad of moldered hay off the fork.

The *grum of* the tractor, the noise from the collecting yard through the cow barn, exaggerated.

- Just one. One wouldn't take it. Just didn't want it. The speckly one.

She was going round the shed, shining the torch at the back ends.

- Well. It's got to have something.
- It didn't want it.

The light in the shed swapped with noise as Da brought the tractor in bale first. He lowered the bale to the floor and let its

48

own weight hold it in place while he reversed and slid it off the spike. Then he came back and used the bottom edge of the spike loader to tip the bale onto its flat side.

He shouted something through the *crrormm*, held up two fingers to tell them he was bringing another bale, then reversed out.

She took the tube out of the basin of boiling water and held it up.

– It won't feed. Might as well have mouthed it, the level of tractor noise.

Da shook his finger and made a gesture that meant wait, put a hand to his mouth, cough, pointed to his eyes then two fingers up to his head, cow's horns, and swung the tractor from the shed.

– It's cold. Its mouth is really cold. The knuckle of her little finger in the lamb's mouth as she cradled it.

– He'll be back now. Thumbed the slide to extend the blade and sunk the Stanley into the wrap.

She turned, angered at him. As if he had something to do with the lamb not wanting to drink.

As soon as the wrap was cut it split of its own accord and the side of the bale breached out.

She looked indignantly down, into the steam rising from the basin, at the tube. There was all the stuff bunched around her middle so she didn't look like her.

– Well. I'm putting it in the box.

She looked the way he'd started to picture she would come to look, while it was *might be*.

    –   I'm putting it in the box at least.

It's better. She likes to do this. She likes the problems, even. She likes to be in the shed. It would have stopped her being able to help, if she had been.

He was misting the stall with hypochlorite when she came back. The barrow was piled with neatly rolled layers of filthy straw. Blood, dung, urine.

    –   Da's not back yet?
    –   Nope.

He heard her put the tea and coffee down on the milk shelf too hard.

A lamb knocked down the feed trough to watch him use the spray, twitched its nose at the high chemical stink.

    –   It's probably the tractor again. Prized the pressure valve, the *spiff* of excess air and the lamb shied.
    –   That's the small tractor. Keeps breaking. The small one.

There was an abrupt smatter of sparrows on the shed rafters, then they went *pinking* out through the gaps in the boarding.

    –   The scraping tractor.
    –   Did you see your mum?

50

Her eyes showed red in the glow of the heat bulb. The tags and medical things skidded off the lifted lid of the warming box.

–   Fuck's sake. The speckled lamb floppy, ropey. Eyes aimless. Its stomach a concave. I knew. I fucking knew this.

–   You'll have to do it.

She wasn't tender with the lamb now, held it down along her legs, its throat stretched sacrificially straight. Loose socky rolls bunched in front of her hands, the lamb's skin too big.

I don't know what I'm doing.

–   Just wait for your dad.
–   We did.

I don't know anything about how to do it.

–   Isn't your mum coming out?
–   There's Lemsip everywhere.
–   What?
–   Chill. Or something. Throat. She wouldn't go back to bed.
–   Okay, so she'll be out.

The lamb was unresponsive.

–   Maybe.

It was too late then. She'd seen he wanted to say some things just. *Now I have to. Now I have to do it.*

–   I don't know what I'm doing.

    – Just don't put it into his lungs.

He tried to *see*. He didn't look at the lamb's mouth he looked away, to some half-understood guess at its insides.

    – Not in his lungs.
    – I know.
    – Well.
    – Please. Crouched, the bark of his bad knee. The still-warm tube extra softened between his thumb and forefinger, the lamb gurgling, soft chin in his other fingers, the hand that also tried to keep the witless mouth ajar.

She can't accept it. She always wants to affect things.

Then the lamb wriggled suddenly. *Christ.*

    – Hold it!

It coughed horribly.

    – You're in his lungs.

I can't be. It would have hit the bottom of them. There would be blood. Wouldn't there, if.

Then there was a gurgle, a tight gastric stench up through the tube and the lamb suddenly goggle-eyed.

    – Okay, okay.

This should be calm. I should be calm. Just look. Just do. You just have to do it.

He fitted the small funnel into the tube and reached the bottle. Dry on the ground a dismembered bat; then recognized parts of desiccated thistle extracted from the straw. The world bent through a capsule. He, her, the lamb.

– How much?
– Tiny.

Undid the cap.

– Don't flood him. Bits. Tiny bits.

What if I pour scalding milk? What if it's too hot? Right into it.

The lamb now looked alert enough to understand.

He put a finger in the milk.

– That's not clean. You're not clean.
– It's fine. It was hardly in. I hardly even.
– You've been doing the stalls.
– Just. Please.

She started to mutter. She started into some litany.

– Stop. Please. Stop.

I don't need this. I don't need any of it. I'm not going to stay in this, always. Stop.

Stop.

It's just everything. She thought it. I did. We really thought it.

53

He tipped the bottle against his wrist, warm circle on his lifted pulse. The faint net of his skin, and, she is right, yes, rimed creases in his hands.

- You want me to use the other bottle? The tube going into the stupid animal. Crouched, the knee burned.
- Just.

The lamb looked at them both now, somehow, at them both.

- Pinch it. As he dropped a little milk into the funnel.

It's just everything.

Let the milk through bit by bit, release, pinch.

- More.
- Okay.

What they got into the lamb felt futile. It had gone into a horrible shake. That flattened his anger. He just felt sick.

- I'm sorry. The coffee stone cold. Sorry I snapped.
- Shall I warm that?

It's okay. That's her thank-you. That's her sorry. That's her thank-you.

- No, it's okay. Let's just go in. I want to do my hands properly.
- I can't believe nothing's lambing. She tried to be light. It's you. It must be you.

One more check. She'll want to do one more check now.

54

– Well. We'll do one last check.

And there'll be something.

He didn't want coffee anymore. He'd gone past it. But he wanted to go in. He nearly said, no, I want to go in. He swallowed down adrenalin. *She wants to be out. She wants to be busy.*

– It's good that we could come and help.

He watched her assess a ewe gurn and lip her teeth.

– Is that one up to something?
– It wouldn't really have been the ideal time.

It didn't seem to penetrate her. She just stared at the ewe with a look of conviction.

He had a foresense something was going to happen. He had the foresense and then her father came into the shed, finally, with the look of someone who had conceded something, and said, I've got a problem with the cow. Can you help?

The cow stood kept tightly upright in the bars of the crush with her neck through the pinning gate. Only one leg was out of the cow, the pulling rope still twisted round the calf's foot. Webbing straps went in a V from the pulling rope to the corroded bars of the run that led along the breeze-block wall into the crush. He guessed for extra leverage.

The one big leg came out wetly and slathered, the size more like something from a tree.

55

    — She keeps slipping the other leg.

There was the one big giant leg like a saucepan handle and, barely out of her, peeped, the other. It appeared to duck protectively away when he saw it, then protruded slowly again, only the curious sensory hoof.

He didn't know anything, but to him even the one leg looked convincingly too big.

A prolonged low came from somewhere deep within the cow, didn't really leave her properly. Her dun flank bulged in the galvanized uprights. He had the horrible sense it would be possible to saw bits off the cow. That you could saw off her legs and she'd just stand there suspended, no different, just her legs sawn away on the floor.

The yard was thick with muck the rain had corralled into piles, formed dams of, with bare channels where built-up water had riddled away through it. The boot prints behind the cow gave a record of what had already been done to try to get the calf out. Sometimes splayed boot shapes imprinted the others, looked formed with more force.

Da got his hand inside the cow and did something telescopular. Rotated the hoof out.

    — Hold it.

It gave a greasy suck. Tried to slip back in as he took the hoof from Da, got his grip around what he could only think of as the ankle, his finger joints against the rope. It was like trying to hold something thickly soaped.

    — Pull. Can you get it? Get it alongside.

The white hoof, split in two sharp ovals, ogled at him, were like cartoon eyes. Her father was doing something incomprehensible. He was climbing up on the metal run.

– Keep the leg out. Dry cough.

Then part-balanced on the wall he stepped off the run and onto the webbing straps.

The exposed leg lurched with a wet fart. The leg in his hand wanting to recoil as if the sound had scared it. *Jesus!*

– Keep the leg out.

The engorged udder, bulged with veins.

Da started to bounce with gentle insanity on the webbing straps. Brought a kind of ongoing *rrorl* from the cow. A bass mammalian sound amplified into something otherworldly as it resonated through the hollow metal structure of the crush. The hoof wide-eyed with surprise.

He instinctively leant back with it. The other leg, against the back of his hand, had been exposed so long it was cold. It was solid. It did not feel like an animal thing.

He read the sports brand on the ridiculous straps, slack, tight, slack. A mark on his wrist, the coat ridden up, tiny flecks of sleeve fabric in the sticky milk residue.

Do I speak? Do I say something? It isn't moving. I don't think it's moving.

The cow reduced to a device. The great slit of her vulva. The pronounced architecture of her pelvis.

57

She should be primal. She should be animate. The bent gate that led into the run and her imprisoned as if in punishment for doing it. As if in some corrective penury.

Slap, the splatter of wet muck. Da down. *Cough*.

   – Needs us both.

We should get a vet. Surely. This needs a vet.

   – It seems pretty big.

The cow looked gargoyled now.

   – Da. Her voice from the edge of the collecting yard. The
     ewe's not good.
   – I can't help.
   – She's not good. She cradled the speckled lamb.

The racer that was on the yard in some seeming comradeship with Da pigeon-stepped away across the roils of muck.

   – I can't really help.
   – Well. I'll have to get Mam then.
   – I can after. Leave Mam. Let her sleep. We don't want her ill.

They wouldn't get through the lambing. They won't get through if they're ill.

   – She's already up.

Da had a look, he was out of time. Lambs out. The bad bale taken in. But now he was out of time.

She'd come over enough to see the leg properly now, and the rigged-up straps.

58

    – It's too long. I'm getting Mam.

Her face looked very small with all the farm clothes bunching around her and her hat down.

    – No. Look.

It's huge, that leg. It was like some wet algae-covered limb of wood.

    – I'll come, after.

There was livid blood on the ground and down around the cow's back legs now.

    – Da. What are you doing?

Muck patterned in the clear shape of partial boot prints on the webbing straps.

    – Dad?
    – She'll come.
    – Well.
    – She'll come.

The calf, cow, her mum?

    – It doesn't look right. Anger folding, her face.
    – Why don't you look after the shed. Sharp.
    – Da. You need a vet.
    – We're in it now.
    – I'm getting Mam.
    – No. Look. Watch the shed, *cough*. I'll be, after. Dry cough.

The cow could not move. The crush held her so all she could move was her head. She was trying to look round to see what was being done but the crush didn't allow it.

59

Her blood was coming now in unashamed trails.

You'd have to watch. You'd have to watch this.

She made as if to sound a deep static noise but no sound came. It seemed to push the other sounds out of the collecting yard. She knew they were going to do it again.

    –   Get up.
    –   Da, what? Eyes flashing.
    –   It's got to come out.

Her eyes. *Just get on it, and then it's over. It'll all come down. He won't have to admit it himself.*

    –   What are you doing? Fuck's sake.

Just watch your knee.

When he put his weight on the strap it was obvious to him the calf wasn't coming out. He was horrified the leg would snap before the calf came out.

    –   Fucking hell. Fuck's sake. Fucking hell. Her shout the same time as the cow's roar.

He was already a meter and a half up on the wall to be there to catch the calf when the vet guided it out. He had to be up there, not next to the vet, because there wasn't much room to work with the open side of the crush so near the edge of the yard.

But. What about his thing?

The vet had sent him to the shed for a bucket.

His thing, with needles.

Her mum sounded hoarse, still flushed from the shouting.

> – *Well. Da can't. He's on the ewe.*
> – *But.*
> – *It's only needles. He's okay with other stuff.*

Da, prostrate by the breaching ewe, didn't see him come through the gate.

> – *It has to take effect. First. He'll have done it already. He won't see it. Dry cough. Dry cough again.*
> – *I don't know why he brought more hay, why did he bring more bad hay in?*
> – *The vet needs a bucket. Is there a clean bucket? Didn't say, he wants it for the placenta.*
> – *Ma. Still cradled the speckled lamb. It's just needles. He's okay with other stuff, as he left.*

From the elevation, a sheen was on the yard. A sheen too on the slates of the old outbuildings.

He looked down at the cow. The vet's plaid shoulders. The tan line on his nape as he *ruzzed* the shaver over the flank. Skin strange, colorless. Rich curls of dun hair feathering to the ground.

From where he stood, he saw over the hedges to the green fields. To a grey ash that seemed to be singing, then the starlings came off in a pointillist cloud; the ivy, cut, dead and hard, that roped on the trunk, like the cow's bulged veins.

When the vet ran the scalpel against the cow to score the first incision she flinched. The flank tightened like it was its own animal. She seemed to lose stability, even within the crush. She was a big cow with big bands of muscle.

The vet hissed something. Inaudible. Broke into a mutter.

He could not see the vet's mouth, just the tense muscles compact at the back of his jaw.

The very faint pink line in the cow's skin began to bead drops of blood. Then the vet stood from his bag with an oversized syringe, the needle in the vial. The needle was as long as his forearm.

He felt the breeze-blocks soften.

The vet pulsed the oversized syringe, watered squirts of anesthetic topically on the cut. A fuzz of numbness.

Don't faint. Mummy. He'd latched onto the mummy thing as something in itself. *You can't. You can't do that.*

He saw a faint spray from the bright point, the vet's spread fingers on the shaved cow, actually heard the *pop* of the cow's skin.

Don't fall. You can't fall.

Do not take your eyes off.

He thought if he looked away that the world would lose anchor and he'd spin off it. Into the rubble and rusty metal and entangled barbed wire, the bramble, broken blocks.

He swallowed it back. *Just look at it. Look.* Tried to deal with it like car sickness.

Now the cow was open. Her exposed organs steamed in the cool air. Bags and bulbous insides kept slipping from the longitudinal cut that divided the cow's flank. The vet fielded them to keep them in, palmed and pushed, appeared to rearrange them somewhere inside the cow's grey middle.

A cow has four stomachs. A vet has two hands.

He still couldn't look away. It looked like the vet was trying to stop things falling out of an overfull wardrobe.

He waited for the wet *thwack* of something vital hitting the floor.

– That shouldn't be there.

With his arms and hands bright-oranged with iodine and his white apron streamed, it was as if the vet had done something tribal to himself.

A cow has four stomachs. A vet has two hands. A pale blue bag palmed up and somewhere into the depths of the cow.

He felt grey, the nightmare of being horribly immobilized while someone did this.

She doesn't feel it. She can't feel any of it.

The muscle was peeled back around the cut. Had taken repeated slicing. A line of dun hide, rim of white fat, then the thick muscle that had hampered the anesthetic.

It looks like steak. It looks like steak. Look. You've got to keep looking. Like steak. Because it is.

There was no blood. He knew we're not filled with blood, not a bag, but to see into the cow and there being no blood made the cow less real.

The vet talked to himself. He was talking rhythmically. The muscles bulbed behind his jaw.

The cow just stared quietly out, through the gate, over the track at the fields. As if she wondered where the rest of herself had gone.

You're going to fall. You're going to fall and break something. You're going to break your neck.

He thought of the cow not feeling half her body.

Just look. Just look.

It's fine. There's nothing. There's no reason. It's okay. You don't have to go through it yet.

A cow has four stomachs.

The cow opened her mouth, seemed about to ask something, but instead there was a horrible, elongated wheeze. It was like she sucked in a great deep breath, to power some earsplitting uncowlike howl. But nothing came.

The precise pink scalpel line in the very top layers of skin. The line. Pink line. Cold sweat getting colder, damped across his back.

Do not look away. The vet had the womb. The calf's bulged eyes. The uterus stretched, opaque.

The fat pink tongue lolled inside the cloudy bag, looked stunned and wounded. The tiny whorls on the calf's brow wetly printed against the membrane where it strained with the big head's weight.

The vet supported the weight, the head, had arranged the cow how he wanted her, *a vet has two hands*, reached back for a knife.

He held the knife with his thumb and forefinger; precisely held the blade with the shaft under his palm and unhesitatingly drew it across the bag, amniotic water *slapping* onto the ground, a smell, the calf launching as a dead weight out of the body.

   – Down!

He jumped. A white flash from his knee but the huge calf was there, under its own slip weight, and its head in his hands.

   – Under the shoulders.

Sluiced. The protruding limb drawn through the open cow and out to him and he carried, half-crouched, the slick weight held on his thighs to keep the calf from hitting the ground. Heard the *splotht* of the placenta into the bucket behind him.

It lay unresponsive. Its tongue lank. The leg that had protruded— it looked dislocated—stuck stiffly out and awkward.

He rubbed the calf roughly, fingered slime from its mouth, patted at its chin. The things he knew to do with sheep, lambs. Dragged the calf, the muck bunching, closer to its mother. *Clean it. Come on. Come on*, even as she was being sewn up. Saw the vet's yellowed arm appear and disappear repeatedly over the ridge of the cow's back, drawing the thick black thread.

The suds in the basin of iodine, each somehow individually colored, rainbow bubbles, the oils of the pigeon's neck.

The cow leaned as far as she could in the crush, seemed to look at the calf without interest.

She didn't feel it come from her. She didn't feel it come out.

   – Lift it, the vet said from behind the cow.

The calf's upward-facing eye opened. A dark globe endlessly deep in the pure white surround.

Stain spreading in the water.

He tried to raise the inert, slipping weight of the calf. Lifted its back legs as high as he could off the ground, tried to swing the calf, to loose the fluid from its lungs; but the calf was too long. *It died. It died inside her*. With all his might he lifted it, arms above his head, but the calf's head still lolloped dumbly on the ground.

He began to jiggle the calf. *Come on*. His knee barked. Shook it like he'd empty a sack of sand. And there was a splutter. The calf coughed, and suddenly it pedaled its front legs briefly. As if it tried to run into the sky. He let it down. Began to rub. Rubbed.

Come on, he begged. *Come on.*

66

LINNEA AXELSSON is from Porjus in northern Sweden, but now lives in Stockholm. She studied humanities at Umeå University and received her PhD in Art History in 2009. Her debut novel *Tvillingssmycket* was published in 2010 and in 2018 the acclaimed epic *Ædnan* won the August Prize, Sweden's highest literary award. Her next novel *Magnificat* will be published in March 2022.

SASKIA VOGEL is a writer and translator from Los Angeles, now living in Berlin. Her debut novel *Permission* (2019) was published in five languages and was awarded the 2021 Berlin Senate Grant for Non-German-language Literature. *Ædnan*, forthcoming with Knopf, is the focus of her work as Princeton University's Fall 2022 Translator in Residence.

from *Ædnan*

LINNEA AXELSSON
TRANSLATED FROM THE SWEDISH BY SASKIA VOGEL

IV

Meanwhile at Lake Gobmejávri. Spring 1913
(as told by mother Ristin)

That spring
longing tasted of
rainwater

–

On a wing
we had ridden

made of the heat
of skin
and voices

–

In the reindeer antlers'
woolly tines

we were caught

There we were left hanging
driving in the wind

While the tundra of work
settled calmly
between us

–

It was the herd
that nourished my blood
it shaped me
with its world

–

The wellspring
of my life's design

A rhythm of tasks

that flayed and
beat out their path
from the reindeer

—

Unhairing the hide
sewing of the hide
making use of the meat

—

Carrying with us
this animal body
in remade parts:

Products nutriment
garments tools

In the evening
the stars flocked

–

They appeared and
were reflected in the embers
in the center of the tent

–

I snapped a
stick and fed
the embers

Brushed a
straw off our
younger boy's arm

Then Nila's face churned
wildly around its core

–

He shook
his head

staring tossing
his hair

–

He who could
be so careful
and soft

–

When he held
the sugar tin
the bentwood box

My friend beside me
sat spinning
with her daughters

–

They pulled tendons
from the reindeers' legs
between their teeth

and twined them
into thread against their cheeks

–

The embers shifted in color

And they spun you
who were with the calving
cows

The sun over
the calving grounds
they spun soothing

to the steaming new
bodies

–

Thought through
fully developed
calves

woven through with
heartbeats

–

A new continuation
of our life

As if absentmindedly
Nila's fingers scratched
my back

while my friend
and I told
her girls:

–

Let the fire
keep you company

Remember that those you
are missing who are at work
far away

are looking up

76

at the same stars

—

In the same dying
embers their tired eyes
are coming to rest

—

Our dark-haired
son's crown

—

When Aslat was born

Never had I seen
so dark

and thick a wreath of hair
as Aslat's

V

The accident site
(as told by father Ber-Joná)

And Aslat
opened his eyes

and he screamed
suddenly out loud
and cried

–

I didn't understand why

but I had
dragged him a ways
along the cliff

–

And twilight
filled the valley

Darkness spilled
down the slopes
towards the plains

where the men
were running in their soft
buckskin shoes

–

The wet snow
began to freeze

–

Someone said

that the unease would cause
the cows to panic

That they must
be set in motion

up the other
slope

—

My brother had
been standing on his own
a while

—

I felt
my eyes tear up

When he came over
and started talking
to me:

We have to help
Aslat up onto
the food sled

–

We'll have to
transport him
that way

VI

The women break camp
(Ristin)

Gently

I bound up
my memories

–

Treacherous company

coming and going
as they pleased

–

Both stood up
and knocked me over

–

The snow crust gleamed
and I shouldered
our packing

Our weak boy
waited calmly

on his own skis

–

He too lifted up
the backpack
of his heart

and stacked
the logs
with care

–

Perhaps

he did

The squeeze of baggage

reminded me of
when our boys
were small

—

When we still migrated
together

wandering
in heavy rain

—

I hold the weakling
by the hand

For long stretches
Nila walks on his own

like his brother Aslat does

–

The water seeps
into his clothes
which darken

and we struggle
against the wind
as we raise the tent

–

Then we lie down
and wait out
the rain

–

The clothes
are hung to dry

And I wipe out
the coffee cups
with a piece of cloth

place them
in the large *kisa* box

–

Inside it I feel
the bag of flour
the silver brooch

–

In the evening
Ber-Joná wakes
very slowly

The sun had been warming
all day

And he lies still

While his thoughts
grow very clear

–

Aslat sits and
listens to the pack reindeer
grazing freely
near our camp

–

One is so tame
it sneaks up
to the tent

it nudges
the canvas

and Ber-Joná
mutters at it

Then he asks me
to mimic a grouse

–

Does this memory

gnaw at him too

–

Once

I tied Aslat
to a rock

I was working my way
across the cloudberry mire

–

It grew difficult
and I took off my
bottoms

knotted my pant legs
and filled them with berries

–

The shawl and the smallest kerchief
I could tie up
the backpack

Full of berries

A black pool broke
through the moss

and the water was cold
pleasant on my neck

–

The golden eagle
dove darkly
from the sky

its eye yellow
and black

–

In that yellow eye

was a different reflection
of the world

It reached out its claws
and dove towards Aslat

I dropped the berries
and ran screaming
arms raised

–

Watched the heavy
bird of prey rise up and off

–

Everything was as usual

but this cast a shadow

–

And Nila he

had been born grimy white

–

Face like a rag

this cast a shadow

–

My friend had laid
that thin figure
across my chest

–

She stretched out
those small limbs
and filled his hands
with her thumbs

But he did not grab hold

He lay but still

arms outstretched

–

I watched his frail
heart quiver
under the skin

I saw the shadows
and that fine
rib cage

–

All the shadows
grabbing hold of
his chest

in an impassive game

All those feeble
soft parts I saw

all that was giving
way in him

–

All that

as soon as
he had arrived
betrayed him

–

I said:

Take him out
into the air
we must rouse
his ire

The cold usually riles
them up

–

And my friend lifted
Nila out of the sugar box

–

His fragile head
just drooped

Legs dangling slack
and head lolling
in her arms

when she stumbled
in the snow

Then I lay there a long while

and met his face

–

The waves sank
and surged again

that broad forehead
those wide-set eyes

–

My own traits
rising and rising

and my mother's traits

–

In the cheekbone
the eyebrow

I felt that I was smiling

–

Perhaps I had
always been searching for
traces of my mother

outside of myself

VII

Through the Rosta River Valley from Lake
Ádjávárddojávrrit. Past the Tamok River
and the Great Dápmoteatnu River
(Ber-Joná)

My brother and I
Aslat
we sang nothing

no longer sang forth
the land and
memories

–

Bowls of song
cupped by the voice

When words were not
enough for the lives
we were living

–

They had sunk
through hate

They had waded in sorrow

–

But they did not make it
through this freeze

we sang nothing

–

Just watched as the mountains
and the old migration routes
retreated

from Aslat's body

–

From the one who is not able

The streaming belt of cows
wandered eagerly
up along the cliffs

–

To feel them breathe

to be left to dissolve with the sea

–

We moved on slowly
after several daylong
breaks

–

May Day passed

and then we could cross
the border

The patches of bare earth spread

and the pregnant
cows waddled on
in a dense pack

–

With a few
single calves
born
along the way

–'

An impatient courage
had come
over the animals

who wanted most of all
to fall into trot

Our son's dog ran
barking along
the edges of the herd

Both our dogs
had to obey
my hand now

–

And the cows
calved

–

One calf was
stuck and we had to
pull it out

It was wedged
so very hard
dead

a big one

–

Many were calmed
by the others birthing
within sight

but some
withdrew
and wanted to be
alone

–

We sang nothing

–

The silence
from the food sled
where Aslat sat
reigned

In the legs
and groin:

an unyielding
baggage

–

Evening came

And I fed
him much
reindeer stew

–

With each spoonful
he disappeared deeper
into the new

silence

And I let him
take out his sorrow
on my arms

my chest

OLGA TOKARCZUK is the recipient of the 2018 Nobel Prize in Literature. She is the author of nine novels and three short story collections and has twice won the most prestigious Polish literary prize, the Nike Award, for *Flights* in 2008 and for *The Books of Jacob* in 2015. Her most famous novels include *Primeval and Other Times* published in 1996, *House of Day, House of Night* published in 1998, *Flights* published in 2007, which, in a translation by Jennifer Croft, also won the 2018 Man Booker International Prize and was shortlisted for the National Book Awards in Translated Literature 2018, and *Drive Your Plow over the Bones of the Dead*, which was published in 2009 and, in a translation by Antonia Lloyd-Jones, was shortlisted for the 2019 Man Booker International Prize and several other awards. *The Books of Jacob* was published in English by Fitzcarraldo, Riverhead, and Text Publishing in 2021 in a translation by Jennifer Croft. Her work is translated into more than fifty languages. Tokarczuk lives in Wrocław, Poland, where she is establishing a foundation offering scholarships for writers and translators and educational programs on literature.

ANTONIA LLOYD-JONES has translated works by several of Poland's leading contemporary novelists and reportage authors, as well as crime fiction, poetry, and children's books. She is a mentor for the Emerging Translators' Mentorship Programme, and former co-chair of the UK Translators Association.

The Masks of Animals

OLGA TOKARCZUK
TRANSLATED FROM THE POLISH
BY ANTONIA LLOYD-JONES

I find it easier to bear the suffering of human beings than the suffering of animals. The human being has its own extended ontological status, broadcast far and wide, which makes it a privileged species. It has culture and religion to support it in its suffering. It has its rationalizations and sublimations. It has God, who in the end will save it. Human suffering has meaning. For an animal there is neither consolation nor relief, because it has no salvation ahead of it. Nor does it have meaning. An animal's body does not belong to it. It has no soul. An animal's suffering is total and absolute.

If we try to look into this condition with our human capacity for thought and with sympathy, the full horror of animal suffering is revealed, and by the same token the unbearably shocking horror of this world.

In ancient, pre-Socratic Greece there was a trilogy in force—three simple imperatives formulated by Pythagoras and his pupils: honor your parents, honor the gods with fruits, and spare the animals. As laconically as possible, these rules identify the three most important spheres of human life: first, the most basic social ties; second, the religious dimension, in the broadest sense; and

109

third, fair treatment of animals. They do not identify any specific forms of behavior, but they point the way. They are precepts rather than prohibitions, and within the areas where they apply the individual is granted freedom of interpretation. Failure to keep them results in a sense of guilt, shame, or moral discomfort. They do not actually need to be spelled out in detail.

While the first two refer us to well-codified systems—social and religious—and rely on clearly set out, generally transparent norms and rituals, the relationship between humans and animals is not organized in a similar way (except perhaps for the lucid list of dietary taboos in the Old Testament), and as a result it is left to human conscience. That is the very reason why it is "ethical," meaning that it prompts one to consider what one should and should not do.

HOW HAVING REASON MAKES US BETTER

The Pythagoreans believed that animals are rational creatures, while the anarchistic Diogenes even claimed that they are superior to human beings in many regards. However, that was not a universal attitude.

Judeo-Christian tradition clearly says that the earth and all species of plants and animals were created purely to serve the interests of the human species. At the very beginning of the Book of Genesis we find the emphatic statement that God gives man mastery over all the creatures on earth, because it is man who has been placed at the center of creation, while the purpose of nature is to serve man.

A similar thought was being developed independently in Greece by the philosophers. Aristotle devised a very persuasive argument for such a hierarchically constructed edifice of creation—man was the only one to be gifted with intellect, and the power of reason is the most important and most significant of all human characteristics. Any creature with a lesser ability to reason is naturally lower down in the hierarchy (Aristotle used the same logic to justify the slave trade, maintaining that some people are slaves "by nature").

The ultimate form of this idea was provided by Augustine, who in commenting on the biblical commandment "Thou shalt not kill," maintained that we should not make the mistake of extending it to creatures deprived of reason.

Whatever indisputable statements can be made about early Christianity, we should be aware how many different visions, ideologies, and interpretations lay at its foundations. We can be sure the prevalent attitude to animals at the time was biased and hostile. Thomas Aquinas, who from the scattered early Christian polyphony built a cohesive, refined philosophy, continued and at the same time went beyond the ideas of Augustine. He maintained that animals are not only mindless, but also that they lack an immortal soul, and so their death is—in the broadest scheme of things—entirely without significance. We have no direct moral obligations toward animals, because only a person (meaning a creature who possesses reason and self-control) can be the subject of obligations and laws.

This was undoubtedly a very radical way of putting the case, which in the future would lead to the mass breeding of animals for meat. We can also say that for many years this father of the Church absolved people from killing animals. We still had the clear commandment "Thou shalt not kill" in our minds, but—thanks to commentators like Thomas Aquinas—it was surrounded by so many conditions and exceptions that the original meaning of those words was totally ignored. In most ancient cultures eating any meat other than sacrificial meat was taboo. To eat an animal, first it was necessary to sacrifice it; this gesture cleansed the killer of the sin of taking another creature's life.

In Descartes there first appeared the terrible vision of the animal as a machine that functions according to quite simple mechanical rules. Man was distinguished by reason and an immortal soul, while animals were more like automata than living creatures, and as a result not just eating and killing them now became ethically neutral, but also practices such as vivisection.

Animals also had Kant acting against them, who wrote in the late eighteenth century that we have no direct obligations toward them because they are not self-aware creatures, but just a means to an end. And that end is man.

The Catholic Church too has consistently denied mankind's moral obligations toward animals. This is why, in the mid-nineteenth century, Pius IX refused to agree to the founding of the Society for the Prevention of Cruelty to Animals. It appears that in the *Catechism* the modern church does in fact recommend being kind to animals and not causing them unnecessary suffering, but at the same time, the text posted on the Vatican website states: "Animals, like plants and inanimate beings, are by nature destined for the common good of past, present, and future humanity."

In biology, on the other hand, the principle is still binding that was formulated in the late nineteenth century by C. Lloyd Morgan, a pioneer of research on animals. Known as Morgan's Canon, it states that "in no case is an animal activity to be interpreted in terms of higher psychological processes if it can be fairly interpreted in terms of processes which stand lower in the scale of psychological evolution and development," which means that it is more accurate to explain animal behavior by referring to reactions and instincts than to ascribe thoughts or higher emotions to animals.

112

Yet it would be an injustice not to mention the great minds that held a different opinion. Saint John Chrysostom, who in a way anticipated Darwin, argued that the origin of animals is exactly the same as ours, and so we should be gentle and kind to them; Saint Francis of Assisi promoted love of nature, but above all he called for treating animals as if they were our brothers and sisters. Montaigne, a great mind in every respect who was ahead of his own times, believed that placing oneself above the rest of creation results from a poverty of the imagination, and is the prejudice of a limited intellect. However, the greatest service to animals was done by the eighteenth-century philosopher Jeremy Bentham, who on the issue of attitudes to animals was undoubtedly a precursor of modern ethicists. He was the first to formulate an idea that appears obvious to many today—that unquestionably in many respects human beings are more advanced than animals in matters including reasoning or level of self-awareness. But for Bentham these differences were not morally relevant. "The question is not, Can they *reason?* nor, Can they *talk?* but, Can they *suffer?*" he wrote in 1780 (in Chapter XVII of *An Introduction to the Principles of Morals and Legislation*).

REASON AGAINST REASON—SINGER

Peter Singer is the most radical of the modern-day ethicists. He is well-known for his dazzlingly logical chains of arguments in favor of animal rights. For years he has been demonstrating that basically our attitude to animals is irrational and illogical. His method is that of a philosopher—to establish the order of reason wherever we are ruled by prejudice and inconsistency.

Singer makes the assumption that the fundamental principle underlying the equality of all human beings is the principle of equal consideration of interests. Anyone who regards racial discrimination or discrimination against women as among the most important moral and political issues will agree with it. It could be said that today no one remains in any doubt that such discrimination is morally wrong. But Singer goes further, demanding the extension of the principle of equality as the moral basis for our relations with other people to our relations with animals. Why? Because our concern for others should not depend on what sort of people they are, whether and what abilities they possess (though obviously what we can do for others will vary depending on their various traits and characteristics). After all, the fact that somebody does not belong to our race does not give us the right to exploit them. Thus the same applies to animals—the fact that they do not belong to our species does not give us the right to inflict suffering on them.

Singer is a utilitarian, which means he regards as ethical actions and conduct that have the best possible consequences for those whom they affect. By "best consequences" he means whatever generally favors the realization of their interests, and not—as the classical utilitarian Bentham maintained—things that only increase pleasure and reduce pain. Following Bentham, Singer identifies the capacity to suffer as an essential characteristic that confers on every living creature the right to be placed on equal footing with other suffering creatures, including human beings.

Buddhist philosophy embraces the concept of the "sentient being." It is also used colloquially to define both humans and other living creatures. This is a special, unique category that has nothing to do with possessing reason, but defines the capacity to experience suffering and pleasure, to participate in the world both physically and mentally. Our Western philosophy only discovered this sort of approach two hundred years ago. This is exactly how Singer understands the capacity to suffer, and he owes much to Buddhist thought. At the same time, he believes in resolving the contradictions and misunderstandings in our thinking about animal rights with the aid of reason. In *Animal Liberation* he offers his readers methods for *logical*, rational discussion of his reasoning, and suggests specific defense strategies. He believes that if one can prove to one's opponents their illogicality or lack of consistency, their views will change.

To sum up, we can say that what Singer actually demonstrates is that our extremely cruel attitude to animals is in fact thoughtless. It is based on prejudices and has nothing to do with logic. It is an error in logical thinking, which upholds the selfish, primitive desire to preserve the privileges of ruthless exploiters. And if only we were to make full use of our reason—as it deserves—we would perceive how very primitive and incoherent Descartes's logic is.

INSIGHT AND EMPATHY:
CAN THEY BE COGNITIVE TOOLS?

Let us move on to a book by J.M. Coetzee. To me, this is the kind of literature that by simple (or apparently simple) methods calmly and consistently tests everything that seems obvious and certain. The result of this plutonic bookkeeping usually turns out to be shocking.

The Lives of Animals is a special book in many respects. The story of its origin is particularly unusual. When the prizewinning author J.M. Coetzee was asked to give a lecture on any topic for Princeton University, instead of a talk he wrote a novella about a female author who arrives at another first-rate university to give a mini-series of two lectures. Thus he brings to life an acclaimed seventy-year-old author named Elizabeth Costello. From then on Costello is every bit as real as the author Coetzee. And in fact she is even *more* real, because in a way fiction is more powerful than

115

reality, and its characters are more real than living ones. This is the great mystery of literature. Coetzee, the master of detachment, is fully aware of this, and retreats from his own lecture into the shadows, behind the stage that he creates for our eyes.

In her lectures Elizabeth Costello talks about animals, though the audience might have expected a more literary topic. We accept her appearances as real events, as we follow her line of reasoning, but also—thanks to the reader's privilege—because we have the opportunity to be aware of the psychological and biographical context of these lectures. In this way Coetzee seems to be saying that you cannot separate someone's views from the actual person; their judgments and convictions can only be examined in context, in the full light of what sort of person they are—including their connections with the world, their emotions and actions. Thus any expression of views is bound to be subjective, despite what is taught at universities, despite the whole vast institution of learning as knowledge striving toward the utmost objectivity. Our communication is significant and profound as long as it is a mutual exchange of things that are subjective, and thus not entirely communicable. And he is also saying that only literary fiction is capable of relating such a state of human subjectivity; only fiction, with its capacity to construct an entire person, has an advantage over the arguments of reason (and thus over the traditional form of the intellectual lecture).

The heroine of the book is an elderly female writer who has achieved fame and reached the stage of life at which she is bringing the things that matter most in her life to a close rather than starting to explore new ones. She probably agrees to give the lectures out of a need to say something she regards as personally essential, something she feels and thinks, without caring what impression she will make on others, or about prestige. That is why she can afford to be radical and does not

116

shrink from pathos or dramatic comparisons. The topics of both lectures—"The Philosophers and the Animals" and "The Poets and the Animals"—are really an excuse for expressing a very personal, highly emotional, if not indignant attitude to the way people have been treating other living creatures for hundreds of years. How can we possibly fail to see the cruelty that we constantly inflict on them, and how can we fail to react? How does the rational distinction of human beings and animals work, on what philosophical premises is it based and are they trustworthy, if they make us indifferent to obvious facts?

Man's war against animals has been won, says Costello. Now they are our captives and slaves, whom—to justify this abhorrent attitude—we have deprived of the rights of subjects. In doing so, we apply reason, which we consistently deny to animals. "Of course reason will validate reason as the first principle of the universe—what else should it do?" she asks. "Both reason and seven decades of life experience tell me that reason is neither the being of the universe nor the being of God. On the contrary, reason looks to me suspiciously like the being of human thought; worse than that, like the being of one tendency in human thought."

Costello demonstrates how human reason has trodden down and marked out its territory through the example of some famous pioneering research into chimpanzees conducted in 1917 by Wolfgang Köhler. Costello tries to reinterpret it, looking at it from the viewpoint not of the human being, but of the ape being studied. This reveals hidden, probably unconscious, anthropocentric assumptions that entirely undermine the significance of the research. We do not know if apes have reason or not, and whether it is the same as ours or completely different. And if it is different, does its dissimilarity justify our actions?

The two lectures are not just a debate with the philosophical arguments that lie at the foundations of the Western attitude to

117

animals, or just a reinterpretation of the research of ethologists. Through Costello's words—as I see it—Coetzee demands full appreciation for two forgotten, underrated, and marginalized ways of experiencing the world: insight and empathy. He raises them to the rank of equally legitimate, or maybe even more "human" cognitive mechanisms.

In the final scene of the novella, as Elizabeth's son drives her to the airport, he asks her why she has become so intense about animal rights. Her answer is unclear and unsettling: "When I think of the words [I want to say], they seem so outrageous that they are best spoken into a pillow or into a hole in the ground, like King Midas . . . Is it possible, I ask myself, that all of them are participants in a crime of stupefying proportions? Am I fantasizing it all? I must be mad! Yet every day I see the evidences. The very people I suspect produce the evidence, exhibit it, offer it to me. Corpses. Fragments of corpses that they have bought for money . . . Yet I'm not dreaming. I look into your eyes, into Norma's, into the children's, and I see only kindness . . . ."

Costello appears to be one of those people who have seen, realized, or maybe it would be better to say *glimpsed* the basic, horrifying nature of the world, because the word "glimpse" assumes the one-off, individual nature of the act of perception. The fact that we fail to notice horror on a daily basis, that it eludes us, and that we do not freeze in dread, is astonishing. Do we really have such powerful defense mechanisms—all those popular, pragmatic arguments, as well as the ones we find in the works of Descartes or Thomas Aquinas, for example? Could it be ordinary human fear of shock, the habit of being perceptually idle, thoughtlessness, the comfort of ignorance? It is simply enough for us that the world is a given thing, it is as it is. But our perceptual passivity has moral significance—it consolidates evil. By refusing to glimpse it, we become complicit in evil and jointly to blame. Thus a moral effort is actually a cognitive effort—we must *glimpse* in a new, painful way.

Anyone who has glimpsed the full horror of what people do to animals will never be calm again. "[W]e are surrounded by an enterprise of degradation, cruelty, and killing which rivals anything that the Third Reich was capable of," says Costello. This comparison immediately stirs protest and outrage, but Costello does not actually defend herself.

The comparison with the Holocaust that prompts indignation involves not just equating the slaughter of animals with the extermination of the Jews, but also a reference to the problem of mute witnesses to crime, all those who, without killing with their own hands, were silently present when it happened—Germans, Poles, Americans, Britons, all unwilling to believe what they saw in photographs.

Insight is the sudden, comprehensive, spontaneous realization in one go of the essence of what we are perceiving. It is a particular form of perception—multidimensional and simultaneous. What, where, how, why, and with what purpose fitted into one; it is intellectual, emotional, and intuitive recognition all at once.

Insight is a one-off experience. It is a moment, yet it has its consequences that exist in time—it is no longer possible to return to the previous state. The new awareness might be painful and terrible, it might mean the experience of horror that can only be spoken into a pillow. From then on, every event will be added to this new sensitivity and the world will be seen anew—as radically cruel. And one will have to live in it. Costello finds her own way: having once "glimpsed," the only thing one can do is learn to apply her "sympathetic imagination," fellow feeling, or to use the terminology of Western psychology, empathy.

It is empathy that is the topic of the second lecture, and a large part of the debate in *The Lives of Animals* revolves around the

119

topic of empathy. Costello points to philosophy and literature as fields capable of going beyond rational and practical language and becoming a means that enables the human being to understand other beings. Science has led us up the garden path. Despite all the research and scientific experiments, we have not found out, and probably never will find out what goes on in the mind of a cow or a dog. We will speculate and support various suppositions, some of which are deceptively similar to prejudices, by conditioning dogs or constructing labyrinths for rats, while at the same time allowing the machinery of death and cruelty to keep working at full steam.

Why do we accept that animals have no reason or consciousness? asks Costello. As we do not know that, we might just as well assume the exact opposite, right? But we do not.

Anyone who finds themselves in a similar situation to Costello, and thus who has realized that they live in a world where millions of animals are killed on a daily basis, feels the same way as she does—alone, or perhaps insane. They are aware of something that others cannot see. They experience their own helplessness; what can one do? Other people don't even want to talk about it, perhaps because somewhere deep down they do in fact feel guilty. "This is life," Elizabeth Costello reassures herself. "Everyone comes to terms with it, so why can't you? *Why can't you?*" she wonders.

One can talk. In her lectures, Costello tries to say it all at once. She does her best to organize her lecture into calm, logical arguments. But her truth is greater than the argument, it cannot be encapsulated within an academic framework. Her reasoning seems unconvincing to the university members, well-versed in debating; it is easy to refute, mock, cast into doubt, comment on—as Norma, Costello's daughter-in-law does—as just another ego trip. And yet this personal refusal to take part in this extended

120

Auschwitz, ignored by the majority, is an act of heroism, all the more since Elizabeth Costello appears to lose. She fails to convince anyone. Her listeners feel disconcerted.

Like all of us, Costello belongs to a world that enjoys testing and invalidating every possible taboo. But this single, final one keeps us firmly at a distance. Talking about animals, about the suffering of animals often prompts embarrassment, it is "fanatical," like vegetarianism or demanding rights for animals. It is placed in the category of eccentricities, troublesome idiosyncrasies.

The book's ambiguous ending unexpectedly offers yet another way of interpreting it. The consoling, reassuring remark whispered to Costello by her son, who says: "There, there. It will soon be over," could be read as an admission of guilt, but above all as an admission that we are all aware of our own cruelty and we regard it as an integral feature of human existence, a quality of the world. We know that, but we say nothing. At this point Coetzee's work takes on an entirely different, sinister meaning—it becomes a Manichean recognition of the fact that human existence is entangled in a darkness from which the only way out is death.

The publisher of *The Lives of Animals* has supplied Costello's quasi-lectures with commentaries by well-known academic authorities. Thus the situation in the book has been repeated—now Costello's lecture, as written by Coetzee, is being commented on by others. We can see how inspiring and rich his text is, what a variety of reactions it prompts, and how many different ways there are to read it. Isn't that how we should always read a book—in good company? Especially Coetzee's books. Full of gravitas, outwardly very precise and limpid, his prose only seems intellectual, didactic even, at first glance. In fact it uses situations and images that are never fully resolved, and that appeal to the emotions, to common sense, as well as to intellectual debate.

Costello's lectures appeal to other cognitive tools, and the form of Coetzee's lecture—literary fiction—does not provide a starting point for a down-to-earth philosophical discussion. "Coetzee doesn't even have to worry too much about getting the structure of the lecture right," complains Singer when asked to comment. "When he notices that it is starting to ramble, he just has Norma say that Costello is rambling!" Being subjective, and thus also a "complete" person, Costello is bound to be more extreme in her views, and it is also understandable that she uses a different method of argument (if the postulate of the "sympathetic imagination" can be called convincing for a philosopher). To discuss Costello's arguments, Singer contrarily uses the form of a fictional dialogue with his daughter, in which he defends philosophy against Costello's attacks. "We can't take our feelings as moral data, immune from rational criticism," he says, and in doing so refuses to treat empathy as a moral and cognitive category.

Empathy has a relatively short biography in the history of humankind. It probably appeared somewhere in the East at least six centuries before Christ. At any rate, before Buddhist teachings no one ever named or fully appreciated this new attitude—to regard another as if they were oneself, or to mistrust the apparent borderline that separates us from others, because it is an illusion. Whatever is happening to you is happening to me. There is no such thing as "someone else's suffering." Not only do these illusory borders keep people apart, but they also divide people from animals. This is how Costello understands empathy, in the Buddhist way. Between the lines we can hear echoes of Buddhist atheistic tropes: awareness of the situation in which we all find ourselves puts us up against the wall, because not only is there no hope, it also looks as if the world was not created to be good—instead, its foundation is suffering that cannot be avoided. And although we do not know why that is the case, in this vast sea of hopelessness we should behave decently—that is what makes us human, not our DNA. We should behave as if it mattered, as if principles and norms existed, as if some salvatory good existed that will save us and make our actions meaningful.

REASON TURNED UPSIDE DOWN, OR A REVERSAL OF PERSPECTIVE: MICHEL FABER'S *UNDER THE SKIN*

In this novel the demand to apply empathy as a cognitive perspective is given the full literary treatment. The method is very simple. The architecture of meanings to which we are accustomed and that we never think of questioning is completely changed by Faber, who radically reverses our viewpoints.

The book starts with the following situation: we are witnesses to a hunt. An individual from one species is hunting individuals from another. After hunting them down, it subjects them to a special breeding program, treating the hunted body like an object, a potentially valuable, sought-after foodstuff. Once its meat attains a satisfactory quality, the farmed individual is killed, and its body is divided into portions to be sold to consumers.

An everyday story. What is shocking about it? Farming another species is a fact nobody finds surprising. It is a situation well-known to nature—some species exploit others.

But *Under the Skin* provides a different context for the familiar pattern of "A farms and eats B." This seemingly minor alteration changes the book into a horrifying nightmare: it is the human being, homo sapiens, that is the farmed creature here, and another, nonhuman (but also not animal) species is farming them. These creatures are closer to dogs or wolves; their recognition of the differences between their own kind and human beings (whom they call vodsels after the Dutch word for food) is basically superficial— but how very familiar to us. Since they are four-legged, they think

123

of sheep as being closer to them than two-legged, hairless humans. They would never put the flesh of a sheep in their mouths—they would feel that sheep are "too close" to them. But the human being's external features render it "edible."

In fact, we know this feeling. We do not eat monkeys, because they are too similar to us.

Under the Skin essentially casts doubt on the simplest, most atavistic division into *us* and *them*. Faber steers the story in a way that makes us involuntarily identify with the other—the alien. He takes advantage of our common sense and our emotions (including our capacity for empathy), making them yield to the rationale of the alien. He disorients and fools us, causing us to drop our perceptual customs and betray our own species. Like this, he relativizes our moral habits and shows how easily we could get used to accepting the greatest of nightmares and crimes. All it takes is the typical human arsenal, including reason, habit, identification, and rationalization.

Faber presents the greatest paradox of empathy: by abandoning ourselves, we may have the only chance of becoming something that is our antithesis. If otherness is not radical, as one would expect it to be, it loses its magical, threatening power. "The other" becomes someone whom we can understand. In fact they cease to be "other"—there is no "us" and "them." We are all "us," so any evil we do to others, we are doing to ourselves.

MASKS: BEYOND REASON, IN OTHER WORDS, THINGS WE DO NOT KNOW, BUT THAT WE SENSE

In a far-eastern city there is a museum of religion founded by Buddhist monks. It is ultramodern, so technologically advanced that even European visitors, usually quite self-satisfied, suddenly lose their sense of superiority. It is the most extraordinary museum I have ever seen. Each of the great world religions has its own separate room, but plenty of space is also devoted to noninstitutional expressions of human religious feeling. At the end I came upon a room filled with screens showing interviews with people from various parts of the world and various cultures, including scientists, artists, and engineers, each talking about a profound experience that had changed them, a critical moment in their life, what a humanistic psychologist would call a "peak experience."

I was deeply impressed by Jane Goodall's contribution. She described how she had watched some chimpanzees bathing under a small forest waterfall. She saw them not just playing, swimming, and communicating, but also sitting still, watching the flowing water, and observing the falling drops and waves in silence.

Goodall spoke with great emotion about the feelings she had at that moment. She felt as if something profound and vital was happening inside those animals as they gazed at the current, as if they were jointly experiencing change, and thus the passage of time. Of course, although words like "contemplate," "think," or "wonder" instantly come to mind, and it takes a mental effort to avoid them, I must be alert and abide by Lloyd Morgan's memorable instruction about interpreting the behavior of animals. But Jane Goodall did not worry about the recommendations of that Ockham of ethology, and clearly expressed her supposition—as she watched the chimps, she saw in their behavior a kind of thoughtfulness about motion; she saw that they too have the capacity for reflection, for "being in time" in a deep, acute way. And that maybe they experience something similar to our religious feeling.

Research by ethologists is constantly bringing us new information about the psychology of animals. The latest I have heard is about their ability to anticipate events. I have also read research that ascribes to animals something like a sense of humor—a tendency to mislead others for fun.

When I was little, I started to think that animals were a sort of disguise, like a mask, and that their hairy snouts and beaks were concealing another "face," someone else. I spotted this in the case of Saba, a stray dog that led a successful, independent life by taking advantage of our school kitchen. She was one of a kind, very smart, with a highly distinct character. I have never seen it as clearly again, but the suspicion has remained with me to this day.

Have you never thought that perhaps animals have masks, that somewhere behind their ears there are hidden straps or zips used to attach them, and that these masks are just as enigmatic, mysterious, and in a way emblematic as the masks worn by people? So who is hiding behind the figure of the neighbors' cat, and who is that jolly little Yorkshire terrier I see in the stairwell every day? Who are the pig, the hen, and the cow?

Can I put the question that way?

Singer shows us a wide route—this is a road for everyone. We all have the capacity for reflection, and we know how to apply our own common sense. His reasoning can be taken forward so that it becomes understandable for people from various cultures and of various ages. I can also imagine a version for children who study ethics at school.

Costello's road is narrower, as she is fully aware. Why does something that some people find repellent and horrifying fail to move others at all? Perhaps we are psychologically constructed in different ways, perhaps we experience the world on different levels, perhaps our sensitivity is innate and cannot be trained. Perhaps in the end not everyone has the capacity for empathy, and many people simply do not understand what this elderly, in fact nonexistent writer is talking about.

And finally, Jane Goodall takes a very narrow path reserved for those who bring sensitivity, their senses, reason, and the honesty to the task of penetrating prejudices and illusions—and looking through those strange masks and glimpsing beneath them those other, mysterious creatures, our kindred beings that are animals.

Baroque, Montana

RICK BASS

We're larger than most deer, smaller than an elk. Definitely smaller than a musk ox, smaller than a moose. But those are ungulates. Let's slide over a click, away from the hoofed clan, and into the family of the like-minded, our fellow omnivores. Here, suddenly we are giants. Of our terrestrial kin, there really isn't much that's consistently larger—in the continental United States, only grizzly bears. After that, what: otters, coyotes, foxes? Stockbrokers might call us dangerously overexposed. We are the largest, balancing on one foot atop the so-called pyramid in an increasingly high wind.

What I am trying to say in a gentle way is that we are pretty much fucked. It would be so lovely, right about now, waist-deep in the tar pit of the Anthropocene, to look away from the facts, and consider ourselves immune—vaccinated by nothing more than luck, or grace—from this most elemental truth of conservation biology, which is: large-bodied animals go extinct much faster than smaller ones.

In the Paleozoic swamplands, rot was the sweet breath that kept the blue earth spinning before our subsequent arrival. Our creation stories, our myths of that first garden, or rather, our belated entrance into it—are slow-moving, ecologically indulgent.

RICK BASS

The color and mood is green, the theme is biological diversity—
two of everything, whether fishes in the sea or fowl in the sky
or beasts upon the earth. The languor of rot, destruction from
within, which we might view as the fatal flaw to the concept of
eternal life, is in retrospect not a flaw it seems but a catalyst that
propels the whole shitaree of the world forward, and which makes
the elegance of respiration and absorption possible.

Flash forward a few chapters to the *now*. It has taken us a
good long while to get here—three billion years, give or take a
couple thousand sunrises—but we have gone from Day One,
and the sweet first corruption in the garden, to Day Seven: the
apocalyptic, revelatory Time of Fire. All that hullabaloo, all those
sky-is-falling false proclamations that the end days were upon
us—centuries of declaration and lamentation by one tinfoil-hat
sidewalk preacher or two-bit reverend after another, and, look,
they were right: we have finally reached the destination toward
which—or so it was prophesied—we have long been traveling.

And what is rot—what was it ever—but a slow burning?

Let's play the Big game a little longer. Condors? Oh dear. Eagles?
Recovered, for now, but—like us, sponges for the heavy metals
in their food, in the water, in the world, with the lead in their
bloodstream and in their marrow and in their muscles pulling
them down, slowing their reflexes, until they are fast on their way
to becoming something in between an eagle and, what, a cement
gargoyle above a stone courthouse, scowling down at the living
who enter and exit each day?

Vultures? Still here. Plenty of food, it seems. Ivory-billed
woodpeckers? *Ah.* Dodo? Well, *shoot.* Whooping cranes? Ah,
dammit.

Robins; sparrows. The meek are still with us. The large are
always vanishing, and we ourselves have become so—large.

130

*   *   *

As a child, I saw the immense dinosaur footprints near Glen Rose, Texas, and the fiberglass and papier-mâché T. rex approximations in one museum after another—Jurassic gigantism growing upward and outward to the max. There seemed to be enough space in the world for everything to keep getting larger, more dramatic, more specialized—faster, stronger, more cunning, more amazing, body and brain size growing—but then came that darned asteroid, which was *not* in the earth's plans, and the giants went away, leaving the world to start over again, which, since the sun was still shining, it did, enthusiastically, if with fits and starts.

More pertinent to our own story than Jurassic dinosaurs would be the Eocene, and the rise of the age of mammals, the decidedly unmeek, dramatized in museum dioramas of the La Brea Tar Pits—of tooth-and-claw scrum. The fanged meat-eating giants sinking their saber-toothed teeth into the bulging haunches of wild-eyed prey: meat, all of it, galloping beneath the sun, comprised of sun—the epic bounty of equatorial heat, swampland, veldt and fen, meadows and marshes, grasslands to the horizon—rolling, liquid sun, spilling out each day with each shake of the dice. Both prey and predator were made of sun, and warmth, of heat, and there seemed to be enough space in the world for everything to keep getting larger—more cunning, more amazing—and then those giants went away too, mastodons and saber-toothed cats, both predator and prey, the result of another asteroid of sorts, but not one from outer space or a universe beyond, but instead a homegrown kind of asteroid, an experiment still very much in progress: the self-titled, self-anointed *Homo sapiens*, replete with a reassuring roster of gods and demigods.

Naked to the world we worshipped, blindly and understandably, at first, the most primal, irreducible elements: earth, wind, fire, but then, as we became more intimate with the earth, we turned toward the greater, older beings amongst us—wolf, raven, lion, owl. Bear. The one most like us. We'll come back to that one later.

And then we refashioned our demigods into a more user-friendly one-size-fits-all God—in Christianity, at least, an omnipotent dude pretty much in our own image, or the image we liked to project as our best look.

I don't know what comes next. Or if there is anything next. I think after that omnipotent being, all there might be would be one another. And when that's gone—hell, maybe that went flying past, last year—only loneliness. The emptiness that well might have been the seed that started it all off.

Why are we here? We are, I believe, of the earth: which is to say, we are carbon and phosphorous, we are hydrogen and nitrogen, oxygen and calcium—really, nothing all that rare or complicated. We are not made of moon rock nor even, somewhat sad to say, stardust.

Let's look at the flip side of our make-it-up-as-we-go theology: that we did not build our god, are not in the process of building our God, but instead, as one prominent religion suggests, we are the build-ee of a home, constructed of clay firmament and fed by this one green garden we inhabit; the one sea, one sky, one continuous forest that we call earth.

Whether God-in-the-stars or God-in-the-dirt, in the soil, in the stone: it seems fair to say that if this planet desired to create life, desired to create a thing larger than the sum of its scattered chemical elements we currently portage across our 72.6 year lifespan, or our species' 180,000 years and counting—

If it desired and conspired to produce, so late in the game, yet another work—yet one more of so many, and us leavened with enough of our tendency toward destruction, chaos, disassembly—then what is our responsibility? Isn't that another way of asking what are we here for? Some days I don't think even the world or God that made us has figured it out yet. I know for damned sure we haven't.

What are we here for? Maybe it's the wrong question. Christianity has tasked a holy triumvirate with saving souls through sacrifice and, well, there's no other way to describe it, blood violence. I'm not here to hazard a guess whether a god made us, or we made our God, or if the relationship is somewhat of a collaboration. Instead, I want to go back in time to the previous administration: but what I mean by previous are the demigods whose best qualities we revered and once looked up to. For if we have gotten a bit off track as a species, metamorphosing our One-God into an eternal field marshal for what I hope is not unending generations of Christian soldiers marching as if to war—it might be worth pausing for a moment to look back at our previous demigods, what few of them still remain; searching the past in the manner I suppose of a man or woman who has dropped something important—eyeglasses, or maybe keys—in the grass, and who has become lost. The grass being the last place we can collectively remember being before we got lost.

One example would be the buffalo, a ceaseless, protean orchestra of ecosystem renewal, redistributing sunlight across the prairie and never staying long enough in any one place to damage the land, but instead stimulating and fertilizing it: so much so that this continent's indigenous people referred to the rejuvenating qualities of wildfire as "the red buffalo."

The end was coming but we did not know it yet. We would learn, dammit. The American ecologist Aldo Leopold said, one hundred years ago, in essence, that to possess an ecological awareness is to understand that we live in a world of wounds.

133

The wolf: pack-loyalty and endurance; the grizzly: power, maternal wisdom, and a keen sense of play, keen sense of joy, rarely seen that much in our own brooding, benumbed, frightened species.

I grew up in Texas, playing in the forests along Buffalo Bayou where I always hoped to find a buffalo skull in one of the bayou's ever-sloughing banks, but never did. I was born in the late fifties, was a child then of the sixties and seventies—my God, the music. Music was one of our deities and demigods, as recently as sixty, even fifty years ago. So too was the moon, particularly in Houston.

I'd been born in Fort Worth, free-spirited country cousin to neighboring uptight Dallas, where, I was reminded for long decades, JFK had been assassinated. Only in recent years has that line of accusation become blurred, but it had a sharpness back then, particularly to a five-year-old. *I didn't do it. We didn't do it.* But we did. We all did. We did it with a handgun, and with a rifle. Texas—Dallas—just happened to be where the needle stopped. As it stopped for Bobby Kennedy in Los Angeles. For Martin Luther King Jr. in Memphis. For Medgar Evers in Jackson, Mississippi. For George Floyd in Minneapolis.

Back to our demigods. Even in a land of myths, the moon was a really big deal in Texas in the sixties. Apostate daughter, big old chunk of rock blasted off from us, floating and adrift, it is theorized, related to the earth by blood chemistry but with no visible means of support, no water, no oxygen, no photosynthesis, no gravity, no fire—just a lovely frozen-ass lifeless place. It was a place just beyond our reach, so *of course* we had to try to walk on it, and to worship the attempt.

And once the moonwalk was achieved, we forgot about it. In Houston, ours was no longer a moon-crazy culture. *Conquered*, we told ourselves. Onto other hobbies. So that demigod, too, once mighty, fell from our portfolio of myths and dreams, and we realized soon enough the distance had never really been all that impressive after all: that a well-heeled Delta Platinum traveler, in circling the earth several times in but a single business season, might just as easily have gone to the moon.

As storytellers, we would do well to reconsider the role of the animals that were once our demigods, looking back to do so, to a time when we were more attentive to the natural world that supported us. Tolerated us. I'll note again that we were most drawn to the charismatic megafauna—buffalo, wolves, grizzlies—whose habits and histories we knew through our keen attention and our interest in them. Not coincidentally, these big animals are ecosystem drivers: influencing and shaping pollination, hydrology, population size and demographics of prey as well as predator, forest type—in short, doing what gods do: shaping, lathing, sculpting. *Creating.*

To pay attention to such details is to treat them with the dignity and respect any living thing—ourself included—deserves. Now, alas, we use them not even as symbols for those qualities we no longer know they possess, but instead merely as mechanisms for the sales of Arctic Cat ATVs, Grizzly chewing tobacco, and Elephant Car Wash.

A bit of a pagan, I like to think our demigods were actually true gods—what the poet Jim Harrison called "little gods"—and that when biblical directives warned us against worshipping false gods, they were referring to the gods of commerce, not grizzlies or wolves. There is nothing at all false about a grizzly.

We have eradicated, or are in the last stages of eradicating, the giants above us—in the sky, our condors and cranes, and upon the land, our grizzlies, musk ox, and polar bears—there are giants beneath us, though they, too, are so imperiled, where

I live, in northwest Montana's Yaak Valley, one of only about one hundred fifty people, and *maybe* twenty-five grizzly bears. There are immense sturgeon a few miles to the west in the Kootenai River, and paddlefish, large as submarines, just to the east in the Missouri River. It takes a lot to support a giant fish, giant bear, giant hope, giant dream. It takes space, time, shelter, food . . . But it works both ways. The big animals—the demigods—cannot exist without the ecosystem intact, and yet the ecosystem cannot exist without them. Depending on whether one is an optimist or a pessimist, one might view this elegant, balanced equation as either a miracle or a conundrum.

What some might call a conundrum, however, a poet might call beauty. These demigods make the natural world—our world— possible. Grizzlies aerate the alpine soil that would otherwise develop into impermeable hardpan and pollinate forbs and huckleberry bushes. They direct the flow of all things. My friend Doug Peacock says the four paws of the grizzly pin down the skin of the earth to keep it from blowing away. Wolves keep herds of elk and other ungulates from overgrazing riparian areas, so that songbirds coming up from Central America, chips and flecks of color that reawaken our souls, can nest . . .

I do not believe the world is about us, or our souls; I want to be clear about that. We have barely arrived at the party. We are new here. We have no function or purpose, yet, other than to be who and what we are, bipolar schizoid wrecks of good and bad, sublime and ridiculous, angels and renegades, beautiful and monstrous. We are new, we are rookies destined to ride the bench for a while—several hundred thousand more years, or a few million?—until the world figures out what to do with us and how, or if, we may be of service.

Our survival depends upon this decision, this fix, this answer— if there even is one.

All we need right now to survive are manners, and yet we are failing even at cultivating those.

And yet, always, paradox: the world desires things—big things—things that will be big and raucous. Things that hurl, yawp, leap, plunge, rip and roar. But remember: we are, or were, somewhere in the middle. We need to honor—in our stories and in our lives—the demigods. To learn from them. To grow toward them—not to seek advancement by cutting them down and erasing them. What a ridiculous notion. We are not yet ready to become gods or even demigods. We just got here. We just got here.

I want to talk a little about the Kootenai National Forest in northwest Montana—specifically, the Yaak Valley—the last place the ice left, when it last went away. A chunk of public land about the size of Yellowstone National Park, but with no federal protection. A land of fire and ice—the most northern and western valley in the state, yet also with the lowest elevation. It's the wettest valley, and—this is important—the most biologically diverse.

It's a land of giants. Great gray owls with wingspans four feet wide; pileated woodpeckers with three-foot spans, hammering the spars of fire-gutted larch trees that were birthed a thousand years ago. Lynx, moose, mountain lion, elk, wolves, wolverines, and, oh yeah, grizzly bears: twenty of them remain. It's the rarest population in the world.

We will remember that Darwin, when writing about this jackpot we're in, used the phrase "*descent, with modifications.*" Not *Lateral Branching With Modifications*, not *Horizontal Exploration of Various Opportunities*, and certainly not *Ascent, With Modifications*. He knew the drift of things. He saw in the Galápagos—in his short five weeks there—what he was afraid of seeing, and what he wanted to see. A way to reconcile the six days of Eden and the hand of God.

137

He saw a business plan that would allow a rank newcomer like ourselves the hope for, well, shooting the moon, gaming the system, winning it all, despite being mere rookies at the gig of life. What he overlooked was how newborn the Galápagos were: the islands, barely ten thousand years old, were still steaming, like a cake just taken from the oven.

What he saw however but did not know he was seeing was not the hierarchy of man atop all-else nature, but instead a doctrine, or doctrine-to-come, of diversity. There just wasn't enough diversity there yet for him to see it or know it. It was all still too new. He couldn't yet be expected to know—not in the Galápagos, at any rate—about sophisticated societies of cooperation rather than the brute muscle of so-called "fitness." He saw what he saw: the Patriarchal Deity School of—*wait for it*—Survival of the Fittest.

What few species were in the Galápagos, building nests with their funny beaks and waddling around with different-shaped turtle shells—were not the fittest. They were the luckiest. Someone seems to have forgotten their theology for a brief idyllic equatorial vacationing moment. The Galápagos tortoises he saw were just the ones that got lucky and floated to this strange little brand-new island at the nexus of three major ocean currents. They were simply lucky the sailors coming back to port in Peru and Chile tossed them overboard, having a few extras whose throats they did not need to cut for either moisture or meat.

There was not diversity, yet, in the Galápagos; hence, there was no need yet for the intricate systems of cooperation that are the gearworks, the great engine, of life, and the signature of time. The determinant as to whether a species goes extinct, or advances, a little further and farther into the light.

* * *

In the Yaak Valley, there is diversity. Fully twenty-five percent of Montana's species-of-concern are found in this one forest. Forgive me, in this, a literary lecture, for dragging in natural history yet again. Long ago a creative writing professor told me that people don't want to read stories about trees, or beavers, or raccoons, or any other kind of animal, they want to read stories about people, about people like themselves. I understood what he was saying and believed him but did not follow his counsel and so began for me a lifetime of poverty and literary estrangement. But oh, the things I see, in the woods.

When you have a lot of diversity, you have a lot of social cooperation. You have to. There's no room for greed. Greed is so 1980s, or, in the case of the Galápagos, so 8000 B.C. The ravening exploitation of every available space *was* a thing—despite his short stay, Darwin did see what he saw. But he saw Day One in a blissed-out Garden of Eden. Days four, five and six were, as they say in Texas, where the nut-cutting began. Where imagination, creativity, leverage, stacking, integrating, cooperating, time and resource management, came into play. Social unity, where when one thing quivered or shuddered, everything else felt it. It was the way of the world before we blundered in. It was, once the world became full, the only way. What Darwin saw was a snapshot of the earth at birth—not the complicated, mature, paradoxical, immense seven-day wonder it would become.

And I wonder: what comes after the fire—after the big fire, the one we are already in the middle of? The only thing that can follow fire is ice. We came to this land, traveling across a bridge of ice, and funneling down the coast, and along the Rocky Mountain Front, still walking atop a shell of ice, hunting and killing all the big things before us—mammoths, mastodons, whatever—until

139

we had killed them all, the last being the plains buffalo, and then we turned to farming.

It all went by so fast.

Who are we, and what stories do we tell, now that the giants are leaving, and we—formerly the meek—have inherited this still green but definitely fraying-around-the-edges earth?

There is more fire coming, but the ice might also be coming sooner than we think. The earth spins on a tight axis, due to the polar caps clutching each end tightly; the earth rotates the way a hard-boiled egg spins more tightly than does a yolk-sloshy raw egg. As the polar caps melt, however, the earth will tilt a fraction of a degree off-plumb, which will change dramatically our rates of exposure to solar radiation. Things could—will, I believe—get very cold, very quickly. As if a loving god had decided, finally, to turn his or her gaze away from us for ten thousand years, or a billion, whatever,

Only ice can follow such fire as that which we now approach.

Spinning as fast as we are, of course we are dizzy. Our points of reference, points of attachment, are shifting. String theory indicates we are all but an extraordinarily high degree of probability, vibrating like crazy—shimmering, is how I imagine it.

How fast the world spins, though surely not as fast as the humming, vibrating coil that is *probably* us. Maybe that's how time gets away from us—in the disparity between our hum, and the earth's. Make no mistake, the earth is winding itself around the axle at a pretty good clip: 460 meters per second, or 1000 miles per hour (it's rotating once every 23 hours 56 minutes and 4 seconds—if anyone can figure out where all those leftover fractions go, I'd love to hear about it). I imagine the earth, bobbing in the dust and ice of black space, being lathed, spinning in the firmament of time, throwing off more dust, and occasional sparks. To get a real sense of how fast a big thing can move, watch a trumpeter swan flying across a river sometime. It seems to be merely *flying*, like any other bird. And when seen high overhead, their slow wingbeats seem leisurely, almost as if they are but floating. Watch one pass right by you, however, traveling down a swift river, catching up with and then passing some spinning plate of sunlit current, and you see how each double oar-pull of white wing carries the immense bird forward such a great distance at a pace that's disorienting: the swan seems as fast as a cheetah.

Let's talk about cheetahs, about ghosts. There was a cheetah in North America that made its living chasing antelope, but then the antelope outran them all and the cheetahs went extinct, so that now the antelope wander around not knowing what to do with all that speed—an echo of the thing that made them who they are. Who they were.

It is a rule of paleontology that once an organism begins developing baroque adaptations to an increasingly narrow niche, or an increasingly vulnerable social network, it's fast on its way to extinction. You can see it in the trilobites in the Wellsville Mountains in northern Utah; you can read, in the layers of stone, the increasingly desperate, ostentatious, futile efforts to fit into a place that no longer wants them. They have become lost.

Let's talk more about the bizarre: the sudden arrival, the experimentation, of a hairless mammal with no claws or fangs, who could not and still cannot last more than three days without water. We are the lost.

Geology suggests that in hard times simplicity is pretty much the ticket to survival. The beast of time does not seem to pay as much predatory attention to the simple, but relishes the baroque. As do we. Time the destroyer; humankind the destroyer—of everything, and therefore our selves.

＊　＊　＊

There are perhaps twenty-five grizzlies left in the Yaak. I've always been partial to burying the lede—maybe it's the geologist in me—but we lost one of the most vital, an adult female, last November, to poachers who, after shooting her, tried to cut off her paws, but found the task too hard, and dumped her in a driveway and fled.

There were local rumors that the female had been seen earlier with three—three!—cubs. A miracle, that number—usually the most they have is two; grizzlies are the second slowest-reproducing land mammal in the continental United States. The government says she didn't show any signs of having cubs, but if they were old enough they wouldn't have been nursing. So it's possible we lost four—one-quarter of the entire population and, as well, a devastation, for no young bears' bodies were found. No orphan cubs were sighted wandering the forest. Maybe it was just her, enormous. Maybe it was all four of them, enormous. There's no way they could have survived winter without her. She was killed the day before grizzlies traditionally go into hibernation.

I *do* want to write stories about people. I do. People can be interesting. But really, we are so new, so plastic; so undeveloped, yet. The old ones—the demigods—are, to me, so very much more interesting. I watch them. I try to watch them closely. I try to listen. Attentiveness is a kind of love, and, I think, a kind of prayer, too.

We must protect them.

Without them, we are lost.

CAMONGHNE FELIX, poet and essayist, is the author of *Build Yourself a Boat* (Haymarket Books, 2019), which was long-listed for the 2019 National Book Award in Poetry, shortlisted for the PEN/Open Book Awards, and shortlisted for the Lambda Literary Award. Her poetry has appeared in *Academy of American Poets, Harvard Review, Literary Hub, PEN America, Poetry Magazine*, and elsewhere. Her essays have been featured in *Vanity Fair, New York Magazine, Teen Vogue*, and other places. Felix's next book, *Dyscalculia: A Love Story of Epic Miscalculation*, is forthcoming in February 2023 from One World, an imprint of Penguin Random House.

In Some Thousand Years

CAMONGHNE FELIX

The rats
and the jellyfish
will survive.

The roaches and the
capybaras
will survive.

The mosquitos, the fruit flies,
the puggles and their soft beaks of
post-apocalyptic adolescence

will certainly
survive.

It's us—malignant tumors of
ominous origin, contagions
of hominid conceit—that won't.

And, anyway, of what use
would it be if we did?

Another dreadful century
gone

to vainglorious apathy and
glamorous afflictions, gone
to the silver nostalgias of war.

In some thousand years, the stars
will be too far to see, the negative space
of the sky a new bruise on our progeny.

In some thousand years, a child
of my blood will gaze up
at the bowl of the night and long for a memory.

Humans live
to find meaning, to make fine record
of some urgent, collective Why.

Imagine, then: a dusk
not littered with stars. Can you?
And, anyway—of what use

would meaning
be then?

LILY TUCK is the author of seven novels, three story collections, and a biography of the Italian writer Elsa Morante. Her novel *The News from Paraguay* won the National Book Award and she is the recipient of a Guggenheim Fellowship.

Let the Memory Rise

LILY TUCK

I

The little girl and the bear walked into the wood. The wood was dark and deep. Soon the path the little girl was on disappeared and soon she was lost. The little girl had to climb over fallen branches, push her way through prickly bushes, once she had to wade through a cold stream. Hungry, she ate a few bright red berries then retched them up. Night fell. Exhausted and cold, she sat down, her back against a tree. Overhead the sky was dark, racing clouds hid the stars. Above her, an owl hooted. Something slippery slid over her leg. Clutching the bear, she finally fell asleep. The bear was stuffed.

The girl went missing for three days. Notices with her picture were posted all over town. The local radio made several announcements. A search party combed the area where she lived. How far could a little girl have gone? Rumors spread. A crazy person must have abducted her—raping and torturing her and leaving her body in a ditch or on some abandoned road. Wasn't a known pedophile living over in the next town? What was his name? A crime. The search party continued to search. Her parents were more and more despairing. Holding hands, they appeared on television making a plea to the suspected abductor. The mother was in tears.

Polly T., who lived not far, saw one of the posters as she was leaving the grocery store. She stopped to read it. She thought: "What is this world coming to?" Once home, she called her friend, Marcy K., who spoke at length about the state of the prison systems in America and the lack of efficient safeguards against potential criminals, etc., etc. That evening, Marcy K. also spoke to her friend Melissa V., who offered: "If the kid is lost somewhere, she would have died of hypothermia by now."

II

The little girl, Laura, now a young woman—clearly, she was found—has no memory of the event. None. Her parents do not speak of it. And since they have moved to another town—her father was relocated—no one there speaks of it either. In the past, her parents had consulted a psychiatrist who had advised them not to mention the incident. "Let the memory rise," is what he had told them. But so far it had not.

Dr. Heilman, the psychiatrist, a Freudian, normally said very little. In this case, he had to say something. "Let the memory rise" seemed only appropriate.

III

Married with two children of her own, Laura lives in yet another town, a big city actually. Her husband works for a well-known advertising firm. One of his clients is a well-known paper company that specializes in feminine hygiene products. For some reason that she does not want to think about or explain to herself, Laura finds this embarrassing and wrong. What could he possibly know about menstruation? She herself uses the cup. To taunt him perhaps, she often leaves the cup in the sink.

Before Laura married and had children, she also worked in advertising—although at a much smaller firm—and it is how she met her husband. Her products were mostly specialty foodstuffs—rice crackers, seaweed snacks, dried exotic fruits—items that had a short shelf life. Now, officially, she is a homemaker. Sometimes and particularly when the children were very little—a boy and a girl only fourteen months apart—and she was exhausted and resentful, she thought bitterly of herself as merely a homebody. Ha.

IV

Now, again, many years later and in her mid-fifties, Laura is divorced. She has declared herself gay or, more correctly, queer. She has cut her hair very short, wears shapeless clothes and ugly, sensible shoes. She is a caricature.

She has also begun to write poetry. Ah! Her poetry is not bad, but not very good either. A few of her poems have been published in literary journals. One of the published ones goes in part like this:

> A foot to stand on
> The man exclaimed
> As the rain fell in sheets
> As the grasses greened
> The woman sat silent
> Her legs folded neatly
> underneath her like shelves

Laura does not use punctuation if she can help it.

V

Amanda, Laura's partner, works at the local college, in the admissions office. Her mantra is "Diversity! Diversity!" If it was solely up to Amanda, no straight white students would ever be admitted.

VI

Laura's children are grown. The boy is a stage manager for a theater company in Minneapolis; the girl works in a bank. *High up in a bank, or just sitting in a little cage, totting up things?* Laura, quoting Noël Coward, is tempted to ask her but does not. Her husband, ex-husband, is retired. He is also remarried to a woman named Nancy. Nancy? Such an ordinary name.

"No," she tells Amanda, "I am not upset that he has remarried. I've told you this again and again. I am not angry either," she adds. Although she sounds a little angry when she says she is not angry. Why is that always the case?

"I am not angry," she repeats to herself, practicing not sounding angry.

Nancy is a highly paid lawyer at a prestigious white-shoe firm. And both children like her.

VII

The phrase "white-shoe" comes from the white bucks worn by Ivy League college students in the fifties. It alludes to a stereotype of old-world firms populated by the WASP East Coast elite. The term has antisemitic and racist implications. Or did. Or still does.

Best not to get Amanda started on Nancy and her career.

152

VIII

Abandoned years ago, in the woods—still one must not forget—
the teddy bear and the little that is left of him? of her? (Are all
teddy bears automatically thought to be male?) A brown-and-
yellow glass eye.

IX

Besides writing poetry, Laura works at an independent bookstore.
The pay is minimum wage and she often complains. She also
complains about having to lift heavy cartons of books—books
she has never the time or opportunity to read. Her favorite part
of her work at the bookstore is advising clueless customers:

*I have to get a book for a sick friend—she doesn't really read
a lot, but something to cheer her up . . .*

*My niece is graduating from college and I want to get her a
book—maybe a cookbook . . .*

*It's my turn to choose a book for my book club and I want
to choose something that isn't too long . . .*

*I can't remember the name of the book or the name of the
author but it's about this young boy whose father . . .*

Laura ignores these requests. Instead she recommends books
by:

Lorrie Moore, Alice Munro, Susan Minot, Natalia Ginzburg
(she is Italian), Louise Erdrich, Tessa Hadley (she is British), Amy
Hempel, Joan Didion, Isabella Hammad (the family is from Palestine), Zadie Smith (she too is British), Joy Williams. All women.

X

Usually, weather permitting, she bicycles to work.

153

XI

Laura's favorite poets are: William Butler Yeats, Philip Larkin, Elizabeth Bishop, Keats, W. H. Auden, Emily Dickinson, and Gerard Manley Hopkins. She likes poems that have a narrative— is how she puts it. The poetry, for instance, of John Ashbery, Anne Carson, Louise Glück intimidates her. She does not understand it and "No one likes to feel stupid" is what she tells Amanda if she speaks of it.

Amanda's favorite poet is Billy Collins. Amanda particularly likes his poem: "Fishing on the Susquehanna in July"—in fact, she can quote the whole thing by heart. The reason Amanda likes the poem so much, Laura suspects, is that Amanda likes to fish, although the poem is purportedly about not ever going fishing.

XII

Amanda has what is called an eidetic memory. She can look at or read a page and instantly know it by heart. Amanda can remember exactly what she wore, what she ate, what she said at such and such a date. She can remember each student's application form, name, date of birth, etc. This too intimidates Laura.

XIII

On the other hand, Laura worries that she is losing her memory. Especially her memory about little things: Did she remember to lock the front door? Did she already take her vitamin B12 pill? Did she . . . now she can't remember what she was going to do. To try to remedy this condition or what she perceives as a condition,

Laura does crossword and sudoku puzzles, she subscribes to Luminosity, she attempts to memorize poetry.

XIV

Speaking of not remembering—Laura does not remember what drew her to Lucie Brock-Broido's poetry. Perhaps her obituary and the look of her—her long blonde hair.

> ... *I am born into the dark*
> *rococo teratogenic rooms of the underground.*

What, Laura wonders, does the word teratogenic mean? (A teratogen is an agent that can disturb the development of the fetus—halt the pregnancy or produce birth defects—such as radiation, a maternal infection, a drug.) And what does that verse mean exactly?

The poem is based on a real-life incident—that is the part Laura likes. On October 14, 1987, in Midland, Texas, eighteen-month-old Jessica McClure (according to Lucie Brock-Broido's endnote) was playing in her aunt's backyard and fell into an abandoned well shaft. She was not rescued until fifty-eight hours later. Her ordeal was highly publicized by the media.

XV

Laura does not show the poem to Amanda. She is not sure why. Only that she wants to be the only one to have read it. She wants the poem to be hers. This cannot be true since Laura knows that many other people—perhaps hundreds or maybe even thousands (she does not know how popular Lucie Brock-Broido was, only that she taught at Harvard and won prizes)—have read it. She also wonders if Jessica McClure read the poem later when she was older and whether like the psychiatrist claimed (again according to Lucie Brock-Broido's endnote) Jessica, although physically battered, suffered no psychological trauma from the experience and would have no memory of it.

XVI

Polly T., who lived in the same town from where years ago Laura disappeared, now lives in a nursing home. She has Alzheimer's and recognizes neither her family nor her old friends of whom not many are left. Mostly she is incoherent when she speaks although, from time to time, she does say Laura's name out loud and repeats it in an insistent way, but when a nurse's aid or one of the volunteers at the nursing home asks Polly T. who this Laura might be—a relative? a friend?—Polly T. falls silent or is again incoherent. Marcy K. died several years ago of an aneurysm. Her death was sudden and swift: one minute she was slicing peaches in her kitchen, the next she was lying on the linoleum floor dead. The only one left of that threesome is Melissa V. who conceivably might still remember the incident and who if one really stretches one's imagination and if one really believes in coincidence might—might just—on one of her rare visits to the city where Laura and Amanda now live, might also just happen to go to the bookstore where Laura works. Once there, Melissa V. might ask Laura if she can recommend a book about the city—a guidebook—since she is fairly new to it and would like to do some sightseeing, and Laura, who is by nature friendly and fairly inquisitive, might, in turn, ask Melissa V. where she is from. Melissa V. would then tell her.

Oh. I lived there as a child with my parents. My father was an engineer. He did a lot of the buildings in town, says Laura.

Oh, interesting. What was your father's name? I've lived in the town all my life. I know practically everyone, answers Melissa V.

Laura tells Melissa V. her father's surname.

Melissa V. repeats the name slowly.

Yes, the name means something to me. Let me think. Oh, I know—

Melissa V. pauses and looks hard at Laura before she continues to speak.

XVII

It had started to rain on the day that Laura spoke to Melissa V. and, on her way home, on the wet pavement, Laura's bicycle skidded into a delivery van that was making an illegal U-turn. Laura fell, hitting her head and breaking her arm. In the emergency room of the hospital, it is determined that Laura has suffered a concussion and that the bone in her arm, the ulna, needs to be surgically realigned with a plate and screws.

Dr. Sanchez, the attending physician, is very reassuring. Before leaving her, he pats Laura's good arm in a familiar way. Summoned, Amanda arrives right away and she, too, is consoling. In great detail, she describes to Laura how she once broke her leg while skiing Gunsight, a black diamond run at Alta in Utah, gesturing with her hands to show Laura the run's steep entrance slot. Amanda was taken down the mountain on a sled by the ski patrol and that, she tells Laura, was almost the worst part—the pain while she was being jolted along at high speed. The ski patrolman's name, she also tells Laura as an aside, was Martin.

An unusual name and another reason Amanda remembers it now, thirty-or-some years later. Martin was Swiss, Amanda continues, and good-looking in a Swiss kind of a way. (Laura wants to ask Amanda what she means exactly by "good-looking in a Swiss kind of a way," but she does not have the energy to ask.)

XVIII

On account of her concussion and the severe headache that accompanied it and the Percocet she was taking Laura could not remember much about the bicycle accident. She certainly could not remember the name of the paramedic who had lifted her from the street onto the gurney and put her into the ambulance. She could not even remember, she told Amanda, trying not to laugh, what he had looked like. As a matter of fact, come to think of it, Laura said, she could not remember much of anything that had happened to her that day.

XIX

Asleep—Ambien induced—Laura dreams that she is walking by herself in a wood. The wood seems familiar and, in the dream, she is not lost or frightened. Instead, she is enjoying the solitude and quiet as she looks up at the tall trees, wishing she could identify them more easily—oak? beech? maple? Bushes and brambles line her way but do not impede it. Some of the bushes have red berries on them but she knows enough not to touch or eat them as they might be poisonous. She comes to a little stream and taking off her shoes she crosses it. The water is cool and pleasant on her bare feet. Deeper and deeper she walks into the wood but, in the dream, Laura is still not frightened. When night falls and the wood is completely dark, Laura sits down, her back against a tree, to rest. Above her, an owl hoots. She shuts her eyes then quickly opens them again when she hears a loud rustling noise. Unexpected, and standing large and dark in front of her on its hind legs, is a bear.

XX

In the dream, Laura and the bear converse:

You haven't changed at all, the bear tells Laura. *I recognized you right away.*

Me, too, Laura replies. *You look exactly the same.*

XXI

Laura wakes to a sharp pain in her arm. The surgery is not scheduled for another two days and she wonders how she will cope. Thank God for Amanda. And she wants to tell Amanda about her dream before she forgets it. A peculiar dream, she thinks, and she wonders what it could mean.

"Did you have a teddy bear when you were a child?" Amanda asks when Laura does describe the dream to her—although part of it is already half-forgotten.

"No." Laura shakes her head. "I had a lot of stuffed animals, but no bear."

"I had a bear," Amanda volunteers. "One of those expensive German teddy bears. I adored him. Hansi Schmidt—I gave him a German name," Amanda laughs. "I made him clothes—pajamas, a hat, all kinds of stuff"—Amanda pauses to again laugh—"And I took Hansi Schmidt with me everywhere," she continues. "I took him with me to college and even when I got married—"

For some unclear reason—maybe she is afraid that Amanda's talk about her own teddy bear will further erode the memory of her dream that she would like, at least for now, to try to keep a little intact—Laura does not let Amanda finish her sentence. Instead, she interrupts to ask Amanda, "What is good-looking in a Swiss kind of way?"

XXII

Back at home, Melissa V. wondered whether she had done the right thing by telling the woman at the bookstore how she must have been the little girl who got lost in the woods and how it was front-page news and all people in town talked about for days. The woman had looked so surprised and was so uncomprehending that Melissa V., embarrassed, had tried to backtrack and had stammered something about how perhaps she was mistaken and how her memory was not always reliable on account of her advanced age. Then, she had hurried out of the bookstore without buying a book.

XXIII

Laura is tempted to tell Amanda about the old woman in the bookstore—how strangely she had acted and what she had said. Clearly, the woman was deranged. But the odd thing, in retrospect Laura thinks, was how, right after the woman had hurried out of the store, Laura suddenly remembered an incident in her childhood. She must have been five or six and she and her mother were having tea with a relative, a great-aunt, who lived alone in a large house, and she had had to use the bathroom during the visit and the great-aunt had given her directions, up the stairs.

"Shall I go with her?" Laura's mother had asked.

"No, no, she'll find the bathroom by herself," the great-aunt had answered. "She must learn to be independent."

Laura had found the bathroom all right. She shut the door and without thinking she turned the little lock above the handle, locking the door. Afterwards, when she tried to open the door, she could not turn the little lock. It was either stuck or she was turning it the wrong way. Panicked, she began to cry.

In the end, someone had come—two men. They had knocked out the lock and made a mess of the door. The men had been sympathetic and had made light of the situation—they even had laughed about it—but her mother was furious. Laura does not remember the great-aunt's reaction, only that they never again went back to her house. But she remembered, clear as day and as if it was yesterday, that feeling of claustrophobia, that feeling of being trapped.

SAMIYA BASHIR is a writer, performer, librettist, and multimedia poetry maker. Author of three poetry collections, most recently the Oregon Book Award–winning *Field Theories*, her honors include the Rome Prize in Literature, Pushcart Prize, Oregon's Arts & Culture Council Individual Artist Fellowship, and two Hopwood Poetry Awards. Sometimes she makes poems of dirt. Sometimes zeros and ones. Sometimes variously rendered text. Sometimes light. Called a "dynamic, shape-shifting machine of perpetual motion," by Diego Báez, writing for *Booklist*, Bashir's work has been widely published, performed, installed, printed, screened, experienced, and Oxford comma'd from Berlin to Düsseldorf, Amsterdam to Accra, Florence to Rome, and across the United States. Bashir's poem "Here's the Thing:" erupted through a collaborative choral process with composer Julian Wachner for The Washington Chorus. Its debut performance is forthcoming. An Associate Professor at Reed College in Portland, Oregon, Bashir lives in Harlem.

Here's the Thing:

SAMIYA BASHIR

Here's the thing: things fall apart.

I am sort of sleeping then
I am on fire. Undone. Burned.
Stripped of skin I feel so
raw these days. Flattened.
Full of doubt. Numb.

Rats thrive in sewers so
maybe I'm thriving. It may seem
simple enough but my dreams don't
say so. This I think I know: no one
notices me. Lost. Alone. Blind
as a sewer rat. Six feet back. Gelatinous.
Raw as a baby rat. Shook. Underdone.
Too-full rat still hungry. Rich rat swimming
sewage. Breadline rat. Baker rat. Transformed. Stuck
in a well. Thriving. Burned into brick
road. Milepost. Sign.

Triumphant. I scream but
words burn like skyfire. Clammy.
Street rat. Fell in a hole. Stuck
in a well. I rattle the cages of our
children. Everywhere else
is empty. I am fluent
in fire. Fluent in indigo miseries.

I am fluent in the absence of heat.
A rat on the street. Sudden and melt.
I am fluent in how time presses
a body. Here's the thing I'm not
supposed to say I saw others skulk
the dark like me. Simple enough.
I skulk away a little more each day.
Maybe there's intelligent life
but I'm not it. How will we survive this
having a body? Trying to be
intelligent life? Fireball struck and stuck.
I study the crows who know this—having
a body to fly.

Almost a dream. A sign
you're not supposed to notice. A path.
Who can I be? Blame the apocalypse.
Its melt. Its bends. It never ends.

Thing is: things fall apart.

I am not saying I'm a prophet but
I know the meaning of a moment
like ours. Burning. I'm almost sure
I'm here. Transformed. Torn apart.
Average. Boring. Humdrum. No sound
stays innocent. Numb. Every day

the end of the world is now again. Normal.
I burn and remember having a body. How
it feels. Cold. If I hold no beauty in this slapdash
world, then tuck me away from the heat of the day.

Alone. I burn. Blame the humdrum
numbness of the end of the world. I listen
for the wind. Intelligent life: where is it? No sound
an innocent means. Route. Way. I am

not saying I'm a prophet but I always travel
slightly singed. Pressed by time. Six feet back
I find the me who's tall as a gum tree, the me
with copper hair. Causeway me. Opening.
Expanse.

Eyes open, heart full of doubt.
I strike my fireballs and burn. Sort of
dreaming. Now volcano. Now oil-slicked
river. Stripped of skin. Fluent
in the press of time. Body clammed. Voice
raw and syrup stripped. Eyes open. Sewer rat.
Thriving. No sound stays innocent. Rats.

Footpath. Corridor. Clearing and
yes the bushes burn like skyfire. And
I decide to survive. Claim every sunrise.
I am dark as earth. Now I am me with the
bright yellow hair. Me with a normal
girth—wait—

Normal? Do I know that word? Did I ever? Is it
normal to hang from a tree? Is normal an ability
to breathe? Are normal these panic attacks?
Does normal stand whole bodies back? Tucked
away from the heat of the day, listen for how to survive
this body. Face twisted. Slightly singed. Fueled
by my own crisped flames. Condemned.

I know the meaning of a moment but here's the thing:
Am I intelligent life? Pffft. How could I tell? The crows know.
I know I'm not road. I'm doorway. And when things fall apart
again I'll be here—my rectangular shade of blue. I'm not
supposed to talk about transformation though. Not the me
with the hollow cheeks. The me with the bloodred stride.
Fluent in the need to dance.

Me with moles in fourteen places. Here.
Having a body. Me with three nose rings. Normal.
I grasp for a branch. Normal. Me with the war wounds.

I thrive. Gutter rat. The burning quiet of stars.
Who else can I be? The crows know.

SASHA TAQʷŠƏBLU LAPOINTE
is a Coast Salish author from
the Nooksack and Upper Skagit
Indian tribes. Her memoir *Red
Paint* is available through Counterpoint Press and her collection
of poetry *Rose Quartz* is forthcoming from Milkweed. She lives
in the Pacific Northwest.

First Salmon Ceremony

SASHA TAQʷŠƏBLU LAPOINTE

"What kind of Indian are you?" my uncle asked as he dropped a thirty-pound fish into my arms. It was Christmas Eve. I was seventeen. He had instructed my cousins and me to join him in the driveway, and we dutifully lined up alongside his car on the icy pavement. Our gifts, he told us, were in the trunk. One by one he presented each of us with a massive salmon, straight from the trunk of his car, frozen and unwrapped. We exchanged nervous glances, bit down on our lips to keep from smirking or erupting into laughter. We probably wanted Discmans or gift certificates to the skate shop. We wanted something from the mall. We were teenagers. But instead we held in our outstretched arms King Salmon. I stood there, snow lightly falling in my blue hair, breath puffing out from my black lips in cold clouds, and said to my uncle quietly, "Uncle, I'm a vegetarian." The statement is what prompted his question. He shook his head as he turned around, asking once more before lumbering back up the driveway and into the house, "What kind of Indian are you?"

My uncle was an artist, a carver, a painter. He danced in the longhouse. He had an art studio in Pioneer Square. His voice boomed when he spoke and he wasn't afraid to yell at the kids. He called my mom "Jilly Bean," and though he was often so

169

stoic he was almost unapproachable, there was a softness about him, a deep care for us. He was ridiculously handsome too, a white woman once told him he looked like "a real Hollywood Indian." From a young age I'd been driven by an insatiable need to impress my *cool* but terrifying uncle. I drew him pictures. I wanted to be an artist like him, I'd say, before presenting him with stacks of what I thought passed for art. Once I even traced every page from my *Beauty and the Beast* coloring book, a small lie to impress my artist uncle. As I stood there in the snow, holding the salmon, I felt shame swell up in me. I wondered, *What kind of Indian was I?*

Shortly after that Christmas I sat in my Seattle apartment still wondering. The salmon was in the freezer, next to the vegan chicken nuggets and the Tofutti Cuties. I called my cousin, an engineering student at the University of Washington. He took the bus across the city with his sister, his backpack carrying his own fish and a six-pack of winter ale. Together we baked and ate the salmon. We laughed about pulling fish from the trunk of a car on Christmas. We reminisced about running barefoot along the Nooksack River as kids, building forts, putting on elaborate circus performances for bored relatives. We talked about the city, his school, my job at the busy restaurant. We'd both made it so far from the river. The salmon was *good*, good like when we were kids, good like we were transported back to summer gatherings and surrounded by family, good like in the backyard of our great-grandmother's house, good like it was done the traditional way over a fire on ironwood stakes and not in the shitty oven of my basement apartment, no uncles or fathers tending coals, nothing but the posters of Nick Cave and Joy Division watching over us. We finished eating and drinking, played the last record on my turntable, and my cousins helped me clean up before we said goodbye. The fish had been my favorite gift that year, but I told no one, not my vegan roommates, not the vegan drummer I was dating. I kept my dietary transgression secret. The next day I threw the bones away so no one would see, but the question remained. As I closed the lid to the trash can I knew I had done something wrong. I had been raised better than that.

My Coast Salish ancestors believed in honoring their food. It's hard to believe I am descended from people who celebrated their food so beautifully when I'm devouring a bowl of ramen, bought in a package of four for a dollar, unceremoniously on the couch while watching bad eighties and nineties movies in the dark, but that's my ceremony. Coast Salish tribes are salmon people. It's one of our main resources. The first salmon of the season was meant to be honored. The fish was carried on an ornate plank dressed in cedar boughs and sword ferns and brought into the longhouse with songs and dances. There was always a big feast following the ceremony in a tribal gymnasium where everyone came together, laughing, sharing stories, but most of all eating. Paper plates piled high with potatoes and greens, soft dinner rolls bought in bulk, and a giant piece of fish. I'd run through the grass along the water, climb the bleachers, horse around with the other kids. We'd line up along the big buffet tables. We'd wait for the elders to get their plates, then we'd rush the table in frenzy, salivating over the metal chafing dishes, the piles of pink fish inside.

I have always been a shitty eater. As a child I favored plain cheese over pepperoni. I never wanted toppings. I picked things off my plate to dumb down the food. If it was Taco Bell I only ever wanted a bean and cheese burrito, no onions. My palate didn't change as I reached my teens, but I did become vegetarian. When I was eleven I spent a week out at my uncle's home on the Nooksack River to visit my cousins. The land was big and curved along the river. Stretching meadows and old-growth forest made up the property, and my cousins and I swam in the river, ran along the trails, and picked berries. We found salmonberries and thimbleberries. We filled our fists with wild huckleberries and snuck into the raspberry fields across the farm road, filling up big metal mixing bowls that we would beg my aunt to turn into a pie. I have berries tattooed on me. Right next to my tattoo of the cassette recorder Agent Cooper uses in *Twin Peaks* I have a stem of thimbleberries inked into my skin. I also have blackberries and huckleberries, and a half sleeve of sword ferns decorating my body. Along with the terrible punk tattoos of my early twenties I have adorned myself with the things that mark me home. I didn't plan them out. It's as if my body knew it needed a map, a way to remember where I came from.

When I went to visit my uncle for a week when I was eleven I met a woman named Dream. My aunt and uncle had let her build a yurt on their land. My aunt and uncle had hippie friends and the tribal land was big enough to let families build little cabins, homes, and yurts. Dream was intoxicating. Looking back I may have had a small crush on her, this radical white woman with a sweet name who lived in the weirdest house I had ever seen. Dream was cool, knew about music, and had a nose ring. When dinner came Dream did not have salmon, but salad. Only salad. I was inspired by this. She was a strict vegetarian and that night out on the Nooksack I passed on the fish that I loved and became a vegetarian. Perhaps if I could pass on fish I could pass on the bad things too, like the trailer we lived in on the reservation, the times we had no power or running water, the times we only ever had things out of cans to eat. Perhaps if I could stop eating animals I could grow up to be a woman alone, in a yurt, with a nose ring and a cool name.

My new diet stuck, even when Dream did not—she eventually packed up her yurt and went on to whatever new, white hippie adventure lay ahead. Maybe she went to Burning Man. Maybe she went to Santa Fe. My staunch vegetarianism remained, much to my mom's dismay, who let out a sigh and an eye roll every time her now twelve-year-old daughter said she couldn't in fact eat chicken enchiladas with the rest of the family.

My diet grew more strict as I left home. At fourteen I met the first boy I loved and together we figured out how to eat vegetarian as teen runaways. We asked for spare change until we had enough for a bag of forty-nine-cent burritos from Taco Bell. I remember the first home-cooked meal I made him, a cheese and pickle sandwich in our friend's kitchen at midnight.

The first girl I loved had a more refined palate. Together we'd sit on the curb of the Skagit Valley Food Co-op eating a picnic of French bread and spinach dip, hummus and figs laid out at our feet like we were Grecian goddesses. In Seattle I met punks and activists. I fell for anarchists who devoted entire afternoons to making huge pots of lentils to supply whatever Food Not Bombs event was in the neighborhood. At the shows I went to I learned about PETA and heard stories of radical activism while a band's music rang out into the parking lot. While punks emptied entire cases of beer into themselves they told me about factory farming and the evil realities of the dairy industry. Eventually I became vegan. It was only a matter of time. Still whenever I returned home to attend a gathering I smelled the salmon baking. I eyed it along the buffet line as the elders went before me, huge servings of fresh pink salmon steaming on their paper plates. Everything about the fish made my mouth water, the silver skin and its scales, the white bubbles of fat oozing from its tender flesh. I would quiet the hunger in me with the tales of overfished oceans, of orca whales dying. I was doing the right thing, I told myself. But still the question clung to me each time I would politely mouth a *no thank you* to whomever was about to serve up a portion of salmon onto my plate. During the feast I'd look down at my sad

173

meal, the iceberg lettuce, the mashed potatoes, and the Costco roll, my plate full, but still so empty. I'd close my eyes to my uncle's disapproving face.

I ate hummus, I ate it all the time because I was always hungry. I didn't know what else to eat. I would come home from an eight-hour shift of waiting tables, stand over my sink, and shovel handfuls of baby carrots and broccoli into my face. All the while this huge fish-shaped hole began to grow in me, no matter how many kale salads I ate I was starving. This is how I passively fell into a colonized diet.

My ancestors' diet was also colonized. Pre-contact they existed mainly on salmon, shellfish, wild berries, and bracken root. They ate things like elk. On reservations they were given commodity foods, things they had never had before, like lard, flour, salt, and canned beef. Once someone asked me what our traditional food was. *Indian tacos, right?* They were amused by this. *Fry bread? Right?* Wrong. This food was introduced to the first people post-contact. It's a colonized food. The people who lost their lands, their hunting and gathering places, the places they fished, were introduced to these foods by the United States government. Fry bread was what they came up with. It's a defeated food.

The first time I recognized commodity foods on television I was watching *Roseanne* with my white roommates. It was late. A band was sleeping over and we all huddled on the couch in my communal house in Seattle, sharing vegan pizza and beers. On TV, Roseanne opened the cupboard and yanked out a bag of chips in a white bag with big black lettering that read POTATO CHIPS, bold and simple. "Oh my god," I laughed and pointed. "Look, reservation Lay's!" My mouth fell open in a dumb smile. I looked around at my friends, waiting for their joined laughter, that sound of a roomful of people all getting the joke. But the group was silent. Eventually a friend chimed in to say something about television series not having the rights to name brands. Something about licensing and endorsements. Something about Pepsi. The conversation shifted, but I couldn't stop thinking about the black-and-white cans of food, the black-and-white boxes and bags. I had seen the same label, the same black lettering against a white backdrop when I was growing up on the reservation. Fruit cocktail in black-and-white. ORANGE JUICE, SHREDDED CHICKEN, APPLESAUCE, and even just MEAT in a can in a cupboard with dozens of other identical cans in my friend's house in the third grade. We had opened all the cans of peaches that day and ate them in her driveway. That night I took some cultural inventory. Each of my friends, my weirdo, disenfranchised, misfit, *white punk* friends had never seen a cupboard like that. I think of this every time one of my vegan friends examines a label, holds it close to their nose to read the long list of ingredients to determine whether or not the food in question meets their standards. This is a privilege. This is a luxury.

I learned how to stay quiet. I learned how to stay hungry. I went to vegan grocery stores looking for what I craved. They had plant-based chicken, beef, and duck. They had every cheese imaginable made with cashews. But they never had salmon. The closest thing I ever found was a thin, unnaturally bright pink sheet of lox. It was like a salmon-flavored fruit roll-up. It was awful. Still I spread it out on a bagel with vegan cream cheese, underwhelmed. I felt lonely as I ate it. I looked at its odd pink color and wondered how they made it. It's easy to accept that your diet has been colonized when you think you've chosen it. In my teens and twenties I convinced myself that if I somehow denied the part that made me Coast Salish, the part that made me Indian, I could be as carefree, radical, and punk as the people around me. That I could be more *White*. I didn't know how badly

175

being hungry would quiet me. I was quiet at dinner parties and on dates, at vegan potlucks and brunch outings. It always came back to, "See, you don't have to eat animals, look at what they're doing with soy and tempeh."

I hadn't realized how lonely I had been in my diet until my second year at the Institute of American Indian Arts, when I accidentally ate venison. I had joined the Students For Sustainability Leadership program. I had a crush on the teacher, who maybe slightly reminded me of Dream, but she was cooler, like cared-about-wolves-and-listened-to-Neko-Case cooler. We planted traditional medicine gardens, raised campus awareness on climate change, and held recycled-fashion shows. Once a month we'd have a potluck, and at one of those I accidentally ate venison. When a vegan accidentally eats meat it's usually followed by a stage-four meltdown, a fit of rage, and most likely a bad case of the shits. None of this happened to me. I was cruising along the buffet line, chatting with my teacher crush, and absentmindedly scooping things onto my plate. Grilled veggies, beans and rice, a tortilla, and finally a cup of red chile stew. We all sat at the big table in the student lounge excited about our upcoming projects. I took a giant spoonful of the red chile into my mouth, then another, and another. It was *good*. Halfway through my meal I began to wonder why my fellow sustainability leader was talking in detail about killing and dressing a deer. He kept motioning to the stew. With my mouth full of the delicious red chile it occurred to me he had brought the stew. I sat with it on my tongue before swallowing. I looked at my friend as he continued his story of how he learned to hunt, how he was part of his tribe's hunting society, how he knew to use every part of the deer, even the hide.

With the stew still in my mouth I closed my eyes to the only memory I had of seeing a deer carcass. I hadn't yet moved to Seattle, but I was dreaming of it. Instead I had only made it twenty miles from the rez and into the woods, to a kind of punk rock never-never land. The white guys who'd built the cabin had also built a skate ramp, a huge half-pipe in the middle of the towering old growth. They held bonfires, punk bands played, and people partied. They prided themselves on living off-grid, on sticking it to the man. They had their own water system rigged up, a generator for power, and were even working on a woodburning soaking tub in the middle of the forest. One morning after a party I walked the trail that led to the creek. I stopped in my tracks. In the hot midmorning sun a deer carcass was swinging from a rope above me. The smell rushed my face like a punch and I quickly covered my mouth, a fistful of vomit caught in my hand. I trembled before stepping back, unable to look away. Its dead eyes were dull and black, like two dark plums, dry and rotting. It hung from a tree in a cloud of flies, eviscerated, its flesh and guts pouring out onto the ground. A wave of nausea hit and I threw up again, this time onto my shoes. I ran to the creek still shaking. I fell to my knees and plunged my hands into the cold water, sobbing. The people who killed the deer were staying at the cabin sleeping off a hangover inside. They had come to sell drugs, and party, and apparently to shoot things. I looked around my surroundings, at the old Icehouse cans, cigarette butts, and motorcycle parts littering the forest. What the hell I was doing out there? My *cool* friends, hellbent on living off the land, making their own place in the woods, off-grid, had trashed the place, had killed something just to kill it.

I blinked the rotted deer out of my mind and came back to the table, to my friend talking about his tribe's hunting society. He talked about how to properly dress a deer, how he had taken his time, how he had thanked the deer for its life. Then he talked about the stew itself, how he had roasted the chiles, as his grandparents had shown him. I swallowed the stew. I wasn't grossed out, or suffering from a stomachache, or any guilt about having eaten the deer. Instead I felt nourished in a way I hadn't in a long time. Like I was back at one of our tribe's feasts. I knew at that moment that I wanted to decolonize my diet.

My time at tribal art college in New Mexico opened up my diet to a world of traditional foods. I only ate meat if it was prepared indigenously. At the grocery store I still bought vegan, but through my school community there was an abundance of indigenous food. I tried elk and bison, and whale cut traditionally with an ulu. I drank Douglas fir tip tea and found a book about traditional Coast Salish foods. I learned how to harvest nettles for stew and felt closer to food than I ever had.

But when I graduated and moved back to Seattle I was no longer surrounded by my indigenous peers. I tried to maintain my diet. It was useless. I found myself at a dinner party with friends. We all enjoyed a vegan stir-fry and I told the story about the venison. "Ew," the girl next to me interrupted, "that's horrible! You didn't spit it out?" A shame so big and heavy swelled up in me that I went quiet. I didn't know what to say, the faces of my friends, my nonindigenous friends, stared back at me. There was no indigenous meat around me. One morning, I found myself staring at a package of bison meat at a Whole Foods. I held it in my hand, twenty dollars worth of grass-fed, organic buffalo. I hated it. I hated the wild caught salmon, the overpriced vegan options. I hated the looks on my white friends' faces whenever I talked about fish. I had no idea how to decolonize my diet from this city. I went back to my vegan ways.

When people ask me if I'm vegan I'm still unsure of how to answer. I still don't support factory farming, or the dairy industry, and even if it were safe for me to eat I have no desire to eat a thing once living. Except salmon. I am wired to want this food. Like the genetically inherited high cholesterol passed down to me through my ancestors, I have inherited an appetite for salmon. I cannot shake this craving.

Last January I took the Californian I have been falling in love with to the beaches and rivers of the Pacific Northwest. I wanted to show him the water up here. He grew up tropical. He grew up in the sun. I wanted to share with him the grey stony shores of my childhood, the midnight-dark waves crashing on the jagged rocks. We drove to the Nooksack River first and camped along the water in the meadow. He met my favorite cousins, I picked him salmonberries and thimbleberries and he shivered when we jumped into the icy waters of the Nooksack. "This isn't California," I teased. My cousin showed me an ironwood stake he had carved, and we talked about the summer gatherings in our grandparents' yard.

Then I took him to the ocean, to a beach I have always loved. On our way we stopped at a trail in the Hoh Rain Forest. Near the northernmost point of Washington state I stood with the Californian in the woods. He stepped over the wet roots and stones. He admired the old growth; the way everything here was draped in moss. I stood at a small wooden sign at the base of a berry bush. Carved in wood the sign identified the plant, both in English and in the Quileute language. It read "Salmonberry." I smiled at the word. As my date snapped photos of giant cedars and dew-covered sword ferns, I crouched down. I bent at the sign as if in prayer. My stomach rumbled for something that was not packed in our cooler full of fancy vegan snacks and kombucha beers.

We left the trail and headed to the beach. As the coast came into view we listened to moody synth music and snacked on hummus and crackers, but I couldn't stop thinking about salmon.

We neared a small reservation. I began to notice handwritten signs for smoked fish. I snapped like a rubber band. I pulled over and turned down "Catacombs," by Cold Cave, on the stereo. My date eyed me suspiciously, curiously looking around, and asked me, "What's up?" I took in a breath. The Californian was a devout vegan. He had been for over a decade. I worried what he might say. I worried about judgment. An embarrassing memory flooded my thoughts, still stinging though it had been years. I'd brought smoked salmon to my ex-husband's family for dinner once. I was raised never to arrive empty-handed to a home where someone has invited you for a meal. I had brought my grandmother's smoked salmon dip. Proudly I set the dish on the counter and laid out the crackers. An exaggerated gasp came from the room over. "Ewww," my ex's mother complained, covering her nose and wafting the air dramatically with her hand. "Something stinks, did someone just open fish? It stinks!" There was emphasis on the word *stinks*. Quickly and shamefully I tucked the offensive dip into the fridge, next to all the bougie Whole Foods groceries typically found in well-to-do white people's fridges. The fish spoiled in the fridge over the weekend. Before my ex and I packed up on Monday I washed the bowl out in the sink when no one was around to smell it. The hot water and lavender-scented suds erased the fish from my fingers.

Now with my new date on the side of the road next to the grey ocean I felt tears forming in the corners of my eyes before I launched into my statement. "I miss my family," I blurted out. "I miss my great-grandmother and my uncle. I miss my cousins and my grandparents' backyard." Cold Cave still droned in the background as my date looked back at me, concerned and curious. "I miss the way my uncle baked the salmon on the fire before my great-grandmother told stories." Tears were now streaming down my face. "I know you planned to make vegan clam chowder, and you know what, I *am* excited about that. But I want to eat a fucking salmon!" I said it defensively, poised for battle, my face red like children after they cry.

180

The Californian laughed. It was a warm laugh, a sweet laugh. He shook his golden hair to one side and smiled at me. "Let's get you a frickin' salmon, babe." And just like that he eased the guilt, the shame, whatever had been growing in me since I was a teenager. My whole body had been stiff, rigid with defense. I felt it relax.

"Oh." I was stunned. "You're not grossed out? Or like, mad or whatever? I'm totally breaking veganism." The Californian explained he not only understood, but that he supported it. He knew this was important to me. I was shocked, so used to the disapproving looks and combative judgment from my hard-core vegan friends. The Californian had surprised me. We drove into the small reservation which looked like the reservation I grew up on. Houses too close together, appliances decorating the lawns along with stacks of firewood. We followed the signs that read "smoked fish," until the arrows brought us up a driveway. An old fishing boat and rotted nets lined the garage. I smiled a big smile.

"This is where you get fish," I told him before enthusiastically hopping out of the car. I glanced back at my date, checking for any signs of hesitation or uneasiness. Up until that point I wasn't sure if he had ever even been on a reservation like this before. The one I lived on was tucked into the city of Tacoma, masked in urban sprawl. This was different. This was coastal. Fewer cafes and gas stations. Fewer white people. I looked back to find him totally at ease, working on freeing a tangle from his long hair as he stepped over discarded pieces of fishing equipment. My heart relaxed. An old man answered the door wearing a dirty white shirt and a big grin. We greeted each other and told one another where we were from. He nodded when I told him I was Upper Skagit and Nooksack. I told him I was looking for fish.

"My son's the only one fishing the river here now." He brought out his big plastic bins of fish. "No one else is doing it like him these days, not since I had the last stroke. Four strokes I've had. I'm not fishing anymore," he said matter-of-factly while laying out the different sizes of shrink-wrapped smoked salmon, a sense of pride on his face. I bought two big pieces and thanked him.

That night the Californian made his vegan clam chowder. I spread out salmon ceremoniously on a big dinner plate. I brought the fish out to the towering piles of driftwood and together we watched the waves as they crashed along the shore. I told him as best I could one of my great-grandmother's stories from memory. We drank fancy cocktails and played Scattergories next to a fire. I beat him. Twice. I had two servings of fish and he never mentioned the smell. This fish was good, soft and salty, covered in a thick glaze from being smoked. It broke apart in my mouth, melting. I closed my eyes to a rush of smoke. I was back at the salmon ceremony, I could smell the smoke rising up through the burning cedar, making its way through the body of the fish.

There is no more salmon east of the mountains in Washington state. Some Salish tribes are no longer able to practice their salmon ceremonies because the rivers are too polluted. They have to buy their salmon from someplace else. I thought about my salmon privilege, how foolish I had been to deny it. I walked to the water's edge and stood with my toes in the tide, my belly *finally* full of fish. As the waves ebbed at my ankles the Californian joined me beneath the stars. He put his hand on the small of my back and told me he loved me. This time I heard it differently, heard it in a way that made me feel seen as a Coast Salish woman, as a woman who comes from salmon people.

When we celebrate the first salmon of the season we honor it. We have dances and songs and a big feast. After the fish has been eaten the people walk what's left of King Salmon, his bones, his head, and his tail, back to the water and return him. They do

182

this so his spirit can travel back to his people, to tell them how we honored him, to ensure his return. I began to wonder if my family would always be able to practice their salmon ceremony. I knelt down, with a fistful of the tiny white bones picked off my plate. Crouched down on the beach I emptied the small bones into the waves. I whispered into the darkness, thanking the fish, the man who caught it, and the ocean for its abundance.

This was *my* first salmon ceremony. It wasn't perfect. There were no songs or stories. My regalia wasn't woven from cedar. I stood in rolled-up jeans and a Joy Division T-shirt. Soon I would turn back and join the person I loved in our cabin, where we would play Judas Priest and dance before getting into a giant Jacuzzi tub. I felt a gratitude start to rise up in me, mixed with the faint grief I carried still. I mourned the time I spent looking elsewhere for nourishment, and I grieved for the eleven-year-old kid who longed to be white, *all the way white*, the kind of white that lived in a yurt and knew about animal rights. I grieved for the girl who fell in love with anarchists and tethered herself to their values, for the silence she let herself learn. I grieved for not going to the Nooksack River enough, for not speaking my traditional language enough, for ever missing a single word my great-grandmother might have said. Mostly I grieved for ever not eating the salmon.

I thought about my uncle's question on Christmas.

What kind of Indian am I?

I guess I'm the kind of Indian who will never be vegan, who will never again teach herself to be hungry or quiet. The kind who will bring the smelly salmon dip into your white fridge. I am the kind of Indian who will always be bad at making fry bread, who loves picking berries, and driving along the coast listening to darkwave and synth-pop. I am the kind of Indian who will never hide who she is again, and who will always eat the salmon. As long as it returns to us.

183

STUART DYBEK is the author of two collections of poetry, most recently *Streets in Their Own Ink*, and six books of fiction. His work has received a Guggenheim Fellowship and awards from the Lannan and the MacArthur foundations.

The Art of Breathing

STUART DYBEK

1 *AN UNNAMED BOAT*

A theory on the descent of Man has it
that humankind evolved not from bands of monkeys
in the trees, but from a lost race of aquatic apes.

That's why our skin is bare—better to swim—
and why, unlike baboons, we copulate ventro-ventral,
face-to-face, as dolphins do, and whales, and manatees.

Such fantasies enchanted me. I lived knee-deep
in books about the sea, above a cove where I'd anchored
a boat bought from a descendent of the Huguenots,
one of the clannish fishermen known locally

as Frenchies. His son, Antoine, was in my class.
I left the boat unnamed, as it had always been,
but it was freshly painted, a wooden petal the hue
of a poppy, afloat upon transparent blue.

2   *INITIATES*

That summer, school over, we taught ourselves
to live off what we caught. Grouper heads,
not turned to chowder, baited our lobster pots.
We dove for conch and when the tide was low
gathered seaweeds and sea urchins for their roe.
Our bodies grew leaner. We fashioned cowries
into fishline necklaces we wore, self-ordained
initiates of Yemaya, Mother of Fishes.

I saved for Show & Tell, the teeth
from the tiger shark I found one noon
washed up before a failed hotel, eerily deserted,
overgrown like an ancient ruin on the still wild,
windward shore where I spear-fished alone
as if protected by a goddess, each day free-
diving deeper. My ears cleared effortlessly.

3

Love was like that: effortless, submerged.
We slept to the rhythm of disintegrating waves
below, and the rattle of a wind chime
we'd made from shells stacked like china bowls
before the entrance to an octopus' cave.
But night rose from the bone-deep city
left behind. I was a caseworker again,
my district burning, mothers guiding children
through ash: sirens, gunfire, a lake the blue
of dome lights, lashing a Gold Coast
graffitied in blood. I learned to dive by watching
cormorants flip through the flash between
water and air. I practiced breathing as if it were
the art of making a single breath last.

4

Breath was a secret that the turtle, dolphin,
and cormorant refused to share. I'd never be able
to emulate the great sigh of breaching animals,
but I learned a breath, taken as if to hold a note,
had no time for the past. Call it rapture
of the shallows, yet I swear once off Congo Cay,
a school of spotted eagle rays opened a place,
and I flew, one of a flock. A loggerhead
with a barnacled shell towed me to the drop
beyond Caraval Rock, where I had to let go.
I yearned to hold my breath as if I could break
the habit of breathing, and for a few minutes
it seemed possible to renounce the world of air.
For a few months one summer, I almost learned
to give up wanting more than I already had.

KALI FAJARDO-ANSTINE is
the author of the novel *Woman
of Light* and the short story
collection *Sabrina & Corina*,
a finalist for the National
Book Award, the PEN/Bing-
ham Prize, and winner of an
American Book Award. She is
the 2022/23 Endowed Chair
in Creative Writing at Texas
State University.

Star

KALI FAJARDO-ANSTINE

I was at a different club a couple years earlier when I first heard the story, how a man stepped through the side door in broad daylight, wielding what some said was a Rawlings and others said was a Marucci, but the brand didn't matter, only that it was made of wood, and he marched past the private rooms and white velvet couches, head gleaming pink and bald under red lights, lifting the bat and swinging hard against the first girl he saw, table six, a dancer named Star. He slammed into her left leg once and then heaved upward, the bat blocking the disco ball light as it came down on her face, the blow sending shards of bone through the girl's skull. She dragged herself across the table, kicked at the man with her good leg, her face simultaneously leaking blood outward as her teeth collapsed inward. Another girl pulled him back by his white, stained T-shirt, then another and another, the man swaying like a bear, the girls swarming like hornets. Star got away, hobbled outside into the sunshine parking lot, where first responders found her on the asphalt, belly down and palms out, the tiniest stream of blood leaking from her face into the gutter.

"And the craziest part of all," said a drunk man next to us, a vodka-tonic to his lips, "she kept dancing for a while." He laughed. "Until they heckled her. Called her Half Face."

"I heard," said another man across the table, "they called her sucker punch."

"Still, smoking hot," the drunk man said. "Mexican-Asian or some shit. What a waste."

The men laughed, everyone but Phil who had flown into Denver that morning from LAX. He was heavily bearded, tall, a chemist who worked for cannabis companies. He loved Burning Man, vintage motorcycles, and drugs. I'd found Phil on a dating app, a sugar baby site, really. In our unofficial arrangement, he paid me an allowance twice a month, sent to my Venmo with a black heart emoji. His last name was Medina, his father's parents from Argentina, his mother a white woman from Connecticut. He had never been married, and had a thing for waitresses and strippers. I was a waitress when we first met, but I lost my job during the shutdown, and then I was denied unemployment due to an overpayment five years earlier. Phil was my only source of income, the way I paid rent.

"This exact club?" Phil said, and removed the paper mask hardly covering his mouth and nose to sip from his old-fashioned. He cupped my left knee beneath the table, tried passing a baggy of cocaine between the chairs.

"Stop," I teased, pushing it back. But I was serious. I didn't want to get kicked out, or worse. I had once been an addict, but that was years ago.

"Fuck no," said the drunk man. "In the ghetto, somewhere off Federal." He dropped folded dollars like tents on the table's vinyl edge. Our dancer slinked toward the money, masked and blonde, her top already gone, breasts natural and petite. She collected her dollars, allowed the drunk man to slip them beneath her G-string, an elastic slap.

"Why'd he do it?" I asked.

"What?" The drunk man edged back, directing the dancer to hover her face above his lap.

I repeated my question, and all the men laughed, this time even Phil, who made me feel very far away from him as he did. The dancer came toward me then, asked from beneath her glowing pink mask if I'd like to see something, and I said of course. She moved onto all fours, reaching across the table, stretching her torso until her buttery hair swept the stage, her ass nearly touching my face, the triangular patch of blue fabric covering her pussy pressed outward, centered in a V. Phil placed a twenty between us.

"Probably wasn't getting any at home," the drunk man said.

Phil laughed, drank heartily. "Pathetic."

That night he took me to the Four Seasons. A room near the top, walls of windows in the dark. Beyond the city there were lights across the mountains, glimmering pieces of gold, speckled among the foothills, trailing into the stars.

"Get on the bed," Phil said, unlooping his belt with a clink. He was wealthy and his clothes were heavier than mine. He smelled of clove oil and whiskey. Only in his mid-forties, his skin was beginning to sag, on his belly, under his jaw, and small red veins spiraled his nose.

I smiled in a way I thought he'd like, open-mouthed, lots of teeth.

He came from behind, forced my face into the down comforter. "Play dead," he said.

I did what he wanted, pulling my red dress around my waist and moving my underwear to the side. I lay there, cheek to the cool bed, staring into the open bathroom, the tub an enormous porcelain bowl. He did things to my body then as I thought of being somewhere else, a small boat on a warm lake in the mountains, the sky blazingly white with clouds.

In the morning, Phil stepped out of the bathroom fastening a silver watch to his left wrist. I had Googled the designer while he was asleep—it cost more than the few semesters of college I attended before dropping out. I stood at the window, gazing across Fourteenth, the desolate stream of the city. Barely any cars. Windows boarded up. Homeless staggering over concrete. A crew of kids on bicycles weaving in looping figure eights across the avenue before the empty opera house. The day was bleak with sunlight and in large red letters, written across the sidewalk: "Be Nice OR Else."

"Wish you could stay longer," I said, turning around. I didn't mean it, but it seemed like something I should say.

"Me, too," he said, and pulled me close by the back of my head, his hand pressing into my brightly dyed red hair, a color he said suited me. "But you'll be with me soon, in sunny California."

I had only visited his house once. He lived in gentrified Silver Lake, where the narrow driveways were filled with Teslas and BMWs and fallen palms. He flew me first-class into LAX, picked me up in his vintage truck. His taste in art wasn't notable, but there was an instrument hanging above his bed, reeds pulled together into something musical. When I asked what it was, he said, "Who knows? Cambodian or some shit. Thought it looked sick."

"Just another month," I said, hardly understanding what I had agreed to when I said I'd live with him when my lease was up. "Do you want to see my place this time? It's only a few blocks away."

Phil kept his face to his phone, fingers beating. "No time, Raquel."

An hour later, he dropped me off in the shadow of my building, slipping two hundred dollars into my purse before driving away. "Bye, Little Red."

* * *

My building was named Hornet Moon, built over a hundred years earlier when one mayor or another wanted Denver to be known as the City of Lights. It said so in the lobby. The façade was covered in fixtures, broken and brown lightbulbs, 1910 carved into white stone. The place was an almost-slum. The windows were painted shut, the power was often out, and the pipes were made of lead. The city had recently delivered Brita filters to our doors, explaining they hoped to replace the plumbing within fifteen years, half my life.

That morning, I spent a few hours packing, mostly winter boots and old jackets, stuff I hadn't worn in months or years. My apartment was a high-ceilinged studio with an Ikea princess bed my big sister had given me, a red lumpy sofa, and a kitchen table that I had proudly pulled myself from the dumpster. It was long and green, dark tiles in the center. I loved that table, and late at night, when I couldn't sleep, the world pressing down on me with all its worry and sadness, I'd bead necklaces and earrings at that table, something my grandmother had taught me, something that had come from her grandma before her. Now it was piled with boxes of family photos, my sister and her kids, our parents, a dead childhood dog named Sara, all black with camera-flash eyes. It felt like a breakup, leaving Denver, but I couldn't afford another place on my own and Phil had grown tired of paying my rent, especially when I could live with him for free. He assured me, with airlines practically giving away flights, I could visit often. Plus, he said, "I have status. You can use my miles."

But it wasn't just the distance. It was the way I looked at the city, how every block and church and street sign meant something. After some time, I got tired of packing. I headed for the shower, but when I turned the faucet, the pipes gurgled and spat, as if the building had gotten sick. That's when I realized there was no running water. Nothing at all.

There are reasons, I thought, why people leave home.

"See this," said the maintenance man the next afternoon. His named was Bradley and he was young and short with sleeve-tattoos and a red mask. I thought he was sort of hot in an aging emo-kid kind of way, but I knew not to flirt back. There was a saying *Don't shit where you eat*, though I'd never say something like that. He had cut open my wall, exposed the pipes like human organs during an autopsy. "It's called the solenoid coil. Yours is broken."

"Great," I said, standing behind him in the doorframe. I'd gone twenty-four hours without a shower, dry shampoo flaking my scalp. "How long will this take?"

Bradley held up the broken part, tapped it with his index finger. "I'll need to order a new one. Could take a few days, and with the problems with the post office, maybe longer."

"What do I do until then?" I said. "I need running water."

"I actually have something for you." Bradley patted his Dickies until he reached into his back left pocket, retrieving a brass-colored key. "7C is vacant. At least you can shower."

The elevator opened with a ping, decorative sconces and marble floors, lofty ceilings and dark metal doors meant to slow down a fire. Music blared, heavy bass, a dog distantly barked. I had come to the top floor with a cloth sack filled with a towel, shampoo and conditioner, some face wash and soap. I walked the hallway, searching for 7C, worried I'd startle someone. Hornet Moon was frequented by trespassers from the city's abundant homeless camps. Some of my neighbors walked on edge to the mail room, the trash chute, the subterranean garage. They'd jump with fright when turning corners and happening upon people sleeping in the darkness beneath the stairs. Sometimes they even did it to me, as if I didn't belong there walking the hallways, emptying my trash.

At the end of the floor, the hallway curved and led to a narrow yellow path of sunlight. It warmed the door's handle. 7C far away at the top. I tried the key, twisted the knob, jostled the handle, but the lock wouldn't budge. Like a bad joke, something God does for a laugh, it was the wrong key.

Still, the handle began to turn, abruptly, from inside. The door opened in a slice. A woman was standing in a wedge of space, her face divided by the door's silver chain. She gazed at me from under her black bangs, dark eyes with lights inside them. Only some of her was visible in the crack. Then a black flash. A Doberman, dark and tan, needle-thin, crossing the floor behind her in the creamy apartment. The dog didn't see me, and for a moment I felt unreal, invisible. The animal then appeared at her legs, wet nose glistening in the doorframe.

"What're you doing?" the woman said, her voice musically gruff.

"I just . . . they gave me a key."

"What?"

"My shower," I said. "It's broken."

The woman stepped back, her lips on the left side seeming to drift. "Of course it is," she said, whistling at her dog and closing the door.

"Mom said your shower doesn't work," said my niece Alexi. "Gross." She stood on the stoop of my big sister Michelle's house in a velvet romper, pointing a thermometer gun at my face. She had a strict face with a curving smile. "Can you bend down please." She pressed the button with a chirp. "98.8," she said, nodding for me to come inside.

I thanked Alexi and stepped over the brown welcome mat into the overwhelming stench of scented candles. It was the end of summer, but the house smelled like October, dead leaves, crisp cinnamon, sodden pumpkin.

"We're actually distancing from other people," Michelle said, rocking her newborn wrapped around her in a BabyBjörn. They lived in a bi-level blue house in Thornton, my sister, on maternity leave from a credit union, her husband, Troy, a Wi-Fi installation tech, Alexi almost ten, and the new baby, Therese, named after our grandmother and also the saint.

"Well, Troy's trying. It's pretty hard when he's out on installs."

We had barely seen each other or our parents since March. Our father lived in Albuquerque and had type 2 diabetes, while our mother was down in Pueblo with severe asthma. We were afraid to be near them, worried we'd unknowingly pass them the virus. Michelle asked if I'd like to hold Therese, but I shook my head and my sister placed the baby in her swing beneath a wall of crucifixes, metal and wood, turquoise and gold.

Michelle turned to me in expensive leggings, purchased used off Poshmark or Facebook Marketplace. "You haven't seen anyone else, right? You're not going to bars or anything like that?"

"No," I lied. "I just stay home."

"Me, too," said Alexi, who was in the kitchen helping herself to a glass of apple juice, the jug comically large in her small hands. "Isn't it boring?"

Michelle frowned at Alexi and told her to wipe off the counter, spilled juice shining. "You're always welcome here, Raquel," she said.

"Just don't get us sick," said Alexi, who smiled at me mischievously. "Auntie."

I glanced around the house, a narrow hallway, two bedrooms, one bath. Baby blankets and teething rings, bottles of milk, browning bananas over the faux-granite counters. It had a smell too, physical, tart, the smell of my sister's body. "Oh," I said, "thanks, but there's no room here."

"Of course there is," Michelle said, shaking her head and handing me a towel. "We have an air mattress, duh."

After my shower, Alexi took the baby outside in her carrier and began drawing with a red crayon on printer paper. Michelle made margaritas with frozen strawberries. She winked as she dumped the entire bottle of Espolòn into the blender. "Pump and dump," she said, eyeing Alexi and Therese through the patio window. She told me not to forget that I had to watch Alexi next week. She wasn't allowed to come along for Therese's checkups, one child at a time. "For the virus," Michelle said. "So any word from the restaurant?"

I told her they had closed for good. "Lost too much business during the shutdown."

"Maybe you can find a job in your field?"

"Doubt it," I said. I had studied art education, first at a community college, and later up in Boulder, but I dropped out two semesters shy of graduation. It was the recession, and there were no jobs. What was the point? Besides, just like a real graduate, I was sinking in student loan debt, an enormous anchor, tying me to the bottom of my own sea.

"What will you do when your lease is up?" Michelle asked.

"I don't know," I lied. "Maybe I'll move to another state."

Michelle scoffed. "Yeah right, like where?"

"California," I suggested. "Rent is too high in Denver."

"Sure, and how will you see me or Alexi or the baby? You know," Michelle said, "if you were married, someone could help with these things." She handed me a pink glass, salt along the rim.

"Is that the only reason to find a husband?" I asked with annoyance.

"Or a wife," Michelle said, examining a fissure in her kitchen counter. A few months earlier, she and Troy had gotten black-out drunk and he threw a mug at the countertop, or maybe it was at her. He said it was too time-consuming to replace, and so they left the crack as is. "What're you doing for money anyway?"

"OnlyFans," I joked.

Michelle laughed, but only a little. "Excuse me," she said. "Those girls are entrepreneurs."

Phil didn't know how old I was. When we first matched on the app, I told him I was twenty-four. He believed it, or he wanted to. It made him feel sexier, more valuable, or at least that's what I felt from him. He wasn't the first man with money I had been with. There had been several, a real estate developer I met at a Red Rocks concert, high out of his mind on molly, he took me by the wrist on the sandstone steps. "I think you're fucking sexy. Are you Lebanese?" He lived up in the mountains, a hot tub on the roof. He said he'd buy me a car, but I got sick of him after a while. He owned a lot of guns and had three ex-wives. I don't use this word much, but there was something evil about him. A lot of these men have that. It's like they show a half truth of themselves to the world, burying the rest inside, poisoning themselves from all that hiding.

"I'm so fuckin' hungover," Phil said over FaceTime. "Work blows today."

I was in my apartment, lying on the lumpy sofa. I had put on a lime bralette and matching bike shorts. "Did you go out last night?" I asked, but I knew the answer was yes. That's all Phil ever did.

"Yeah, and I'm becoming an old man." He laughed, and I pictured him on his orange modern sofa, thick abstract paintings ugly behind him.

"What kind of meetings do you have today?" I asked.

"Budget stuff. Not my favorite. Also, I fucked up and spent like 5K on the expense account last month."

"On strippers?" I asked flatly.

"Them and you," he said, coughing. "It's fine. The company never cares." He made a face, angled the phone. Then he asked if the money came through. "Until you come here. Then no rent, Little Red."

"Thank you," I said, unfeeling and quiet. The future didn't feel real anymore. Everything felt like a dead end, some impenetrable woods.

"Give me some dates," he said, "and I'll book a flight to help you pack up. I can't drive back with you though. Too many meetings."

My water went out again that night, but this time I was in the shower, my body lined in red streams, hair dye like watery blood spiraling into the drain. I turned the knob until the thing broke, the metal sliding from the fixture and slamming onto my left foot. "Mother fuck," I screamed, stepping out of the shower. Michelle and Troy had taken the kids out of town, some cabin in Wyoming. I texted her about the spare key and headed for my car.

The basement garage was a horrifying rock cave, the walls stained with waterlogged decay, patches of ceiling eaten away by rats and time. Even beneath my paper mask, it smelled of limestone and gasoline. My shitty car was parked in a faraway damp corner and whenever I went down there, I gripped my mace and taser. The elevator opened and I stepped out with my weapons, but it was the wrong floor. A masked woman stood in the hallway, and I knew I had seen her before.

"Going up?" she asked, and I shook my head as her black dog, the Doberman from 7C, stepped inside the elevator behind me.

"We'll ride down and back up," the woman said.

We rode to the second and first floors in near silence. There was only the clattering gears, metal cords above us and below. The woman was tall and the skin of her arms and legs was a beautiful reddish brown, her long dark hair shiny blue. Her mask was black and her shoes were blisteringly white. The Doberman sat very still and tall at her side. When the elevator reached the bottom of its track, the box sighed and shifted into a minuscule crash. The woman spoke directly ahead, her eyes locked into space.

"What's the deal?" she asked, the Doberman regal beside her.

My T-shirt and hands were all covered in red. I was like one of those stragglers who miraculously gets up from a car crash, walking away fine. "Hair dye," I said.

"I know," she said. "But why are you in the elevator covered in it?"

I laughed, stepping out.

She blocked the door from closing with her right hand. "Is your shower broken again?"

I told her it was.

"If you want," the woman said, softer than before, "you can use mine."

She told me Obsidian's name before she offered her own. "Obsi for short," she said as we walked the seventh-floor hallway, nearing her apartment as she turned back, uttering from behind her black mask. "I'm Clara."

"Raquel," I said.

Obsi trotted ahead, stood guard at their apartment, her nose pressed to the metal door. Clara whistled and the dog luxuriously morphed into a sitting statue.

"How old is she?" I asked.

Clara was turning her key, pushing the lock. "Three. I got her for protection. Didn't I, Obsi?" She patted the dog's long face before pushing inside her apartment.

A brightness shone from the floor-to-ceiling windows like a wave of snowy froth. The room was spacious and our movements imprinted into white carpet as Clara and I removed our sneakers. I was afraid to leak myself onto her things, to smear red over the walls and carpets and expansive kitchen countertops. The room smelled of paint and lavender, an undercurrent of eucalyptus. The apartment appeared to be one massive area with an elongated nook where her queen bed stood in a solid shaft of sunlight. In the corner, above a cow-hide rug, a clothing rack with several outfits, matching lingerie, a black leather harness, something red and feathered. There was hardly any furniture, an ivory-colored loveseat, a glass coffee table with open books.

I pointed to a green paperback, face down. "Is it good?"

"The latest dream I ever dreamed," Clara said, then opened and closed a closet door. She swiftly turned around with a towel, placing it on the kitchen counter. "Keats," she said, moving her dark gaze behind me. "Obsi must like you."

The Doberman had walked toward me through a set of camouflaged French doors opening to a patio. Outside the mountains glowed in their late afternoon golds and blues. I couldn't believe Clara lived here all alone in a room that felt like a church, a steeple in the sky, Obsidian prowling like a cat.

"It was the Chamber of Commerce," she said.

"This apartment?"

"Yeah. This was the main office. The center of all the money."

"How cool," I said. "I had no idea."

"Me either. The ghosts told me."

"What do you do?" I asked. "For work."

Clara removed her mask and smiled. A hole. In the left side of her face, open to the bed of her tongue and teeth, the corner of her lips wrinkled inward, diving into her throat. The wounds were old and seemed as though she'd had several surgeries, the skin layered with grafts, different textures and shades, her teeth white seeds among her red mouth. "I dance," she said, handing me the towel, pointing left. "Shower's in there."

I thanked her, stepping through the French doors, Obsi trailing me like a shadow.

"I met someone," I told Michelle over the phone. It was the following week. A heat wave choked the city. Smoke from wildfires hazed the entire region. I was outside on the fire escape, fanning myself with a paper plate, my eyes burning through tears.

"That's great!" she said. "What's his name?"

"No," I said, "like a friend. A girl who lives on the top floor."

"Well," Michelle said with hopefulness. "She can be your wing-woman or something."

I heard Therese crying in the background, then the sounds of something falling. A bookcase or a table. Michelle yelled Alexi's name before hanging up.

I had meant to tell her about Phil, the house in Silver Lake, my idea that it would be easier to leave Denver rather than stay, but I knew Michelle wouldn't approve.

"You don't even love these men," she had once told me, after I took a call from a boyfriend in front of her. "Why put yourself into this life?" We were outside on her patio. It was springtime. Michelle was very pregnant and her skin was luminous and smooth. Her black hair had grown thicker, deeper since pregnancy. She looked as if she was always meant to make life.

"I don't love them," I said. "I love not being poor. It's like a job."

204

"Well, you're not very good at it." Michelle shook her head, rising from her metal chair with a swinging ponytail. Cottonwood seeds blew around her in the air. "Think of all this time, all these lost years. Don't you want children someday?"

"What?" I said.

There was an apology in her glance, as if she'd said something she couldn't take back. "I'm sorry," she said. "I didn't mean it."

Phil had made it clear, he wanted to have uninhibited sex whenever he pleased, and that meant no condoms in our new living arrangement. The next afternoon, I drove to a women's clinic on the south side of town to look into an IUD before I moved. The intake nurse told me to wait in my car, and I sat inside my Corolla, staring at the dirt-coated sign of a now closed dry cleaner. For a long while I watched traffic and considered where I should take Alexi later. My apartment wasn't fun for kids, and she had let me know this directly, several times. Then the nurse called.

"Hello," she said over the phone, "is this Raquel Gallegos?"

I said it was.

"Wonderful!" She asked my Social Security number, date of birth, and if they could identify themselves as a women's clinic when calling my cell phone.

"Now," said the nurse, "I have a few more questions for our records. Has your partner ever tried to get you pregnant when you didn't want to be?"

"No."

"Does your partner refuse to use condoms when you ask?"

"No."

"Has anyone forced you to have sex in the past year?"

"No."

"Have you ever been pregnant?"

I moved my hand to my belly in the midst of midday traffic. My palm was warm against my stomach, and I thought of myself nearly a decade ago, eight months pregnant, sleeping on my sister's couch. I had placed her hand over the pulsating knocking from inside, the little girl we were soon to meet. "I'll change everything for her," I had told Michelle. "I'll get a steady job, find a place to live. I can do this." Michelle agreed. "You can, Raquel, and Troy and me, we'll help you. With anything you need." Maybe if they hadn't offered the help, I wouldn't have taken it, leaving Alexi with Michelle when she was barely two months old. I drove away that day still high from the night before, crying in pain, my body and my choices unbearably my own. One of her baby blankets lay bundled like a pink puddle across the car floor.

"Ms. Gallegos?" said the nurse. "Have you ever been pregnant?"

Outside my windshield, a police car flipped on its sirens, sliding through the intersection's red light, quieting once it had arrived on the other side.

"No," I told the nurse. "Never."

"With your red hair," said Alexi, "you look like Ronald McDonald."

"That's funny," I said, "because I think I look like Rihanna."

"Her hair isn't red!"

"It used to be. Before you were born."

Alexi giggled. "I have trouble remembering that far back."

I had driven us to a reservoir across the street from Lakeside Amusement Park. We walked the path along the reflective water, not far from a white wooden rollercoaster, dilapidated, with broken shingles and flickering bats. Couples and families strolled around us, their faces covered in masks. There were geese angrily walking, bossy and fat.

"Did you play here when you were little?" Alexi asked.

"Sometimes," I said. "But your mom and me mostly played by our old house. How do you like having a baby sister?" I asked.

Alexi had skipped ahead on the path. She ran in ways I recognized—my sister's stride, my own giddy coordination. "She cries all the time," she said. "Even late at night."

"Babies," I said, "are real party animals." I motioned for Alexi to turn toward the playground, where I took a seat on the bench.

I watched her play for some time. She climbed on the back of a cement dragon painted a seaweed green. I could tell Alexi was pretending to be on horseback, maybe galloping through the mountains and deserts of the Old West. I wondered what she'd look like as a grown-up, and I could see glimmers of seriousness register on her face. The sun was setting behind the mountains beyond the highway, light clouds outlining the high country in oranges and pinks. The lake was part of a system, several reservoirs all in line. From above, I imagined the lakes like a grouping of burns, scooped-out flesh in the earth.

"I thought that was you," said a woman's voice from behind the bench. She had stepped in front of me with her dog on a leash and her hair curled in long midnight waves. Clara, I realized. Obsi at her side. Her eye makeup was stark, large winged tips, blue glitter shadow, dazzling like stars. "I was going to text you," she said. "We should grab a drink, before every bar in this city closes for good."

I laughed, glancing at my niece. "Sure."

"Oh," Clara said. "I didn't realize."

"Just babysitting for my sister."

Clara nodded and took a seat beside me. There was pleasure in being outside at dusk, a calmness that seeped into the colors of the world. Clara asked about Alexi, her age, where she went to school. Obsi protectively followed her with her eyes as she moved from the swings to the jungle gym. "You're like twins," she said.

"I know. We've gotten that her whole life."

"I'd like a little girl someday," said Clara.

I studied Clara for a long time, her eyes focused and bright, and I thought of her scars hidden beneath her mask. "Really?" I asked.

"Yeah, like an extension of me and everything I've worked for, but her own person."

"Wow," Alexi shouted, pointing at Obsidian and sliding from her dragon. "Your dog is pretty!"

Clara smiled with her eyes. "Would you like to pet her?"

Alexi was already charging across the playground, though I hesitated a moment. Obsi was intimidating, shiny black with notches of ribs and a clipped tail, a frightening mouth. But as soon as Alexi had shouted, "Sure," the dog stepped past me on its leash, folding her legs and curtseying into repose onto the gravel.

"Hello," said Alexi, stroking Obsidian's ears. "I like you," she said.

The dog opened its mouth, euphorically panting, a long pink tongue.

"How come she acts so good?" Alexi asked Clara.

"She went to a special school. She's actually British."

"I didn't hear your accent," Alexi told Obsi, who smiled in the obvious way some dogs do.

The night after Alexi went home, Clara and I walked outside, the evening warm, dusty with a coating of leftover day. Buses screeched past us, sending Clara's short fluttery black dress flying. Her nails were painted a neon green, and she walked with a swagger that almost seemed like a limp. Clara was sexy. She smelled good, like roses, and her hair shined with every color inside the black. As we walked, she pulled out her phone, and pressed against the side of a brick building.

"I'm going to see what's open," she said. "Keep an eye out."

I looked around as she scanned the glow of her iPhone. Figures moved in the alleys, formless and void. Down the block, a shirtless man screamed into the air, yelling about Jesus, asking the sky if it was God. A trickle of water flowed down the center of the roadway, shimmering like mercury in the night. As she searched, leaning against the wall, I decided Clara was more than sexy. She was strong.

"Found one," she said. "How about the Oxford?"

It was an old hotel, built in the 1891, a martini lounge with a smokey hue. It's also where I found Phil, mindlessly scrolling on some app. "Sounds great," I said, and we stepped off the wall where we had docked, walking toward the lights.

"See that building?" Clara pointed north, her green nails ushering my gaze to the sky. "I'm moving there."

I was surprised. The building had to be one of the most expensive downtown. "That's incredible. How's the rent?"

Clara stopped on the sidewalk, her heels clicked. For the first time, I heard her laugh. It was musical, low, an engine rumbling. She shouted into the dark, her voice echoing among the canyon like brick walls. "I bought it, bitch!" she said. "A two-bedroom."

She howled with happiness from under her mask, musical sounds gliding from one building to the next, an echo of joy. I couldn't help but smile. I let out a yelp, then a long sonorous woo. Clara joined in and we hollered until we were out of breath, leaning forward, our hands against our knees, tears forming in our eyes. How peaceful, I thought, all alone in the sky with a dog.

"What're you going to do?" she asked after some time. "When your lease is up?"

I grew quiet. The bar's entrance was a few steps away. I shrugged. "I think I'll stay with a guy maybe. He lives in California."

209

"Your boyfriend?" Clara straightened her bra straps, both had fallen down her arms.

"Kinda," I said. "It's a little more open than that."

"Be careful," she said. "Don't want to get stuck far away from family."

"Yeah," I said. "It's just, rent's so expensive here."

Clara walked forward, straight to the heavy-set bouncer who sat outside the hotel on a black stool. He was a white man with a buzz cut, a black collared shirt. He motioned for our IDs. Clara was ready, but I had to search, my eyes to my wallet when I heard the bouncer say, "Pull down your mask, please."

I peered upward, watching as Clara, methodical and smooth, lowered her mask, revealing her face, all of it. The intricacies of her wounds, a warrior's receipt. Then she snapped the mask back around her mouth and nose, as if it were the rest of the world that was broken.

The bouncer turned to me. "Mask down," he said, and I complied.

"Everywhere is expensive," Clara said as we walked inside. "Raise your prices, renegotiate terms. This is your home, and you'll find a way."

Phil came to help me pack up a couple weeks later. It was the first time he'd seen my apartment, and when he walked inside, folded cardboard boxes in his arms, he looked at my green kitchen table and said, "Yikes."

That night, he wanted to visit Diamond Cabaret, his favorite Denver club. He claimed my bed was too small for the both of us, so he got us a room at the Brown Palace, some supposedly luxury hotel that only felt to me like it had an infestation of ghosts. Phil couldn't have sex before we went out, because he had taken too much molly the night before. I pretended I didn't know. I figured he wouldn't like that.

He wore a white button-down shirt and his luxury watch lumpy across his wrist. I dressed in a black midriff with lace cups for my breasts, a red harness bra, roped across my cleavage, matching my bright hair. Though it was late summer, I wore combat boots with my short skirt. Phil didn't like them, and suggested we should go to Cherry Creek the next day. "Get you some real shoes," he said. He liked heels, the taller, the better.

Jack and Diet Coke coated my mouth as we pushed through the club, the lights deepening to velvety red. Phil preferred Latinas and Black women, and he swiftly moved past a table of blondes, their backs against the stage, their pink legs in the air like open keyholes. The club was at half capacity, and both men and women slinked back, some masked and some sipping cocktails, all of them feeling enhanced by the presence of half-naked women.

"This one," Phil said, excitedly tapping the backs of two chairs at table five. He pulled out my seat for me, handing me a wad of cash as I dipped into it. A curly-haired dancer was finishing her set. She wore forest green lingerie, clear heels, and her nose was pierced at the septum. She moved from the stage as a Jeremih song quieted. Phil's phone went off then as he received a text message, his face lighting up with purpose. He stood and leaned over me. "Need to step out," he said, and I nodded, eyeing ahead at the woman's body snaking before me. I knew he was going outside to buy drugs, to sit inside some guy's car, to try it all out before coming back to me. I felt a wave of grief, disbelief at the life I had created for myself. It was a sensation like invisible dirt piling to my mouth and nose, of being buried alive in my seat. I had nothing, and soon I was going to live with a man who when he fucked me, I imagined myself into another reality, my body a kite, tearing through the wind, snagging over treetops and billboards, shredding me until there was nothing left.

I suddenly lost my breath. I pulled down my mask and stood from the table, grabbing my purse from the dirty floor. When I checked my phone, there was a text from Michelle, a drawing in red crayon, two women sitting together on a bench, the squiggles of a dog at our side. "Alexi made this," she had written. The music shifted then, changed into something older, languid. It wasn't a song I recognized, and the DJ came over the speakers, his voice vibrating throughout the club.

"Now at table eight," he boomed, "everyone's favorite nightlight, yours truly, Star."

I turned around from my chair, gazing in her direction. There she was, her abundant body stepping out of her robe like a waterfall, her oil-black heels revealing the contours of her legs. She bent forward, tying her black hair away from her masked face as she came closer, kneeled across the table, crawling to me. I felt woozy with want as she moved near, lying down before me, turning her body so her back was against the stage, her elegant arms fanning through the air as she brought my face closer to hers. "Go, Raquel," she whispered, and my lips shined in her sequin mask, as though I looked into a mirror, our features together in their brokenness, a thousand shards of light, our faces one.

ARTHUR SZE's eleventh book of poetry is *The Glass Constellation: New and Collected Poems* (Copper Canyon Press, 2021). He lives in Santa Fe, New Mexico.

Oxbow Lakes

ARTHUR SZE

Quartz, peak, crowd, junk, tiger, rose—
the audiologist asks me to repeat
the last word to each sentence,
while she slowly turns up background
noise until it obliterates language.
As I listen, a plume of water
laden with tritium seeps,
under a mesa, into an aquifer;
in Point Barrow, polar bears
rummage through trash at the city dump;
as I listen, an Inupiat woman
steps out of her apartment, avoids
needles scattered in the parking lot.
I say *witness* and recognize,
against noise, consciousness
as a river that floods, shortens course,
leaving behind oxbow lakes;
and, in this immediate time,
when I say *convolution*,
we can land a probe on a comet
but can't end hunger across the street.

AMEER HAMAD was born in Jerusalem in 1992. He holds a degree in computer science from Birzeit University. In 2019, he was awarded the Al-Qattan prize in two categories for his first two books: *Gigi and Ali's Rabbit*, a collection of short stories, and *I Searched for Their Keys in the Locks*, a collection of poetry.

YASMINE SEALE is a writer and translator living in Paris. Her work has received a PEN America Literary Grant and the Wasafiri New Writing Prize for Poetry. Her books include *Aladdin: A New Translation* (Liveright, 2018), *The Annotated Arabian Nights* (Liveright, 2021), and *Agitated Air: Poems after Ibn Arabi*, co-written with Robin Moger (Tenement Press, 2022).

Gigi and the White Rabbit

AMEER HAMAD

TRANSLATED FROM THE ARABIC BY YASMINE SEALE

His aunt was coming to visit with her twenty-year-old daughter Gigi: a golden opportunity. He would put them to use. Milk the easygoing atmosphere they brought with them. Craft a careful plan and give them starring roles.

His aunt had married a Dutch supporter of the Palestinian cause (he'd converted in Jerusalem) and after twenty years in America she had turned foreign. Thoughtful like a foreigner, she marked the birthdays of young relatives with expensive gifts. She gave them hugs instead of kisses when she came to visit. And—most important in his eyes—she cared about animals. Her children were allowed to keep pets; once (so she told him) she even let her son adopt an iguana, no matter that its tail gave her the creeps. She had an enormous dog called Poochy whose name was always on her lips and who could do no wrong. When her husband called her on Skype, she would make him hold the camera up to the dog's face, then she'd plant a row of kisses on the tablet screen. Like the dog was her husband.

Her blonde daughter was the envy of the women in the family. Each of them dreamed of kidnapping her as a wife for her son or one of her friends, dreamed that she would leave the United

States and come to live here in Kafr Aqab, in a ten-story building fenced round by other blocks and overlooking the checkpoint.

The girl had pale skin and blue eyes and the build of a Victoria's Secret model. She had American and Dutch passports. She was working on a master's thesis in international law, having completed her bachelor's degree in only two years. Her passions and values belonged to our sun-baked East: she loathed American fluidity (Western men had lost their manliness) and had a weakness for olive oil with zaatar. Everyone would strive to please her and her mother; they'd all blush at the quirky gifts that fell into their hands and at their own halting English efforts to explain to Gigi, when she failed to follow them in Arabic, why they couldn't possibly accept this or that.

Ali, aged eleven, had eyes only for his cousin's delight, her tender way of swooping down on every creature she passed in the street. The neighbors' mangy dog. The one-eyed cat by the dumpster. The poor donkey all the local children used to ride. Deep within him a plan was slowly ripening, drawing on the animal data gathering in his mind—which, like the radar systems of American fleets, was operating for once at full capacity.

Of all the children, Ali was the closest to his grandparents; their constant helper and companion, light of his grandmother's life. Yet even she, like his mother, lost patience with him now that he talked about only one thing: animals. Now that he'd become—as his introverted older brother put it—a bestiary on legs. It often seemed to them that he made up his own language to describe the beasts, just as a tribe who lives on fishing might have many different words for a single kind of fish.

The moment she was in their midst, in Kafr Aqab, Gigi was drawn to Ali: to his kindness, and to the apples in his cheeks which made her want to bite them. Each opened their heart to the other; no language barrier between them since his aunt had made sure to teach her children Arabic and to fill their ears with it when, on visits to Palestine, they'd stay in the old family home. And when some word or other stopped the flow of their conversation, Ali would turn to the internal dictionary he'd built up in English class.

Gigi told him about growing up on their farm in Pennsylvania, about riding her horse which she had named Barq—Arabic for lightning—and about the competitions they had won. She told him about feeding birds and gathering eggs and milking cows, and he listened to this Scheherazade of his with Shahryar's delight, but he was not satisfied with listening, and he told her about growing up in Sinjil, in the Palestinian countryside, where he'd played with goats and ridden donkeys and roamed the mountains in search of hedgehogs. He told her about slipping out of the garden and into the farm of one of his father's friends, and how he had managed to walk the sheep around the field not once but twice, after a friend had bet him that he couldn't.

Mother and daughter spent the first week of their visit confined to the house. Outside, clashes had erupted with the occupation forces. And because the checkpoints, where such confrontations occurred, separated each city from its sister, and often from itself, they had nowhere to go but Ramallah, and Gigi didn't care for Ramallah—a city of retail outlets where Western brands hawked their worst clothing for prices that rivaled the stores of Beverly Hills. Nothing for it then but to stay home and receive the delegations who came to devour Gigi with their eyes, like the front rows feasting on supermodels floating down the stream of fashion week.

That's when Ali seized his chance; his plan was ripe. He went to the couch where his aunt was sitting near his mother and grandmother. Then the idea left his lips: he could take Gigi and Maryam (his little sister) to the new park. A family park—no

219

loitering young men. And full of trees which, by filtering the air, would allow poor Gigi to taste the breeze of her mother's homeland. For Gigi could not have imagined, not in her worst nightmares, that home had come to this: a sun-deprived apartment in an overcrowded neighborhood, which younger Jerusalemites who wished to retain their blue ID cards had chosen as their refuge from the capital and its suburbs, where real estate prices were fantastical and where the municipality restricted what could be built or restored.

The mothers agreed that Ali's proposal was sensible. It would do Gigi good: she who was accustomed to darting like her horse's name from one state to another—each of which was several times the size of historic Palestine, and several several times the size of Oslo Palestine, and several several several times the size of Likud Palestine—faster than it took to go from Kafr Aqab to Qalandiya checkpoint, had become like the neighbors' canary who, put off by the roar of traffic rising to its cage, had ceased to sing, and now only stared mutely at the concrete panorama before it. (It wouldn't be long before they decided to shoot the next installment of *Spider-Man* here, the residential towers being so tightly packed that a stuntman would find it easy to leap from roof to roof.) And with nothing on TV but soldiers, heavily equipped in armored cars or on American horses beating back defenseless protesters, Gigi had lost her appetite. She couldn't, wouldn't eat.

No doubt about it: the kunafa which Ali suggested they take to eat in the park would help restore some color to her cheeks. And try, her mother said—once Gigi had agreed to go, and Grandmother had slipped him fifty shekels—to feed her something more substantial. Shawarma, say.

In the street, Ali excitedly counted the money in his hand. Not that he could have got the sum wrong: he held a single banknote which bore the likeness of the Hebrew poet Saul Tchernichovsky, a spot previously occupied by the Ukrainian Nobel Prize laureate Yosef Agnon. His mind flashed into action—a scientific calculator, full marks guaranteed. Silently and with great speed, he tallied:

Three-and-a-half plus three-and-a-half plus three-and-a-half: transport.

Minus half a shekel: discount (we're three, the driver can't refuse).

Four plus four plus four: half an ounce of kunafa each.

One plus one plus one: a glass of tamarind juice each.

That makes twenty-five shekels, leaving me enough to buy a rabbit for fifteen and a cage for ten.

And having assured himself that the rabbit, which had for so long hopped around his sleeping and waking dreams, and for whose sake he now took advantage of his aunt and cousin, was still wedged in its cage in the pet shop window, and having informed him by telepathy that he'd be buying him today, he looked at Gigi.

It's such a nice day, he said. Why don't we walk instead of squeezing into a Ford? It's only ten minutes away. Fifteen at most.

Before she could answer, he turned to his sister. What do you think, Maryam?

Maryam agreed at once, and Gigi didn't dare say no for fear of seeming lazy or spoiled beside these spirited two. Of course, Ali conceded, they wouldn't want to walk after their play. They'd get a Ford back.

In the old streets of Kafr Aqab, pitted and scarred like the face of the moon, Gigi—slender as a spear, wavy blonde hair down to her waist—became one more reason for the gridlock, the cars crawling along by a meter every two hours. Her toes, their nails filed and painted lilac, were nestled in Tommy Hilfiger sandals which made it hard for her to walk, there being no clear border between paved sidewalk and dirt road. Sometimes the pits brimming with wastewater got tired of vehicles falling into them and took up residence on the pavement instead, for it is preferable—all said and done—to be fallen into by a person than by a giant truck.

Public and private vehicles left the street and sped over the pavement to outpace the solemn single file, grazing Gigi as they passed, dusting her hair with their hoods whitened by their passage in the wake of bulldozers. All heads, even the drivers', craned out from windows to stare at the young body, some silent and some whistling, some venturing to offer the honey a lift. Ali, rising to the occasion, stared them down and, having pushed his fingers into Maryam's ears, flung out insults of the highest caliber. Gigi laughed, not knowing the words but sensing their vulgar power.

When Kafr Aqab lay behind them and they reached the gate of Al-Bireh (above which read: AL-BIREH LEAVES YOU IN THE CARE OF JERUSALEM) Gigi in her broken Arabic asked Ali how long until they got there. Just ten more minutes, he said, and Maryam echoed: Just ten. Gigi pointed out that he had said ten minutes half an hour ago. Because you walk like a snail, he said. If you walked like me and Maryam, we'd have got there yesterday. Maryam was quick to correct him: You don't walk like a snail.

The streets of Al-Bireh were paved, no border disputes with the pavement here, and this brought Gigi some relief. She didn't understand what a "snail" was, but she knew it was something no one should imitate, and walked silently on. After another half hour, Gigi sat down to rest her tired feet on the edge of a flower bed. Ali sighed. You know that every Friday people walk from Ramallah to Hebron in only half an hour? Less than that, said Maryam. Then he pointed to the horizon. See the trees over there? he said to Gigi. That's the park. Let's get a move on. I see it, said Maryam without looking up. Gigi stared and saw nothing, but mumbled that she could see it too, lest her eyesight was also said to take after the snail.

Finally, two hours into their walk, they reached the park. The moment they were inside its walls, hollowed by hunger, they wolfed down half an ounce of warm kunafa each. Delicious— Gigi's verdict. Ali would have liked another slice but could not disturb his calculations, so he hoovered up the remains that Maryam had left on her plate.

Gigi glowed after the kunafa like jasmine in the rain. She threw off her sandals, which had darkened at the edges like her toes, and broke into a run on the sand. Then she was like a girl flying a kite on the seashore, delighting the children around her who rushed to join in. The feather of a smile on her young face, her eyes lit by the mares of her childhood opened up the children's doors to her. They were running, leaping, galloping together. A white horse pulling a cart of them behind her. In the joy of the moment, the white rabbit had crept out of Ali's mind and was now playing alone under the sand.

After their fun, they bought tamarind which stained their lips black. Proof, Ali told Gigi, it was the real thing.

They left the park and the rabbit returned to his mind.

Then Gigi caught a whiff of something wonderful. Her nose leapt out of place and the rest of her followed, then Ali, then Maryam, and when they stood before the restaurant window the smell became a huge shawarma on a spit, spinning around itself as if drunk. The poor girl after her days of hunger strike began to salivate, and her mouth, backed up by the choir of her other features, requested shawarma with tahina sauce—her favorite as a child.

Ali threw her the same look he gave to those who praise the occupation and curse the Arabs. Hang on, he said. Everyone knows this place uses donkey meat. Let my father get you some shawarma from the butcher's and prepare it at home. My father's friend once saw them kill a donkey with his own eyes, didn't he Maryam? Yup, Maryam nodded. Donkey's tough.

Ali flagged down an empty service taxi. Brushing past the driver, he heard him say, How's life, Ali? His father's cousin from Sinjil. He wouldn't take money from them, and took no other passengers so that their guest could rest. His uncle's son's son's aunt's daughter? May as well be his sister. The road home was more or less clear of cars, and Ali wished—remembering Gigi's displeasure and the delicious kunafa—that he had run into his father's cousin on the way there. But he forgot his sorrows when the driver, who hunted in his spare time, told him about his search for porcupines the week before and answered all his questions about rabbits.

When they arrived, Ali told the other two to go on ahead; he had a friend to see. As soon as they moved away he headed for the pet shop. There was the rabbit, giving him what seemed a reproachful look. Ali whispered sorry for having kept it waiting. Freedom was near, he promised.

To the owner, a notorious hothead, Ali declared without introduction that he wished to buy the rabbit in the window. He followed the man out onto the sidewalk, pointed to the animal, and said that he would also take a cage. The seller seized the rabbit by the ears (a surge of anger in Ali) and plopped it inside one. The money was handed over immediately.

Ali raced home, cradling the cage to keep the rabbit safe. Not long now, he murmured. He climbed the stairs to the apartment door. There, he gently lifted out the rabbit, brought it close to his face and pecked it several times between the eyes, then implored it to stay calm. And as he held the little animal behind his back, it worked its legs in vain as if the air beneath it might be grass.

He opened the door and went to where his mother, grandmother, aunt, and cousin were sitting. And like a man springing a ring on his fiancée, with a grin he presented the rabbit to his aunt. Look how lovely, auntie! I got a cage for it, too.

Ali was expecting some encouraging reaction: a long awwww, then she'd take it from him to kiss like she kissed Poochy, and she'd say things like, So cute, and, What are you going to call it?

But his mother was faster and firmer than his aunt. She went into a rage as if it was a bad school report he was holding, not a soft rabbit wriggling about. She started shouting, I've had it with you and your siblings. You expect me to clean up the rabbit's shit as well as yours? And what about diseases! Germs! Fleas! Last thing I need.

Ali's mother looked at her sister.

Drives me nuts. Nothing in his head but animals. He thinks we're still living in Sinjil. He thinks this sardine can we call home's a farm in California. Once he brings me a dove with her nest and eggs. Once it's a black dog that'd scare a jinn. Another time he's breeding cockroaches in a shoebox under the bed. Animals belong outside. It's not right, they need space to breathe. They can't be living with a family.

Then Ali's grandmother took the helm of the shouting ship and poured fuel on the fire.

Once, it's nighttime. Grandfather and I are asleep in God's peace when we hear a sound from the balcony. Someone's crying. With terror in our hearts we go to look, and we find a kitten going meow, and next to her's a cup of milk. And beside it, mortadella. Of course we knew it was Ali, and after two slaps from your father he confessed. Her mother got run over, so he took her in . . .

225

Ali was staring at his aunt, waiting for her intervention—all his plans depended on her reaction to this moment—but the shocking force of these responses tied a knot in her tongue. All she could do was try to calm things down by saying, Hey. Come on, people. It's nothing. He's only a little boy.

It struck Ali at that moment—the rabbit wriggling all the while in his arms—that his aunt had become too much like a foreigner and had learned not to intervene in the affairs of others. He turned his pleading cat eyes to Gigi, perhaps their friendship would help him, but she said nothing and simply rubbed her swollen fingers, tired of her long walk between the pits and scars, and angry at him now it was clear she had fallen into his trap like a little blond bunny.

Having returned the rabbit to the cage he had left at the door, Ali ran back to the pet shop as quickly as he had left it, but this time anger made him forget his care, and he sent the animal crashing against the walls that caged it.

When he arrived, the owner was shouting at two children who had come to return a canary, taking advantage of the state of lawlessness that had descended now that the Palestinian Authority only showed up to arrest drug or arms dealers, and soldiers only swept in for "security reasons." I wouldn't take it back from Netanyahu himself! Ali heard him exclaim. And he pointed to a sign which read NO EXCHANGES OR RETURNS. I have one rule in life, he said. One rule only!

The owner noticed Ali and asked him what he wanted. To return it, he said with a furious wave at the rabbit. The fire in his eyes was now fed by the tapes playing in his mind, a montage of his many failed attempts to convince his parents to let him keep a pet of any kind or size. Startled by this fire, which made Ali's whole body glow with rage until his face seemed to contain not two apples but a whole tree of apples like the one that got our first parents thrown out of Paradise, the man gave him back thirty shekels out of fear instead of twenty-five.

Gigi, who aspired to higher things than sitting at home and churning out babies like rabbits, rejected all the young men of the family one by one; the women of the family, to humiliate her, seized on the story of her misadventure with Ali. They told everyone how a little boy had pulled a fast one on a Stanford graduate—whispers which snowballed through the streets of Kafr Aqab until they reached the ears of the CIA, who opened a file on Ali and began to investigate what they described as a Palestinian teenager (the stone-throwing type) who had scammed an American lawyer by convincing her to donate a "green rabbit" (one million dollars, in Palestinian lingo) to mysterious and suspicious parties.

A year later, Ali's aunt returned with her youngest daughter Bella, who had green eyes and a supermodel's figure, and who very nearly graduated from college after only two years with a degree in political science. Hope returned to the women of the family. This Bella seemed more patriotic than her sister. Her Arabic was better. She wore a shirt that said FREE PALESTINE and a keffiyeh around her ivory neck. And she had dark Arab hair, not Dutch yellow like her sister.

Ali sat with his grandmother and Bella around a table crowded with dishes. They were alone, his mother and aunt having gone to the Hisbeh for vegetables. Barefoot in a black tracksuit, her hair tied in a bun, Bella sat perched on the sofa, learning from her grandmother how to stuff carrots with rice and meat. When her grandmother got up to relieve herself, Ali took advantage of her absence and reassured himself that she would not object to his plan, not if his cousin approved, now that the matter had been quite forgotten.

Throughout the year Ali had attempted several rabbit-driven schemes, all foiled; now he devised one for Bella which drew on all that he had learned, not least with her sister. He inched towards her, praying all the while that Gigi had not told her about the embarrassing incident between them, and was on the point of proposing his new and improved plan (taxi rather than walking, shawarma instead of kunafa, fairground over park) when Bella surprised him by speaking first in her American accent. What are you trying to do, Ally, trick me like Gigi?

And as Ali's gaze darted between her and the full plates, he saw the front teeth of all the rabbits he had tried to bring home collected in a single mouth which swooped down on the hollowed carrots and on his plan.

CHIARA BARZINI is an Italian screen and fiction writer. She is the author of the story collection *Sister Stop Breathing* (Calamari Press) and the novel *Things That Happened Before the Earthquake* (Doubleday).

The Boar

CHIARA BARZINI

The night the wild boar came, I was in bed with a purple rosary. We were living in a house in the city limits of Rome. I had insisted we move there when I was pregnant with our first child because it bordered a natural reservoir. There were woods and hills and pastures on the edge of the garden, no buildings in sight.

When we had our second child we got stir-crazy. All that space and wind and leaves falling all the time. We became nervous and declared things like "I have to take a shit" even when it wasn't true because we knew that saying that meant having ten minutes to ourselves. We remembered tasks with urgency: bills, taxes, taking out the trash. We took long trips to the end of the driveway to place items into their legitimate bins, even though we knew they would all end up in the same dump by the airport. Taking out the trash involved air, a different kind of breathing, four minutes of silence. On weekends we bundled up and took day trips with the kids. Riding in the car was the only thing that made our newborn sleep. We drove to Tuscany and Umbria where the hills were cold and metallic and wolves howled at night.

I bought the rosary in Civita di Bagnoregio. A squadron of men wearing orange vests lined the hillcrests above the forest that surrounded the town. They stood with long sticks in their hands. A guard stationed at the suspension bridge that led to the main square told us they were hunters. It was their ritual: they spread out on the mountainsides, signaling to each other from one ridge to another with hums and whistles. They moved towards the center of the woods to close in on the animals. It was boars they hunted, the guard explained. The wild pigs rustled through the autumn leaves, moving away from the edge of the woods. The hunters bracketed around them until they were trapped in the middle, caught in an ambush, squealing.

The town of Bagnoregio was perched on a plug of volcanic rock, surrounded by trees, deep canyons, and eroded ridges of white clay. Erosion ate away at the delicate village, that's why it was known as the dying city. It was not safe to live there. Landslides had sheared chunks from the town's flanks, toppling stone houses into the valley below. Almost everyone had left. Everything was crooked and unstable, just like the narrow bridge you had to cross to get there. Japanese tourists came, photographed the bridge, laughed at the precarious scenario, and left. They didn't walk to the town, afraid it would tumble down. The bridge was the thing. It looked like the kind of passage that separated humans from dragons, the path to a temple where people with red eyes ripped your heart out.

With the kids we made our way below the overpass into the woods. Edoardo, our eldest child, collected empty ammunition cartridges from the ground. We saw blood on the grass and wondered if the hunters might make a mistake and shoot us instead of the boars. On the back of the mountain a path led into town through a series of carved out tunnels. We listened to our echoing screams as we ran. In the church in the main square was Saint Vittoria's sarcophagus. I bought the purple rosary at the souvenir shop because it had a medal with her face engraved on it, and I liked the color.

Ten days later in Rome, I was alone with the kids in our house at night, and heard a loud bang in the garden and got scared. Out the window I saw a black, silvery mass digging holes in the ground. A large snout knocked everything over and ate what fit into its mouth. Tiny eyes foraged for food. I got back in bed and listened to the bangs. Olivia, in her crib, ignored the sounds, arms outstretched above her head, suckling into the air and looking for a breast in her sleep. I turned the lights off so I could see outside better. It was a boar. The beast squealed and ran into the cast-iron front door I had forgotten to close. I wondered if that was the same sound they made when hunters closed in on them, if they had that same frantic fury, or if the rosary was trying to send me a message. Saint Vittoria had protected her town from a dragon that killed beasts and men. What had I done?

The next morning when I walked into the yard it was like a hurricane had passed. I looked at the signs—the overturned clods of earth, the dug-out roots and half-eaten bulbs, the ravaged acorns beneath the oak tree—and felt that the pockmarked ground revealed a familiar absence.

As I drove Edoardo to school the next morning I googled: "wild boar appearing meaning." I sometimes googled things I found on my path to discern the presence of a higher message, hoping there was a master plan. "Reoccurrence of seeing the number 1111 meaning," "seeing lots of ants meaning," "dreaming of bats meaning." I hoped there was a universe out there that cared enough to try to get in touch with me.

The page read: *If you have the symbology of Wild Boar coming into your awareness then this could be a message that you need to step up and face some confrontations in your life that you have been avoiding.*

Google had turned against us before so I had to be cautious.

"My wife doesn't want to have sex." I had found Nicola's search and all the articles that ensued a few years earlier. We had spoken about it, promised we would do something about it, but I had stopped feeling attractive, stopped emanating pheromones. At night I fed the baby and watched TV series. I liked images of men who rested big hands on the cleavages of beautiful women. I imagined the warmth they exuded. Even if we weren't having sex, even if we hadn't in months, maybe my husband's hands could be the kind of warm hands that would return to my chest. The feeling of having cleavage, of having something that wasn't a feeding device, would that return? An older friend had explained after my first baby: we spend the first few years after having children waiting for our lives and bodies to go back to the way they were. Then we wake up one day and understand they never will. I knew what Nicola thought when he saw my slack belly. I had promised I'd get back into shape after our second, but I hadn't. The day I turned thirty-eight Nicola gave me a basket of face creams and said I made a wonderful forty-year-old woman. Thirty-eight, I corrected him, and he replied it was the same thing, I was one of those women who folded into the next decade early.

Ten months had passed since Olivia was born and I still had an ugly haircut. I still hadn't dyed my grey. There were things I pretended not to see and things I told myself Nicola surely wouldn't notice. Hairy feet, dirty nails, and an explosion of wrinkles, not just crow's feet, but creases beneath my eyes, the kind of wrinkles that made me look sad and no longer part of the world. At night in bed I twirled my pubic hair into little balls and tugged them out. Nicola saw the balls of hair on the sheets, saw me wipe them off, but never said anything in the morning.

❊   ❊   ❊

But after the boar came, after I started spending my mornings turning over clods of grass and mud, the words came.

"Carolina stared into my eyes and showed me photos of herself in a bikini. She was bursting out of her bathing suit," Nicola announced when he came back from dropping our son on the first day of school. "She wanted something from me. In front of the gate she brushed against me long enough for it to be awkward."

Carolina had moved to Italy from Brazil when she fell in love with her husband William, an Irish-Italian with curls and green eyes. Their son Ethan was Edoardo's best friend in school, but I thought she was only nice to us because Ethan had a speech impediment and Edoardo was his only friend. Like me, Carolina was a mother of two, but she was the kind of woman who had flourished after having babies: compact body, taut skin. She never got cold, didn't wear jackets, just upscale sports clothes and tank tops.

"She invited me to go to Cinecittà with her and the kids so you can get rest. William works. It would be the two of us. She understands how tired you must be from all the sleepless nights with Olivia. She gets it, you know? Maybe some other time you could go somewhere with William. Alone, the two of you. It might be good for all of us. She said so too."

We were in the garden and I was putting the hydrangeas the wild boar had eradicated overnight back inside their pots, making sure to assemble the root bits together, hoping they would somehow find each other below the soil and reconnect.

"Does she want to fuck you?" I found the courage to ask as my stomach began to turn.

"Maybe," Nicola replied. "But I think it's more of a couple swap situation."

I imagined Carolina's arm lingering on Nicola's shoulder when they greeted each other in the morning in front of the school gate. She probably kissed him on both cheeks when she saw him, maybe she sniffed him as her nose sunk into his sideburns. "Excluding us, Carolina and William are the only couple in school who are having good sex. We should take advantage of it," Nicola added, ignoring the fact he hadn't been inside me in months.

In October I wore a velvet Sherpa jacket to Ethan's birthday party that I had bought for Nicola at a thrift store in South Dakota during our first American road trip. Unlike Carolina, I was always cold. I had terrible circulation and when winter came I had to sleep with socks and a nightcap. Beneath the jacket I wore a pair of mustard-colored stretch corduroys. They were the only pants that fit me though they gave me a camel toe, which I tried to cover with an extra-large T-shirt featuring the silhouette of the strippers from *The Sopranos'* Bada Bing nightclub. The T-shirt crept up so unless I pulled it over my pants constantly, the camel toe still showed, and with the brownish color of the pants, it looked like an actual camel toe. Nicola suggested I wear a dress, something so that William could look at my legs. "Don't hide your strong suits," he said. "Investigate, smell the air."

There were more parents than children at the party, most of them getting their after-school buzz on. I was stunned by the house. It was the first time I'd been there: a converted barn with sun-filled glass verandas and a garden overlooking ancient pine trees. The sun refracted on a pond filled with red fish and the day felt like a gift, an unexpected dip back into summer. Everyone gathered by the outdoor brick oven where William baked pizzas, charming the school mothers with his Irish accent. Olivia was well-behaved in her baby carrier. As the kids got in line for food I took a look inside. The main rooms had antique Tuscan ceramic tiles, everything beautiful and tasteful, our kind of people, I reassured myself. In a smaller, private living room I found Botero-like paintings of luscious women with huge breasts next to oversized framed paintings of Indian figures interlocking in Kama Sutra positions. I knew Carolina and William rented their place for events. He cooked and she served tables during their dinner parties, but looking at those paintings on the wall, I wondered exactly what kind of parties they hosted. I texted Nicola. "You need to see this house. I think you're right, they're swingers." Nicola texted back with the emoticon of a cactus. It was the first dirty message he'd sent me in a long time. I heard the kids' excited shrills and William's soft voice as he conversed with the other mothers outside. He was telling them about his childhood growing up between Ireland and Italy, a whiskey drinker who loved to cook.

"Pizza! Pizza!" the kids chanted.

The chaos outside was an opportunity to step further into the house, if I got caught I could always pretend I was hunting for a bathroom. In William and Carolina's bedroom there were framed pictures of them, mostly selfies on Brazilian beaches. I picked one up and examined it: Carolina's arms around William's neck, breasts compressed against his chest, nipples barely contained inside the thin rim of a bronze-colored bikini. Was it the same photo she'd shown my husband? I set it back down and examined a portrait of Carolina's extended family. In the forefront one of her relatives in a wheelchair held hands with a woman who looked like Carolina, but older and not attractive. A dated Christmas card from her nephew back home, the drawing of an airplane flying between Brazil and Italy. She missed her home.

"Oh my god. I am in their bedroom. You have no idea. Sex den," I wrote to Nicola.

He replied immediately asking for a picture. I took a selfie with their selfies and sent it to him.

"More!" he begged.

I took pictures of their vacation photos: Carolina in a floral-and-gecko-print sarong wrap staring longingly at the camera, her lips wet with the beer she held in her hand, William's strong arm wrapped around her waist. A photo of Carolina and her golden retriever Jay where she kind of made a sexy face. Another picture of William fishing, the bulging outline of his bathing suit suggesting he might have a big cock.

"Dirtier please. Check panty drawers." Nicola texted two more cactus emoticons.

I walked toward the closet, my heart racing. I opened the first drawer and started fumbling around. It was dark, but I could feel lace and silk and latex on my hands. A G-string made of pearls. Finally I reached something hard, a dildo it seemed, covered by a leathery pouch. I pulled it out and discovered an electric razor. I heard the veranda's sliding door pull open and the sound of the party streamed inside. A kid had peed himself and needed a bathroom. "It would be easier if you just told me when you have to use the bathroom instead of crying like an idiot," his mother hissed, heading straight for the bedroom. I slipped out of the closet, crossed the bedroom, and rushed outside as stealthily as I could.

By the brick oven Carolina was holding Olivia in her arms. She was wearing a low-cut wrap dress and Olivia's cheek was squished against her firm breast. She had found peace.

"She didn't want to be in the carrier anymore," Carolina said, managing my daughter with ease. Edoardo greeted me with a plate of food.

"Carolina made her stop crying," he said.

"Go ahead"—Carolina smiled, pointing to my pizza—"I can hold her so you can eat in peace."

"Thank you." I gobbled the slice and promised myself to skip dinner. William came by and handed me a glass of prosecco. I held my gaze when I thanked him and prolonged physical contact by sliding my index finger into his hand during the glass exchange. It was more of a scratch than a caress, but I had to start somewhere. I ate two more slices of pizza and wandered into the garden with Olivia. There was a pool and a shed in the back where the grass was thicker and tall. I looked through the window. On the wall was a wooden display case with thick engraved glass panes. Inside was a shotgun collection. The guns stood next to each other, perfectly aligned, and sets of camouflaged clothes hung from an open wardrobe. Drills, chainsaws, sanders were organized inside a workshop area created by a few plywood cubicles. Guarding over the tools and guns was a crucifix and a large taxidermy deer head with glass eyes staring into space. Everything was quiet in this part of the garden and it smelled like sawdust and chemicals.

"Cake!" Carolina called out from the main house.

Olivia began to cry and I realized I'd forgotten to give her the bottle. I walked back to the party, prepared her milk, and fed her with one hand as I ate the dessert with the other: a meringue pie with a marzipan Brazilian flag on top.

Carolina looked at me with big eyes and a pout. "Nicola won't make it?"

"Sorry, he's still at work," I answered with my mouth full.

"I'll give you a slice to take home. We'll have to get together some other time."

She smiled and pressed her fingers into the fold of my elbow, and I couldn't understand if she was doing a repeated arm touching, eye-locking thing that swingers did, or if she was one of those people who smiled at everything and dug fingers into other people's flesh. Was she flirting with me, with us, with the possibility of something? Maybe she was just good-natured, but ended up seeming flirty in the process. We sang "Happy Birthday" to Ethan in Portuguese. She taught us the words, then the boy blew out

239

the candles. When it was time to leave, the other mothers knew all the right things to say: the names of the teachers in school and each other's and those of each other's children. I only knew Ethan. Maybe one other kid, though I wasn't sure.

"We should have a chat about Eleonora," the mother of the boy who had peed himself announced, pulling the straps of her red Furla handbag over her shoulder. "It's not a coincidence the kids have a hard time with her year after year."

"She's too tough," another mother agreed.

Carolina nodded. "And she's fat. Fat people are mean."

I glanced at my reflection in the veranda's glass sliding doors and blushed. I hoped it was clear that even though I was over-weight I didn't mean any harm.

It wasn't until after more pizza and meringue pie and two more glasses of prosecco, while I was in the car driving home, Olivia asleep in the back and Edoardo on a sugar-infused rant about his new superpowers, that I realized I was both drunk and sad. I couldn't remember what had initiated the sadness, but it was getting progressively worse with the traffic. I thought about the cake and the hunting shed with the tall green grass and the prosecco and Olivia's cries. Maybe it was the guilt from too much pizza or Edoardo's comment on Carolina being the only one who could get Olivia to stop crying. No, I thought harder, it started before that. I had binged as a reaction to it. As I merged onto the highway, I realized I was sad because of Nicola's message. I read it again. "Dirtier please. Check panty drawers." My investigation into the private lives of Carolina and William had been a thrill to me, I had even felt kinky for a moment. But it hadn't been enough for him. *I was disappointed by his disappointment.* I scrolled through the photos I took in Carolina's bedroom, glancing down at the phone and back up at the road, and saw the images under a different light. I thought of how normal they might have appeared in Nicola's eyes. Maybe I hadn't been brave at all. I felt like I'd done something creepy, taking photos of normal people, squeezing myself inside their private lives for no reason. I scrolled through the library, hoping for something sexier I could offer Nicola upon my return home. I swerved when I realized I was almost crashing into the car in front of me. I put the cell phone away, suddenly sober. Olivia woke in a jolt. Edoardo screamed, "That was cool!"

We'd been through a dry spell before and had found our way back. The year we had Edoardo, Nicola and I took a weekend-long course in tantric massage. We left our nine-month-old with my parents and drove seven hours to a bed-and-breakfast in the foggy plains outside Milan. It was snowing. We didn't know what we were doing, but we knew we needed a change. Our mentors Daniel and Vera were in their mid-twenties and had studied Shakti Tantra in Kerala. They stripped us naked in a cozy, well-heated room and got us to lie on their tatami beds. Candles were lit, Shakti was invoked, chanting followed. A topless Vera massaged my husband while Daniel massaged me in his briefs. They made us come several times in a row and were very professional about it. When they were done, they explained what kind of sexualities we had according to the shapes of our sexual organs. I was a wolf-woman, capable of deep vaginal truths. "Most porn stars are wolf-women," Daniel congratulated me. There weren't many of us around. Nicola was a horse-man, but nobody congratulated him on that. We were deeply compatible, they said, we just needed to find the right level of depth and stimulation. Horse-men sometimes pillaged their way across the sexual landscape, wolf-women needed more foreplay than others. They told us about the tension that got trapped in our genitals. Sex, like money, was a channel for fears and desires. We had to find a way to free ourselves, despite being parents.

When we came back to Rome I downloaded Indian chants and researched tantric centers in our area. We visited an Osho ashram in a garden filled with dead plants in the city's outskirts. An old man with bad breath tried to get me to go down on him. We left the ashram feeling discouraged and ashamed and never went back. We vowed to return north to visit Vera and Daniel, but never found time.

In bed with Nicola I held the purple rosary over my heart. It was made of cloth and the threads that kept it together were starting to unravel. It was looser now, like a piece of stretched-out underwear. I thought of Saint Vittoria and her dragon and the cave she had to enter to find him. She had gone in silently to catch him off guard, but once they were face-to-face what had she told him that convinced him to leave?

"Are you scared?" I asked Nicola.

"I'm excited," he replied. "I think we deserve an adventure."

"What if he can't get it up? I don't think he likes me very much."

"Don't be silly," he said and stroked my face. "What's not to like?"

He kissed my lips and my eyes.

"And what if you fall in love with her? "

"I won't," he said. "It's just a game. We have nothing in common, not like that."

"Good. 'Cause I'd have to murder you otherwise."

He kissed me harder and pulled the rosary away from my chest and flung it to the floor. He got on top of me, spilled a glass of water with his foot, and we made love. It was sweet, our bodies slipped into each other with familiarity, nothing had changed since the last time. We moved with accustomed gestures. I knew when he'd come, he knew when I'd moan. We knew things, we were family.

Later that week Nicola showed up with a bucket of fermented corn and a rectangular iron trap he had bought at the discount hardware store. He was ready to catch the boar, he said. We'd leave bait on the ground, the animal would enter, the door would latch closed, and there would be no more banging sounds of a hungry animal feasting beneath our bedroom at night. We'd bring the boar to a farm, perhaps we could make some money off it. In the afternoon he set up the cage and dumped buckets of corn inside, but by the next morning the corn was gone, the trap door wide open and dented, mats of ground flipped over, the usual roots scattered all over.

Edoardo dressed up like Spider-Man for Halloween. When I dropped him off at school, Carolina and William were pulling in. Ethan hopped out of their huge dark green jeep in a hunter's outfit.

"Ethan's a hunter today. His dad kills animals in real life. When he grows up Ethan is going to be a hunter like him," Edoardo explained.

The four of us parents chuckled as the kids ran inside, Edoardo shooting webs from his hands and Ethan pretending to shoot him with a toy rifle. Carolina's hair flipped back over her eyes, partly covering her face as she leaned into Nicola.

"We missed you at the party."

"Yes, I heard there was great pizza," Nicola said.

"I never saw so many hungry women all at once," William replied.

Carolina turned to me and asked if there was anything I needed help with, Olivia or cooking or just someone to talk to.

William came closer to me and pulled me from a belt loop. "Just ask us for anything," he said, and I told him we had a wild boar in our garden. It came at night and was fearless and dangerous. The cage had not worked, it just sat there in the garden gathering rust, but a hunter, a real hunter, might know how to solve the problem. William blushed when I said that. Hunting within the city limits was illegal and if we decided to go ahead with it, we should make sure our neighbors wouldn't call the police.

"Does that mean you'll do it?" I said.

William glanced at his wife for approval. Carolina clapped her hands and Nicola's face rearranged itself into a grateful smile. I had found a way in, a way to make him happy, and my belly turned warm.

"Yes, come and hunt the boar, please. We'll make a night of it," I insisted.

Then the guys began talking about guns, which Nicola knew nothing about. William suggested he bring his crossbow instead. It was quieter, but the job was dirty because the boar didn't die right away.

"It might run a few meters after you hit it, and then of course it gets a bit tricky when you have to extract the arrow."

Nicola was aroused. He wanted the rifle. Nobody would call the police, he assured William. Bring the gun, he begged, bring your big big gun.

They arrived in a jeep.

"Don't get close to me," Carolina told me after kissing Nicola on both cheeks. "I'm on a breakfast-only diet and my breath smells terrible. I gained six kilograms after summer."

She glanced at my oversized wool sweater.

"Well, it doesn't look like it!" I said. "And if you did, it seems like they went in all the right places."

244

"Yes," Nicola agreed, staring at her cleavage.

I decided her breasts were real and looked over her shoulder as William approached. He came unarmed, a military duffel bag slung across his chest. When he noticed our disappointment, he explained there were several steps involved in a good hunt. "It's not the Wild West, guys," he said with a smirk. He had to scout the territory first to find traces of the boar's passage, possibly a den, he needed to understand how the animal thought and acted.

The sun was setting behind the hills. We walked William to the edge of the woods and entered through a cluster of thorns, bats flying above our heads. Carolina and William pushed away the brambles, scraping their hands. He stared at the ground, examining the path for pockmarks. Nicola had never guided me through these woods with confidence.

"The boar is coming from the valley below. This is good because it always takes the same route," William asserted.

"Yes, they have fixed habits," Carolina added.

William put down his duffel bag and made a clearing around an oak tree that leaned towards the bottom of the hill. He took out a compact camouflaged camera and pulled some metal rods out of the bag. It was a mountable ladder that wrapped around the tree with a boomerang-shaped piece of metal. He fastened each section with molded tree-strap hooks, then climbed up and planted the camera on top of a branch with a nail and hammer. The camera would record the boar's comings and goings. Once a pattern was established it would be easier to know where and when to kill the animal.

From the ground I could see William's shirt roll up his belly as he fixed the camera on the branch. I stared at his firm, tanned skin, muscular and hairless, and imagined resting my cheek on the hilltop of his six-pack. The other fathers who came to our kids' school were hairy, balding, mostly overweight. But he was different and that was one good thing about having to sleep with him.

"Before these cameras, hunters had to wait all night long and try different routes every day. Can you imagine?" Carolina said.

"No, I can't."

"I don't even have the patience to wait for water to boil when I make pasta. It drives William crazy."

"She's from Latin America. They don't know how to cook there," William said with a smirk. Nicola giggled at the joke. I didn't find it funny.

William returned three days later with Carolina to retrieve the footage. I was home alone with Olivia and asked if they'd come in for a coffee, but William went straight down to the camera spot and Carolina waited in the car. When Olivia fell asleep I snuck out and ran down to the oak tree. William was climbing down. With a final jump he was now in front of me and kissed my cheek. He'd never done that before.

"You want to see it? It's huge."

"What?"

"The boar." He smiled, flipping open his camera.

"You got it? Already?"

"Oh yes."

He pressed play. The camera showed night vision footage of the clearing beneath the oak tree. The boar had passed through at two a.m. and again at five.

William inched close to me and moved the camera towards my eyes.

"It's a male," he said. "Look at those tusks."

"Are you sure? Those eyes, the way they search, something makes me think female."

He freeze-framed the video and traced his index finger over the back of the wild pig.

"You see how his butt is shaped like this? You see this curve?" He let out a nervous laugh. "Right under it are his, well, his balls." He chuckled and looked at me like I better trust him when it came to matters of balls and large wild pigs. I did trust him, completely, I just wanted to show him that I too had opinions and thoughts about the boar. I wasn't just some girl who didn't want to have anything to do with his hunting life. Blood didn't scare me. I had seen a farmer drown two kittens in a bathtub when I was young.

As we walked up to the house in the evening air, the outlines of Nicola and Carolina's bodies appeared against the sun. Nicola had arrived and Carolina was now leaning on the trunk of her car talking to him. They were intimate and close, there was a yearning there that had nothing to do with me. When they saw us walk up the hill, they slowly moved apart.

"He's trying to convince me it's a good idea for us all to go hunting with William. I told him I never go," Carolina explained. "I don't hunt, I just don't do it."

"Why?" I asked.

"It's a man's thing. William showed me a boar after he shot it once. There was something about the way the eyes stopped moving, how they flashed from one side to the other, trying to jump out of his body. And then they stopped, wide open, and it looked like they were glaring at me."

"I'll hunt," I said. "I'll go hunting with William and you guys stay home."

"Perfect," Nicola chimed in. "We'll drink the wine, you kill the beasts."

Everyone agreed with this plan and when we said goodbye there were hugs, deep eye-locking sessions, and nods. A pact was made, we tacitly declared the new arrangement of our desires. The wind became cold and the low clouds turned purple and metallic. The warmer October days, when we had lightheartedly joked about promiscuity and couple swaps, were past us. Now there would be a dinner party and a hunt and new flesh inside our mouths. There was no turning back. It had been an unusually warm fall with long days and far-reaching skies. Seagulls and crows croaking in the yard, green and moist and summery, Edoardo running home with rosy cheeks, and the bathtub filled with mud. Those warm days had given us the illusion we could cheat winter, but I knew to be suspicious when things got too beautiful.

That night I made pork shoulder cooked in milk, thinking it would be fun to maintain the pig theme. Carolina reminded me of her diet and didn't taste a bite. She drank wine while Nicola tried to light a fire in the chimney to set the mood.

William explained that the hunt would be great for their event hosting. Dinner guests had actually been requesting wild boar pappardelle. It was fall and people liked strong tastes to get ready for winter.

I imagined wild pig parties in their house, bacchanals with wine and roasted animals and sex, and wondered if we'd be invited. I poured everyone more wine and took a shot of whiskey for myself. Nicola lit a candle in front of Carolina and gazed at her. She smiled back and dug her fingers in the hot wax, then took off her sweater and started massaging her breasts over her tank top. Nicola let out a lusty groan with a trembling voice I found disgusting. Carolina kept touching herself in a way that suggested it was inevitable, like she was being eaten alive by insects and had to rub her breasts continuously to keep them off her.

William slipped into his camouflage gear and threw a pair of old military pants at me. We both changed and covered our faces in a foul-smelling black grease. We had to smell wild and dirty like pigs if we wanted to catch them. I filled up a big iron flask of whiskey. William retrieved what looked like a folded elevator chair and his rifle from the car, returned to the house and nodded at me. It was time. We left Nicola and Carolina in front of the fireplace, drunk on red wine, electricity building, and I thought about the unfair advantage they had over us, covered in manure and stepping into the cold night.

Down the hill, in the dark, I helped William set up the hunting spot on top of the same oak tree where he had placed the camera. He secured the sniper seat on a small platform above the ladder so he could hunt while sitting.

"Will we both fit?" I asked.

William smiled. "We'll be tight, but I don't mind."

Up in the tree everything became silent and we saw the dark world above the ground, its nocturnal insects and animals rustling through the dry leaves. An owl stared at us from another branch then flew away, we heard the lonely cries of dogs barking in the valleys below. I smelled burnt pinewood drifting over from the chimney of our house. It was cold so I offered William some of my whiskey to warm up.

"Are you ok?" I asked as I sat on his lap.

He circled his arms around my waist and sniffed the side of my head.

"Perfect."

William took his phone out and pointed it at me.

"We should commemorate this event," he said.

The flash was blinding. I tried to keep my eyes open. He took three pictures of me and erased them all.

"You looked too seductive," he said.

"I thought that was the point."

"Never mind," he said and we stayed put for a while. I tried to make small talk about the other parents from school, but blanked out on their names.

"I must be getting early-onset Alzheimer's." I laughed self-deprecatingly.

"Let me ask you something: when you dry your hands under hot air machines in restaurant bathrooms, do you notice if the skin on the back of your hand wobbles? If it does it means you're getting old. If it doesn't you've still got some good years to live."

I had seen my skin wobble.

We drank more and I said that I wondered what those other two were doing. He broke the ice and confessed it wasn't the first time Carolina had suggested they become intimate with other people.

"I'm up for it if you like," he said quietly.

"I am up for it too. I wouldn't be here on this tree if I wasn't."

William said we shouldn't kiss because we smelled so badly and our faces were greasy.

I went for his belt to show courage, but he blocked my hand and said we should drink more first. He wasn't good at multitasking except for when he was drunk.

Another swig and William started to stroke his penis on top of his pants.

"Touch yourself," he commanded.

We were too crammed in the chair and I couldn't get in there. He got up, moved onto a branch, and pulled down his pants. His hard-on glowed against the darkness. He stroked himself and I was too cold to really take my pants off, but now there was more space in the chair and I could maneuver my hand more easily.

William was on his own, eyes closed, masturbating on top of the tree. I understood in that moment that killing and fucking were two difficult things to do. I stopped touching myself and offered my lips to William, but he pushed them away and came on his own. His sperm flew out from the tree into the darkness below. I heard it hit the crackling leaves.

When the boar arrived William signaled at me to keep quiet and cup my ears. I thought it would take a while to do the killing. So many hunting stories were about patience and time, but I didn't realize we had already gotten the whole patience thing out of the way. We'd done all the waiting, now it was just the shooting, and that was fast. I thought it was a similar process as going through labor. Everything that happened before a baby came out was painful and seemed impossible, but then it happened and the actual birth was fast and slippery and after a final push you had a new human. Killing was like birthing: you had to wait and it was painful but then it happened fast, from one moment to the next, something that was alive was not alive any longer. Or something that didn't exist was suddenly in a room, crying.

The shot did sound like a bomb. The night birds flew out from the trees nearby. Dogs began howling and for a moment it seemed that everything around us, even the most invisible presences, had woken up in protest. The boar fell over right away, on the spot, just like William had promised, no unnecessary cruelty. I followed him down the tree to the body. I was intent on the eyes, remembering what Carolina had said. She was right, they trembled like they were looking for a way out of the body. I stayed fixed on the animal, kneeling over him, and noticed the sound of a waterfall right below our feet. I thought how silly I had been, insisting we buy a house in the woods away from the city, in the name of our children growing up with swallows and crickets at sunset. I had been obstinate about this choice and yet had never even noticed the stream at the end of our yard, a whole waterfall. As I turned towards the sound, I realized the gurgling was the noise of blood streaming out of the boar's side. It sounded that way for ten full minutes and then it stopped. William hung a hook on a line he set up between two trees and dangled the body there, facedown. He opened the boar in two with a knife, then pulled out its internal organs. I was covered in blood. The blood was hot and it steamed in the night air.

When we got back to the house I heard soft laughter coming from the guest bedroom. Carolina came out, a towel turbaned around her head, in underwear and a tank top.

"Did you get it?" she asked William.

"Of course."

William smacked his wife's ass.

Nicola appeared with a wild, spirited face, his eyes wide open. We had never made love in that bedroom because it was always too cold. He seemed ecstatic and lighthearted. He didn't hide it from me because he wanted me to see and share that joy, just like we said we would. He made coffee for all of us. They smelled like sex and bed and linens. We smelled like blood and dirt.

The four of us sat at the kitchen table and sipped our cups in silence. I realized I was still drunk because of how foreign objects seemed to me. A wineglass was something to drink with, but also a luminous pile of crystals that gathered and trapped light. My fingers touched each other around the cup and my hands felt wrinkly as if they belonged to someone else's body. I thought about what William had said about the hot air machines in restaurant bathrooms, maybe I'd dried my hands too many times. Maybe I was dying. Carolina finished her coffee. I could tell she wanted to giggle to break the silence, but she turned on her phone instead. I picked up a morsel of bread from the table, another extraneous object with dry, uneven edges. I took a bite and started to chew, but the saliva would not gather inside my mouth and I spit it back out into a napkin, into an ashtray filled with cigarette butts. Where did that ashtray come from? Nicola never smoked.

The sounds of daybreak had begun and made us all feel even more ill at ease. And that glow on Nicola's face—once he'd noticed it was not reciprocated on mine—was turning into a constipated expression. His eyes were still wide, but he was sheepish now and he gave me an apologetic glance. I got up and tried to say goodbye to William and Carolina. I was so parched I emitted gasps instead of words. I made my way up the stairs toward the bathroom and let Nicola usher them out. From the top of the staircase I turned around and looked at my husband standing at the front door, unarmed.

I undressed and got in the shower. Carolina had left the hair dryer plugged into the socket by the sink mirror, and I thought I was better than her because I never dried my hair. I was a wilder woman than she was, I had killed a boar.

In the bedroom I slipped into a T-shirt and got under the covers, shaking from the cold, my hair dampening the pillow. From the bed I noticed the purple rosary was still on the floor from the night when Nicola had knocked it over. The small portrait of Saint Vittoria hanging from the loose threads stared at me dumbly. I recognized the soft thumps of the big wheels of William's jeep on the gravel as they pulled away down the driveway. Nicola didn't come up to see me. I knew he'd pass out on the couch downstairs, then wake up with a stiff neck and we would have to talk. I would tell him William and I had kissed and made love on the oak tree, that he'd made my stomach turn and my mouth water, and that yes we were on top of a tree but it could have been anywhere else, nothing could have stopped us.

I was almost asleep when I heard a sound like that of a rabid dog, followed by a kind of wail and a bang. I got out of bed and opened the window. In the blue pre-dawn light I saw something like a hippopotamus, huge and magnificent, standing in the yard. It was another boar, three times bigger than the one we'd just killed. This one had no tusks. Behind it were two smaller boars, the same size as ours. It was a female pig and the others were her babies. They banged against the fence and dug with their snouts, unearthing larger chunks of earth than the previous boar ever had. The big one was looking for her son. He must have been there, somewhere. She could smell him.

MARTÍN ESPADA has published more than twenty books as a poet, editor, essayist, and translator. His last book of poems, called *Floaters* (2021), won the National Book Award. He has received the Ruth Lilly Prize, and teaches at the University of Massachusetts Amherst.

Love Song of the Moa

MARTÍN ESPADA

I strapped my KN95 mask over my ears, ready to brave the grocery store.
Then I turned and saw myself in the grocery window, a tall and spindly
apparition with a beak. I was not man but moa, a large flightless bird
hunted to extinction, mounted in a glass case at the natural history
museum. I was ready to peck on the window with my face when
I remembered your words: *We need a pound of sliced turkey, my love.*
I wandered to the deli counter. Waiting in line for a pound of turkey,
I saw a bowl marked *BBQ Wings.* Most flightless birds have wings,
like the wings of these chickens, necks wrung so we could all have
wings dipped in bleu cheese sauce for the ballgame. A farm girl told me
that she could wring a chicken's neck while the other chickens stood
there, waiting in line, unblinking, as if to say *What happened to Fred?*
There are no pottery shards from bowls of moa wings, since the moa
had no wings and could not even flap as other flightless birds flap,
leaving moa tracks the size of flapjacks for archeologists to ponder.
My shoulders are wingless, so I must be a moa, hunted to extinction
centuries ago, yet picking up a pound of sliced turkey at the deli counter,
and my beak would grow pink with shame if only beaks could blush.
I tell you about the ethics of the moa, and you peck me on the beak,
saying: *But you are not a moa, my love.* This is why I am ready to bang
my face on the glass for you, screeching my love song of the moa,
a tall flightless songbird scaring the other songbirds off the branches.

257

SHANTEKA SIGERS is a graduate of Northwestern University and New York University's MFA Writers Workshop in Paris. Her work has appeared in the *Paris Review, Best American Short Stories,* and the *Chicago Reader*'s Pure Fiction issue. She lives in Austin, Texas.

Lucky Land

SHANTEKA SIGERS

Charles March Farmer IV sat on a bench listening to the whining, chattering, slurping, and guffawing of thousands of people shuffling through Lucky Land amusement park. Above his head, brightly colored containers of humans zipped by like oversized summertime insects, buzzing at the edge of his consciousness, then hyperclose, humming in his ears. Farmer's wife and their friends were riding something called the Rosewood, and he listened to fiberglass logs careen down the fabricated rapids before crashing through pool water to the sound of drumming designed to suggest distant, dangerous savages. Then, there was *the* sound. First, the climbing notes of a hymn . . . then a scream, delirious with victory and finally sharp, relieved laughter. He did not need to see her. He could pluck her delight from the cosmos.

Farrah.

She reminded him of the funk album covers he'd spent his eyesight on in his youth. Rich brownish red sunshine illuminating plump, quivering droplets on the verge of spilling over into sticky slithering trails across collar bones and thighs. His father's record collection had been a catalog of powerfully concentrated, potent women. The *Jet* Beauty of the Week was too studied, too posed. But there, on his knees before the record player, he'd gotten open mouths and delicate veins under tongues sliding over lips. Farrah was a thick and earthy rebuke to the famous sparse woman who bore the same name.

She splashed down on the bench beside him and he was flooded by her smell, spiced and sweet and leafy, cut by chlorine. Farrah wrung park water from her hair, a sandy brown mass of locs that shaped itself according to its own artistic desires. The water, heavy in her clothes, made them droop around her body, made them slurp at the wood and finally release into friendly puddles crossing the bench and saturating the mesh of Farmer's shorts. Even as he greedily inhaled her nearness, he felt the explosive pang of regret that Farrah was not his wife.

Eight years ago, his best friend Leon had rented a huge black SUV and driven around campus pulling up on select acquaintances. Leon drove uncomfortably close, then slowly rolled down the blacked-out windows and growled, *Get in, nigga. We out this bitch*. At the first sign of hesitation, Leon would pull off, making the engine roar and the tires squeal. Farmer could still remember the black truck pulling a dramatic U-turn, bearing down on him and parking a casual, impudent tire on the sidewalk. The passenger door flung open like a wing. Diana, then Farmer's girlfriend, had only been invited, had only gotten in the truck in time because Farmer forgot to let go of her hand. Every couple of years postcollege, they had recreated the now legendary wild hair road trip. This year they'd ended at Lucky Land.

"Your boy almost got us kicked out again," said Diana, molting layers of protective plastic.

"Was this not expected?" said Farmer.

"He got up and ran around the dang ride," said Diana, as she shook her sensible relaxed hair out of a swimming cap. Diana had several more disposable ponchos in her fanny pack. Leon was covered to his knees by a garbage bag.

"Y'all crazy," said Leon. "It was my constitutional right to avoid all waterfalls."

"This has been his creed since we were kids," said Farmer, although he knew that his wife's statements weren't based in surprise but complaint that Leon remained unpunished.

Leon dramatically ripped his way out of the garbage bag to reveal a Hawaiian print, deep green and yellow patterned shirt with matching shorts. The rich colors of the outfit, framed by the thick creamy bands of Leon's light skin and rounded shoulders reminded Farmer of a shampoo bottle.

Leon was the delight of Silicon Valley, the exceptional Black man who had built and sold several businesses, each more expensive than the last. He had never developed the true sense of confinement of a traditional job. His business partners had come to expect a certain disregard for all beaten paths and rules. He ate watermelon with wild abandon in front of white people. During negotiations over the sale of one of his start-ups, he had famously yelled, *I don't know who you took me for, but I'm a free Black man* at a phalanx of lawyers, spun on his Louis Vuitton sneakers, and walked out. The lawyers had recalibrated the deal in his favor and later, opposing council had been seen at one of Leon's cookouts at his family's house in the Hamptons. The family, initially leery of his flashy behavior and refusal to honor a single one of their requests, had been won over by the *Wired* nods and gave him the indulgent leeway of a pet hip-hop mogul.

Diana remained unmoved by Leon's charm, success, and his bringing of his whole Black ass to work. Partially, because he had always refused the responsibility of the Talented Tenth, embracing instead a sense of freedom native to rich white boys. And partially because of the Shirt.

As if to make up for the sudden, unplanned nature of the original trip, Diana tried to impose as much order as she could, including arranging matching polo shirts. Leon never wore the Shirt. And every trip they took, Diana's annoyance with that rebellion flared anew. Hence, no disposable poncho for him this year: instead, the garbage bag. Yet here they stood, telling a story together while pointedly ignoring each other, both unnaturally dry.

"The Mineshaft! The Mineshaft!" cried Farrah, describing the speed and the flinging and the dropping of it with full-armed gestures, sprinkling water everywhere. Farmer's skin puckered into goosebumps.

Diana stomped water out of her tiny sandal.

Historically, the Mineshaft triggered an outsized episode of vertigo and motion sickness in Farmer, dangerously beckoning his childhood seizures and pain from his teenage rugby concussions to return.

"You can't sit outside every ride feeding pigeons like a old lady," said Leon when Farmer tried to beg off. "You and me, in the front."

"You all cannot be serious with this," said Diana. "Who's going to deal with him when he's sick? *Me*."

Leon stiffened and spun backwards, embarrassed to have witnessed this. Farmer caught the scent of Drakkar Noir and Sportin' Waves cutting through the thick sawdusty scent of the prize booths.

"Why don't we just go, and pick when we get there?" said Farrah and lunged in the direction of the path, pointing at all the excitement to be had if they could only move toward it.

This was the difference between Farrah and his wife.

The woman he married dealt in straight-faced information with her arms at her sides. Farrah's body was not subtle. She moved in technicolor, in theatrical gestures and motions that always called his eyes to her.

As they walked, Farmer once again thought about how he got here, a third of the way through the wrong life. He usually started by blaming his teetering-on-the-verge-of-Black Republican family, fifteen years of Jack and Jill, an Ivy League college, the famous prep school where he taught, where he was the only Black man in the building besides Tobias on the janitorial staff. His only rebellion thus far has been his profession. A teacher. Not even a college professor. A teacher.

Farmer had had to dig so deep to stand his ground on that, he'd had nothing left when his parents expressed their overt approval of Diana, her family and her attorney-ness, followed by their desire for him to settle down. Farmer suppressed a grunt of disgust, remembering how eager he had been for his parents' approval, how he had savored the pleasure that Drs. Delphine and Charles Farmer the Third (Farm Tre) took in announcing his marriage to the right kind of girl after he had picked the wrong kind of career.

My son chose a noble profession.

Farm Tre had learned the lines composed for him by his wife, settled upon after the fiftieth time he'd growled, "Well what the hell do you want me to say about this bullshit, Del?"

Farmer looked around now at freer people and dreamed of tiny mutinies, of perhaps growing a bumpy high top fade coming down into a short beard. He dreamed of kicks instead of running shoes. He dreamed of telling his smug family and his liberal friends that they were all predictably and painfully stupid and if there were another way to be, he would be a registered member of that. He often dreamed of teaching in the Blackest, poorest public school he could find.

But these were all things he could not have or be or do. Therefore, his hair was cut low. His face was clean-shaven. His posture was straight. He was fit but not too fit (and was mistaken for a

263

physical education instructor anyway). He did not wear cologne because it gave the vice principal headaches. His ears were not pierced. He wore no jewelry besides his wedding band and most painfully, he did not marry the last girl to get in Leon's SUV so many years ago.

Lucky Land offered itself to Farmer as they passed through highly processed sensory experiences with sudden blunt beginnings and endings. A steamy, leafy prehistoric cave city with the dry raspy smell of stone heated by sun. A general store was a frigid, neutral box of air with crisp edges. A sweet bready scent with a hint of salty fleshy meat, candy apple, and the optimism of fresh-cut grass was nothing if not the county fair of a small town. An outdoor sound system hissed and crackled to life to deliver campy show tunes into the air. The flashes and shudders and tics of an old-school arcade, the friction of sneakers, clicking plastics, and trinkets.

Farmer used the duty of answering work emails to extract himself from the discomfort of being constantly checked by his wife. His phone was almost dead. He would not ask her for one of the chargers she'd brought. Her, going into her purse and pulling it out, the smug look on her face, all too much to bear.

The path to the next ride was clogged by confused adults herding strollers and children. A recording of the Lucky the Lemur song, sung by a children's choir, softly calming them as they attempted an orderly pour into the seats of an outdoor amphitheater.

Everyone knows, that wherever I goes, there's sunshine!
Things go my way, it's gonna be a great day, there's sunshine!
I'm just lucky, I guess!

Leon and Farmer watched Farrah party with a small circle of children, dancing and screaming lemur calls and admiration for their Lucky gear. Leon pointed at a cherub of a girl eyeing the stage eagerly but dressed in a full-out Princess Tiana costume. "That girl is like, yeah, yeah, Lucky, I fucks with you, but your artificial boundaries don't really mean shit to me."

"Fuck your multinational conglomerate . . . I guess," said Farmer, with a high voice and exaggerated shrug, parodying the delivery of the lemur's catchphrase.

The three trumpet blasts that announced Lucky's presence came stinging out of plastic speakers, brushed and painted to look like rocks. Farrah waded out of the children who were sorry to see their playmate go.

Lucky the Lemur's famous hand, an almost random assortment of long, thin, knobbed digits with a suspiciously thin middle finger and an oddly distant thumb, poked between the curtains, gave a shy wave, then snatched itself out of sight.

That peculiar hand had shaken hands with thirty years of American presidents. That hand had been extended in international friendship and overseen the shuttering of rustic puppet shows that told children stories of the greatness of their ancestors. It had made the rough, imperfect fingers of handmade brown dolls sewn from coffee sacks no longer desirable. That hand had held Lucky the Lemur erect as he performed a sort of donkey kick–hand spin in a multiracial breakdance routine that made Farmer grimace in embarrassment every time he witnessed it.

On the stage, a chunky parody of a sneaker emerged and waggled at the crowd of children, who let out a collective scream which appeared to startle the foot. It retreated. The clapping began. According to Lucky the Lemur lore, clapping along with his song was the only way to call him out of his tree. The madness reached deafening levels until finally the entire stage rumbled, the curtains swept open and the entire affair rotated, revealing the famous lemur appearing to drop from a tree. The emerald

265

green, sable black, and safari beige–gray of the stage were repro-
duced in miniature on cell phone screens like a field of abstract
paintings.

Once again, Lucky's ambiguity amazed Farmer. Without the
word lemur it would have been close to impossible to name this
animal. Tree-dwelling beaver-toothed cat-rat? Friendly, fluffy-
tailed wingless bat? His huge head and large cupped ears were
covered in gray and brown velvety fur and his bright round amber
eyes were framed by innocent lashes. His nose resembled a small
leathery package, only suggesting the vulgar ability of breathing,
and his snout angled down to two rodentlike top teeth jutting out
of a warm, eager smile.

Dancers in silver bellhop uniforms were performing a sort of
shuffle skip onstage and let out a jazzy blast of "Just LUCKYYY!"
Lucky shrugged, curtains pouring over his shoulders like a cape,
and with his tinny, auto-tuned voice said, "I guess."

Farrah roared at the stage with glee. Farmer remembered
a week of texts, fast and furious, the two of them one-upping
each other with historical trinkets about Lucky Land. Trinkets
they'd never shared with anyone else. "These bellhops used to be
blackface Pullman porter types," said Farmer now. "All dancing
'round Massa Lucky."

"Oh the whole thing was ridiculous. Lucky shoe shine stands
everywhere," said Farrah, drawing from their shared stockpile.
"Anybody wanna guess who worked at those?"

"You can rub their heads for luck," offered Farmer.

"But you sure don't mind spending your dollars at the Nigger
Rat Rodent revue though," said Leon, as he gave his cell phone
pleased taps with his thumbs.

"Look," said Farrah. "Our whole lives were full of racist shit.
You gotta pick your American poison and I pick the dancing
primate with the bomb-ass rides."

266

Lucky and the children all began a bouncing bopping dance, all to their own unique, out-of-sync rhythms. Without thought, Farmer matched his dance to the high hat jangle of the keys in Farrah's purse.

They left before the show was over, Farmer glancing back to see Lucky high-kicking his sneakers into the air.

One hour and fifteen minutes later, Farmer tried to remind himself that the Mineshaft ride was a simple concept. A massive empty room housed a metal box of seats which were flung about by metal arms, and there were scenes projected on moving screens plus a sudden blast of heat or spray of water to give all the flinging context. That was all it was. But the violent shaking made him acutely aware that his brain was indeed suspended in liquid and had been repeatedly dashed against the side of his skull like a wet sponge. The air was too dense to breathe. The spit inside his mouth was thick as jam. The climbing threat of vomit was expanding Farmer's esophagus. He was dizzy and disoriented even as he watched children race toward the exit, exhilarated.

Diana touched his chest, frowning. "You alright?"

"Farm is fine. Look here, peoples," said Leon, pulling up the corner of his shirt and patting his stomach. "It's about time for some drank."

"I'mma hit that bathroom. I'll catch up," said Farmer. He needed a minute. He needed to breathe. He needed to sit down and squeeze his eyes shut as hard as he could. He hurried behind the wall of artfully overgrown foliage that hid the restroom entrance and was thankful for the aggressive antiseptic that cleared the cocktail of cotton candy, warm caramel, and baby powder scents which had lodged in his nose. He stepped to the side just to breathe the minty acid in, hoping it would fight down the rising muck in his throat, and then he saw the door.

This was not a graceful, employees-only thematic access point, the door of a primitive yurt covered in tiny happy skulls, marked *Sorry, Witchdoctors Only*. This door, and really the entire wall, had the temporary nature of a scab. Thin wood hastily erected to cover repair. But most importantly, this door was deliciously ajar.

The universal warning symbols of danger were posted but if it were really that dangerous, then . . . Farmer didn't have an answer for that thought. Instead, he stared at the warm, beckoning shaft of light pointed directly at the toes of his sneakers.

Apparently, white people snuck around the park with little repercussion, but Farmer imagined himself shot to death, as a headline, as a hashtag. He imagined losing his job. Drs. Delphine and Farm Tre. He thought of getting crushed or electrocuted. He also imagined a behind-the-scenes-of-Lucky-Land Instagram post, where he would be lauded as extra brave because he is Black. So his thought completed itself and became his justification, his affirmation. *If it were that dangerous, someone or something or the universe would be here to stop him.*

Farmer waited for a break in the flow, then put on a can't-nobody-tell-me-nothing face and slipped inside.

He was in a world between worlds, a glowing corridor between makeshift walls so tight he couldn't stretch his arms all the way out. Outside, the midday sun bleached the park but here, it was filtered by a beige tarp creating a buttery yellow light. The walls were whitewashed and free of the constant chatter of the park. Under his feet was an impromptu path of chipboard planks leading toward a metal door. He was nowhere at last, with not a bit of luck in sight.

He took six pictures to get one that properly captured the promise of this voyage. Eight more that included his face, to place him here. He settled on one where he looked handsome and like he was on the jet bridge to an airplane that promised to transport him far from his current location. He should have sent it to Diana. It went to Farrah instead. Then he quickly diluted his transgression by sending it to all sixteen friends currently on their own adventures in the park. Immediately the phone flailed in his hand, alive with a flood of pleasing but battery-draining commentary. He took a few giddy steps forward, easing on down the planks like they were made of yellow bricks.

Farmer emerged into an empty, wide hallway so devoid of color that it made him feel like he was inside a black-and-white TV. He set off wandering, moving easily through the campy uniforms of the park workers and the business casual of Lucky corporate. Farmer was neither. He wondered who they thought he was and how long his luck would last.

He tried the first door he saw without a keypad.

It opened into the industrial innards of the park. Small trucks lumbered past on a boulevard surrounded by squat brick buildings. The Lucky Land laborers swarmed trucking containers, loading and unloading items like pit crews. Familiar orange forklifts maneuvered expertly through it all. The only overblown Luckiness were the golf carts kitted out with sound effects to match the land they belonged to. The carts from the Hitching Post Saloon in the Frontier emitted a deep, thrumming gallop. A high-pitched warble from the silvery carts of the Futurian Moon Expedition. Unlike inside the park, uncurated sound and scents entered and exited in proper disorder, a perfume of trees, warm bread, and occasional sharp notes of gasoline.

Farmer, eager to escape, was headed for the sunshine when he noticed, carved out between the solid blocks of crates and completely hidden from the outside, a tiny apartment.

Farmer stepped inside, eyes wide, taking in furniture scavenged from around the park like it was an opening attraction. A round emerald green rug with a pattern of white lattice within the outline of Lucky's head. A wooden coffee table inlaid with brass keys. High-backed green velvet thrones whose seats had been worn into a soft silvery gray, the arms and legs made to suggest that they had grown directly out of a tree, its plastic branches covered in vines of fabric leaves. Three card tables made a long dining table, lined with folding chairs. There was a small kitchen area with a mini refrigerator, a microwave sitting on a trunk. A haphazard relay of power strips and extension cords snaked toward the wall. A large round clock whose face was Lucky's face had been hung on the wall of crates.

The shade made it impossible for Farmer to get the pictures he wanted. In the dark, there were only unidentifiable suggestions, but the flash created squalor, which felt exploitive somehow. He could not get at the soul of this place, the melancholy of an abandoned dollhouse. Delete. Delete. Delete.

Examining the details of the room, Farmer decided it wasn't an apartment, but a well-appointed breakroom of sorts. Surely Lucky Land provided its workers an air-conditioned respite somewhere. Perhaps this place was put together by bored college students looking for privacy.

Farmer's eyes fell upon a black-and-white photo of opening day at the original Lucky Land featuring Lucky and his creator Miles Matlin surrounded by smiling, white children reaching for the lemur who seemed little more than a child himself. Vintage Lucky had been far smaller, with the simplicity of a Halloween costume. The picture stood in a frame on a small table in the makeshift living room, making it seem like a cherished personal artifact.

What else could be hidden inside these crates? A bedroom? A bathroom? Farmer grimaced at the thought. He wedged himself into a tiny corridor between the crates to see if he could uncover a secret behind the secret.

Like a man coming home from a long day at work, Lucky the Lemur walked into the room. For a brief second, Farmer wondered if this was what happened if someone went AWOL in the park. A one-lemur security patrol. There was no pigeon-toed walk. No bashful tilt of the chin. No bend in his back. The pounding of Farmer's heart made gentle sour waves in his throat.

Lucky paused at a card table covered in stickers and began pulling himself apart. He removed his oversized gloves in the shape of the famous hand and tossed them on the coffee table. He placed his decapitated head carefully in the center of one of the card tables. The neck of the suit revealed the structure the head attached to, wide and round like a mayonnaise jar. Inside that was a man's head. Dark skin flowed, uninterrupted by any suggestion of hair, over the man's skull and the shockingly familial architecture of his face.

There's a brother in there. *Lucky is a brother.*

The unexpected appearance of another Black man in a white setting brought Farmer familiar, marrow-deep relief, soothing an alarm he wasn't always aware he had sounded. *A brother.*

Brother Lucky flared his nostrils and took in the oily air of the loading zone like it was mountaintop pure. He slowly rolled his neck, clenching and unclenching his hands, making the most of his freshly freed body parts. He stretched his arm to the ceiling. He touched his toes. Faintly, Farmer heard the delicate pops of Lucky knuckles. The man pulled a bottled water off a shelf and downed most of it.

Farmer tried to record every image in his mind but each evaporated with the fresh excitement of the next. He did not dare move.

Brother Lucky slouched into the nearest throne. The glow of a mobile phone lit up the interior of one wide sleeve. Farmer could hear a hip-hop baseline, barely audible but fragrant with familiarity. Brother Lucky bobbed his head, curled his lip, and mouthed every filthy word, his tail twitching in angry agreement.

Farmer couldn't return with only words. He slowly reached for his mobile phone, fumbling for the silent lever, covering the screen with his hand. Brother Lucky, legs thrust wide, watched his phone screen with a naughty grin that revealed a charmingly crooked front tooth. The event on his screen culminated in exclamations from a tiny crowd and was mirrored by a cringe from Brother Lucky. A deep rumble thumped about in the barrel-shaped center of the man. A chuckle? Brother Lucky threw his head back and cupped his mouth, "Wooooorld Staaar!"

Farmer blew his stealth by barking a loud, satisfied laugh in response.

Brother Lucky jumped to his feet, spinning in horror. Farmer slowly emerged from his hiding place, arms up to show that he meant no harm. Brother Lucky said nothing, scanning Farmer's golf shorts, Adidas running shoes, the polo shirt, and the lack of a badge or Lucky Land walkie-talkie. Farmer felt embarrassed by his hiding, his desire to collect this man as a memory. He felt like a pervert.

"Hey, hi. I'm sorry. I didn't mean to . . . I got a little turned around, and I certainly wasn't expecting to see you here," said Farmer.

"Oh! Friend!" The castrated, high-pitched voice shot out of Lucky like he'd been kicked in the stomach. The Lucky head typically dispenses a limited amount of pre-recorded and preprocessed phrases, but any comedian worth his salt can do a precise impersonation. Farmer grinned at hearing the voice, *that* voice, at a conversational level rather than an amplified processed level.

Farmer backed toward a velvet, high-backed couch and tried to make the moment last. "I'm invading *your* privacy here, sorry. Just need to catch my breath and then I'll be on my way."

"Oh ho, friend, don't sit there!" warned Brother Lucky. "Some of this furniture is unnnnstable. Wouldn't want you to hurt yourself."

He took small jangling steps, his fingers spread into wide showy paddles as he pushed a woodland throne behind Farmer. "Here. You. Go," he said with a flourish.

"Thank you, Brother," said Farmer. The lemur tensed so dramatically it felt like the air had tightened around Farmer too. Farmer gestured to the room. "This your doing?"

There was silence, then the lemur did a little bop of his heels. "Can I help you find your way back to the Behind-the-Scenes Tour? I bet they're missing you!"

This rebuff annoyed Farmer. "Seriously, they have to have some nicer dressing rooms for you, you're the star of the show."

The lemur blinked. Then he chirped, "I'm not the star! You're the star of the show, friend! Ha-hah."

"You know what I'm saying, though," said Farmer. "Why are you out here with all this shitty furniture?"

"Weelll, yes," said Brother Lucky, making a statement to avoid an answer. "We put the best things out for our guests. Official Lucky Land furniture is of the *finest* play-land velvets and silks. Then, if they've done a good job serving our guests, when those things get a little worn or maybe a little broken, we don't send them to the trash! We bring them back here, haha! And they take care of us and we take care of them. Because that's the Lucky way!"

"I am not here to bust you, man," Farmer said. "You don't have to do all the Lucky stuff, although I appreciate the thoroughness."

"Lucky stuff is all I do, friend!" the man said, exuberant and ridiculous.

"How long you been working here?"

Brother Lucky seemed confused by the question and said nothing. And then, "Since the beginning?"

"Seriously, you don't have to do that," said Farmer. "That was a real question."

Brother Lucky's eyes roved about the room like he was cornered by a maniac and was looking for a weapon. His eyes landed on his own decapitated head. He took a cautious step toward it as though if he moved slowly enough, Farmer might not notice him putting it back on. Farmer tried to distract Brother Lucky, to pin him in place with conversation.

"My wife Farrah, she adores this place," said Farmer, buoyed by how good the lie felt and that it did indeed stop the man in his tracks. "Seriously, this woman comes here so much, she's like, oh the third zebra from the left must be out sick. I'm like, Farrah, come on. But what are you gonna do? Happy wife, happy life, right?"

"Oh, so you're Lucky in Love?"

"I am indeed. College sweethearts. Five years married." The fantasy made him grin and he leaned forward conspiratorially. "Listen . . . she would love a picture of you."

"Well of course!" Brother Lucky said.

Farmer knew he'd been misunderstood by how relieved Lucky sounded.

"No, no," said Farmer. "We have a ton of Lucky selfies. I want her to see that all along, Lucky was a brother inside."

"No sir!" said Brother Lucky, and it was a real no. He softened it with, "Lucky is all lemur inside."

Farmer wondered if he could get the shot and outrun the lemur and as if in punishment for thinking such a thing, his phone died in his hand.

His irritation and nausea and vertigo combined into a nasty sludge and Farmer said, "You know you're not a regular lemur, right?"

"Well GOLLY, I'm not," said the silly voice trumpeting out of the tiny-looking head.

"Well yeah, all that," said Farmer. "But I'm talking about the fact that you're an aye-aye."

Brother Lucky, frowned. "Aye, aye . . . like 'Aye, aye, Captain'?"

"No, man," said Farmer. "An aye-aye is a kind of lemur. It looks like a walking vampire bat with these long, skinny, creepy middle fingers . . ."

Lucky pulled up his arms intending to examine his lemur hands and found a man's hands instead. He dropped his arms. "Surely you don't find your pal Lucky . . . creepy!"

Farmer was talking to a two-hundred-pound squeaking Black man who was asking him not to find him creepy. He almost giggled.

"I don't. Aye-ayes are actually pretty cool," he said. He suddenly grabbed one of Lucky's gloves off the table. Brother Lucky started and a little groan escaped him. Farmer pretended not to notice. He gripped the middle finger and forced it back and forth, surprised to feel the strong resistance of an underlying mechanical structure instead of foam. "This long skinny finger you got? Amazing. Aye-ayes use it to tap-tap-tap-tap on trees to find food. That's actually how my wife figured out what kind of lemur you were, those fingers."

Brother Lucky was on his toes, his too-small hands gesturing for mercy. Farmer stopped waggling the finger but did not put the hand down.

"You supposed to be knocking on trees with that," said Farmer. "Don't they tell you nothing about yourself?"

"Well, you know the story of how my luck began, right?" offered Brother Lucky, never taking his eyes off his own hand, captive in Farmer's.

"Actually, aye-ayes are possibly the least lucky animals on the planet."

"Why would you say that, friend?" the man squeaked.

Farmer was now seated on the edge of the chair, legs spread and confident like he was leading a class in the middle of the year. "They say if an aye-aye points at you with this long finger, you cursed! You gotta kill it or you die," said Farmer, dramatically shaking Lucky's hand back at the rest of his body.

Brother Lucky let out a long sigh for himself. "Maybe I'm not an aye-aye then. Maybe I'm just a regular ol' lemur."

"Well, that's a strategy," said Farmer.

Lucky looked at the clock like it had suddenly entered the room. "Say, friend! I've got a show to get to—"

"So this was the afterlife, then?" interrupts Farmer.

"Say that again, friend?"

"The afterlife," said Farmer. "For the furniture?"

The obtuseness of the statement made Brother Lucky forget to aggressively gentle his face, which Farmer could now distinctly read as *nigga what?* Farmer, drunk off the realness, laughed out loud, startling Lucky back into docility.

"I mean like, if the furniture was good little furniture out there. Followed the rules. Worked hard holding up asses, then the good furniture would make it to the promised land. If you a rebellious piece of furniture? Say, you dropped one of them big, funnel-cake-eating motherfuckers dead on their spongy ass? To hell with you. Right to the incinerator you go. You can burn in hell."

"That's one way to look at it, heh."

"Now you?" said Farmer. "You Jesus in here."

"Not . . . no . . . just Lucky, I guess," the man said half-heartedly.

"No," said Farmer, "look at that picture."

"Why that's the very first—" Lucky began, encouraged by familiar territory.

"Everybody knows the story," Farmer interrupted. "But every-body misses the point. That picture right there. He is God. You're his son. Here, walking amongst the people. Trying to save our dumb asses or at least make us happy." Farmer pretended to hammer a nail into the middle of Lucky's paw. "You die for any sins yet?"

"Not yet," the lemur said.

"This ain't no trick question, but you believe in heaven?" Farmer said. This was a trick question.

"What?"

"Do you believe in heaven?"

"Well one time I went on a wacky romp in heaven after an unfortunate encounter with a steamroller . . ."

"Bruh," said Farmer, irritated again. Ready to pontificate, he gestured widely, and smashed Lucky's hand into the wall of crates. The impact was unsettlingly human, like he had broken his own knuckles.

Brother Lucky was suddenly inches from Farmer, glaring directly into his eyes. He snatched his hand away but stayed, breathing hard into Farmer's face. Farmer wondered if he was about to be punched by a two-hundred-pound lemur and won-dered if he should let him because a black eye would be a suitable souvenir. The touch that made the story of the day real. Also, he was pretty sure he would throw up all over the costume.

Instead, Brother Lucky backed away, gathering the parts of himself. Farmer's adrenaline would no longer keep reality away, a headache bleeding into his skull along with the realization that he was being a dick and he wasn't sure why. He felt like the high school students he taught, ruled by sudden sweeping emotions.

Unable to come up with a suitable apology or farewell, he stood and tottered out of Brother Lucky's nest. His adventure had soured, so he hailed a teenager driving a golf cart sporting long fuchsia plumes that gave the impression of a giant legless flamingo speeding along the ground. Lucky, now reassembled and whole, was visible in the bay, watching him get into the cart. Farmer gave him the nod, the only decent thing he could think to do. Lucky's fingers curled, on their way to fists, then released. Lucky the Lemur raised his arm, tilted his smiling head, and gave Farmer the finger.

The cart sang out with bright, speedy chirps as it swept Farmer back out into the life he deserved.

DIEGO BÁEZ is a writer, educator, and abolitionist. He is the recipient of fellowships from the Surge Institute, the National Book Critics Circle, and Canto-Mundo. His poems and book reviews have appeared online and in print. He lives in Chicago and teaches at the City Colleges.

Yaguareté White

DIEGO BÁEZ

No jaguars wander my father's village, no panthers
patrol the cane fields caged in bamboo fences,

nestled among the Ybyturuzú, what passes for a mountain
range in Paraguay, the Cordillera Caaguazú. You see,

Spanish adjectives arrive after the noun they describe,
clarifying notes that add color and context.

There is history and then there is history, but there are no jaguars
here, only a pool of blood petrified into stone, a place I call home,

tierra of clay so bright it stains orange. This color we call rust in English,
after a chemical reaction used to describe the old, unused, out of practice.

And it's true, no mountain lions roam my mother's home-
town of Erie, Pennsylvania, wasted city of industry, named for the native

people who once combed its shores, called "Nation du Chat"
by the colonizing French, after the region's Eastern panther.

By now, every oxidizing firearm and spearhead and family
charm has moved west or died out, like the Lynch clan,

my ancestors, or the only indigenous word to survive
the Erie people: "Chautauqua," co-opted by enterprising whites,

literally taken to mean a cross-country, faith-based movement,
a cultural accumulation, which does sound awfully familiar.

Don't worry, because I don't know how to pronounce it either,
the Guaraní. I only know Jopara is like Paraguayan Spanglish,

a mixture of Spanish and Guaraní spoken in the hillside villages,
the campos, the countryside. But I speak none of the above myself.

Even English makes little sense whatsoever, hybrid monster
of predominant whites, but this book is not about albinos.

It's not about willow bark or sugar cane or bartered soil.
It's not about the basilica at Caacupé or the spring of the Virgin Mary,

busy with elbows this morning. It's not about anything
real or true. It's not about binaries, ancient or new.

It's not about a tía teaching her sobrino to speak,
spelling out the sound of each color and pointing:

charcoaled remains of last night's fire, *hũ*.
Ash blown and scattered, *morotĩ*.

It's not about mythology, evil Tau
chasing the child Kerana,

fast silhouette of an immigrant couple
racing across the border, seven offspring in tow,

cursed to haunt the forests outside my father's village.
It's not about a story I only learn online:

the death of Arasy, mother to Rupave and Sypave,
the sun and moon, murdered by celestial jaguars.

The siblings avenged their mother, killing all
but one pregnant jaguar, their end and their beginning.

282

They are now entangled, twinned. Jaguars come to represent
the souls of all the dead. Inseparable from each other,

this people and their origin. So it is, and so am I,
here now in the temple.

TESS GUNTY is the author of *The Rabbit Hutch*. She holds an MFA in Creative Writing from New York University, where she was a Lillian Vernon fellow. She lives in Los Angeles.

On Jawless Fish

TESS GUNTY

i.

It was a hot night, a cold fortress, a tense dinner party. Only September and we'd already lost seven species that year, but I tried to keep my thoughts on the food. A medieval chandelier heavened the ceiling, iron tentacles gripping fat wax and chains. It was the kind of party I try to avoid, everyone fracking each other for social capital, but the Host had hired me as an interpreter, and he paid well, and I needed the money. He said there were eels in the moats. He said there were iPads in the bathtubs. I took him as my opposite because he was old and rich, but we shared a lot of sins: long showers, occasional steak, a tendency to skim the news, electricity from the mines, hairspray from the cans. Plus, we were Americans in France—another kind of sin. I forgot the Host's name and never asked him to repeat it, because I felt that nothing mattered, felt that we were safe. Besides, I didn't want to seem inattentive.

I came to Paris one month prior, greeted by shuttered shops and heat like butter. The week I arrived, I couldn't sleep, attacked by visions of man-sized, woman-eating birds. From the corner of my bedroom, the birds stared at me with black eyes and white

285

faces. So I lined up miniature soldiers—childhood toys I'd packed without knowing why—in lockstep on my desk. At the dinner party, I thought of them. Their green plastic weaponry.

The Host wanted to fan the feathers of his new place and boast its emerald plumage, so he served each course in a different chamber, with accompanying facts. L'apéritif in the hunting room, goatskin chairs coarse enough to wake you up. Champagne and figs, duck pâté and ginger jam, sage butter on pumpernickel, a pretty good time.

"My new fortress," he said, "was built in 1179. It's got ties to the Crusades and also to King Richard the Lionheart. Once home to Carmelite monks. Cold as hell, and no bill for that—a big plus, in this climate."

"This climate," muttered a woman in a long braid. During introductions, she had identified as an activist, but did not specify further. She spoke in sacred whisper, like she was performing a hex. "This climate crisis."

Entrée in the dark wood library. Elderberry mead, stuffed pheasant egg, charred ox ear, rainbow roots. I chewed and ogled the books; centuries of spines bewitching me, flaunting all the chemistry I'd never memorize, the philosophy I'd never synthesize, mugging my attention from the table. I was a spacey freelancer, but this time, I forgave myself because my services weren't needed. Everyone there spoke English. "Sixteen bedrooms and five hundred acres of land with stables and woods. A darling little chapel. Hot tub, pool, spa," the Host continued. "No tennis courts though. What can I say—I'm an impulse buyer." And somebody rolled her eyes. Maybe me, maybe the Filmmaker; I often mistake myself.

La soupe in a room of maps and globes. Barley pottage, then raw eucalyptus to chew. "Only three reports of paranormal activity," the Host said. "And all of our ghosts are Democrats."

The whole table laughed.

Plat principal in the chapel, facing a tabernacle that loomed gold and wrong. One seared dove per eater, fanned in crescents of orange and rusts of clove, agave, and purple potatoes. It occurred to me that someone had scooped the meat from each body; that was someone's job. A sphere of flesh sat at the center of the plate, colors orbiting it. My knife and fork hovered above, immobilized. The longer I observed the food set before me, the more it resembled a solar system.

"The reason doves aren't typically eaten," said the Filmmaker, "is that each bird yields about as much meat as a chicken nugget. Not very economical. See?"

"It's very tender," said the Startup Guy.

"Exquisitely so," said the Actress.

"I will murder one of you tonight," said the Host.

Our attention leapt to him. For a moment, I admired evolution's flagrance. Always predators, always prey. Central heating— still so new! Then I remembered the dread, and my pulse joined the kick-line.

"Just kidding!" chuckled the Host, cherry-cheeked and anonymous.

"The food is outstanding," rushed the Startup Guy.

Startup guys know how to rush. We mimicked him because we wanted his language—its math.

"Delicious."

"Divine."

"*Sinfully* good!"

And then we were drunk on champagne and St-Germain, giggling into clay bowls of blackberries and rosewater cream. I reached for a dish of honeysuckle buds and sucked their nectar dry.

The dessert room had Dantean flames in its stone fireplace and a tapestry of a woman riding a zebra while playing the lute and nursing a baby. "She can have it all," I grinned to the fellow beside me, who wore stormy eyeliner and cleaned his nails with a pocketknife under the table. He was the only guest who might've needed an interpreter, but he refused to speak anything at all, so I couldn't do the job. Still, he laughed at my punchlines.

I was the thirteenth guest, an accident. Everyone else was remarkable. A celebrated journalist. An actress. A tennis player. Senator, astronaut, composer, archduke. Faces I knew by screen, voices I knew by podcast. Strangers are stranger when they're famous, because they know you think you know them.

I chewed off my lipstick, plucked a hole in my nylons, sipped from the wrong glass—the Astronaut's. You could tell he had grown into his appeal, features clunky but snug, skin bearing a lifetime of emotional wreckage the way a neighborhood bears the debris of a parade. He looked like the sort of man who grew his own tomatoes. "Merde," I hiccupped, merry and bewildered. The Astronaut called me charming and confiscated my smallest spoon as retribution.

The Host sat at the head of every table, which was not surprising, and announced the calorie count of each course, which was a little surprising, and had a wife, which shouldn't have been surprising, but was. She sat opposite him, bored and extravagantly sun-spotted. An accountant.

The Host hadn't addressed me yet, but just in case, I stored up some contributions to make. Like: *Hedonism is a paradise to its audience, a parasite to its host.* Or: *While molting, ten-to-thirteen percent of lobsters die from exhaustion.* I was waiting for the right moment. Never had the muscle for small talk.

But by dessert, all talk had churned thick and dumb. We were distracted by the word *murder*, and also by the rabbits on the floor. Blinking ones, warm and cloudlike, ears like living adver-tisements for fabric softener. Dozens of them cheerfully shitting and chewing the twelfth-century wood. "Our pets," the Host explained. Didn't believe in leashes, he said. "And cages—just forget it." This was their Friday room. "And not one rabbit has ever wandered into the fire." He said it like a brag.

Feeling weird, the guests took to describing the Host's hat out loud, like compliments but not.

"What heavy brown fur."

"Looks so warm."

"That hat is really something."

They were facts, at least.

"It's made of bear." The Host beamed, each tooth white and correct. "Grizzly. She died of natural causes." He winked.

A rabbit brushed my ankle and I gasped but nobody heard.

ii.

I'd met the Host the day before, both of us rainy and misplaced at a Monoprix in Paris. I didn't see him at first but we were shivering opposite each other between walls of snacks that were neither cookies nor crackers when my phone rang. I answered first in French, then in English, but the line cut out.

Which is when I saw him, white stubble on the jaw like reverse shadow, watching me in pricey shades of beige. He had a face of punctuation: questions printing the forehead, exclamations bursting from the mouth, ellipses dimming the eyes. All inter-rupted by a loud nose.

My hair is long and red and people often spectate, so his gaze was just weather to me. There's nothing less remarkable than being young and female, a temporary condition that afflicts half the population. The attention that men pay said condition isn't personal, meritocratic, or interesting. This I knew, and yet the hail of his stare jolted me awake. He perched a helmetful of apples on his hip.

"Telemarketer?" he asked in English, his accent American.

I looked around, head hot, toes cold. "It was my grandmother. Someone got her a phone too modern to use."

"And how old is she?"

"My grandmother? Ninety-three."

"And how young are you?"

I hesitated. "Twenty-four."

"Should you call her back?"

"I'm sure she'll call again soon—she's been ringing all morning about our book club."

"Book club?"

"We hold a book club at the residence where she lives."

"Oh? Which residence?" Because he thought I was lying.

"La Maison des Parents." Because I wasn't.

"So that's where Paris keeps all the parents." He had the kind of smile that unzips you and then just leaves you there in the chill. He made you want to elaborate, and then made you feel stupid for doing so. "And what's the crisis, if I may ask?" he asked. "The one that prompted all these morning calls?"

I paused. "Well, I'm supposed to purchase the refreshments for this afternoon and she's worried about accommodating all the dietary needs. Irène is allergic to tomatoes, Béatrice can't have salt, Jean-Pierre has no teeth, Clément finds Dijon overwhelming, no sugar for Babette. Pas facile, vous voyez."

"How intolerant our bodies become as we age," the man frowned. "And does the book club have a theme?"

"Eighteenth-century erotica." But now I was lying.

He smiled, cocked his head. "Where are you from?"

"Michigan. You?"

"Where did you learn your French?"

"Good teachers. Nine months in Bordeaux. My grandmother."

"So you speak fluently?"

"Yes," I said. He looked at me so hard I blushed. "And how old are *you*?" I asked.

"I'm from Maine," he said. "What do you do for a living?"

I shifted. I had eighty euros to my name, an untapped linguistics degree, and No Real Future. I shared a three-bedroom in the cinquième arrondissement with two graduate students, one Cavalier King Charles, and a human baby. They let me stay there for free, provided I nanny, clean, cook, walk the dog, and do their shopping on weekdays. I also had to affirm them every time they insisted that their baby was advanced.

"This and that," I said.

"How adorable."

"I study economics," I added defensively.

"Oh? At which university?"

I twitched. "I study it—recreationally. What do you do?"

"Energy," he said, swatting his hand at my question. "But how boring! Look, I'll cut to the chase. My interpreter's had a bit of bad luck. *Bat* luck, you could say." He chuckled.

Medjool dates, baby shampoo, rodent bedding, and eleven adapters cradled inside his shopping cart. I admit I was intrigued.

"My interpreter sleeps in an attic, see," he explained. "He prefers it. His childhood—no matter. Point is, he took a vampire bat to the chest last night. Now he's receiving the first of several rabies shots."

I'm very sorry to hear that would have been the right thing to say, but I watched the phrase steam and fade from some cognitive mirror, watched the man step toward me and noted his baby-skinned longevity, a lack of visible senescence, characteristic of lobsters and the wealthy, who age without loss, never swapping time for anything vital like fertility, muscular resilience, or metabolic health. It's obvious what preserves the rich but not so obvious for the lobsters, who can live well into their seventies and beyond. My money's on the telomerase: an enzyme that repairs long sequences of DNA. Most vertebrates express telomerase in the embryonic stage, but lobsters express it in their adult tissue, too.

His hair was gray and smelled of sex.

"I just bought a fortress," he said. "In the Dordogne region. Near Limoges. You know Limoges?"

"I don't."

"Porcelain city. You'll like it. You look fragile and—painted."

Which I knew to be an insult but felt to be a compliment.

"Anyway, I have this housewarming thing tomorrow night—a sort of dinner party. Normally my assistant does the errands, but she forgot a few things and I felt like a ride on the old vespa. I'm just a regular man at heart, you know? I do my best meditating in the middle of a crowded supermarket. But I digress. The point is I invited a few francophones to my little soirée, and they're not all comfortable in English. Who knows if they'll show up, but since poor Enzo can't make it, I'm short an interpreter." He took a step back. "You've got the right look."

It was my Year of Yes so I asked how much he paid.

"It's very casual," he said. "Have you interpreted before?"

"Yes." And I had, but not formally.

"How much do you charge?"

"Three thousand euros per engagement." Though I'd never.

Recalling the cornichons and tampons in my basket, I briefly lost but regained power, like my mother's farmhouse in a tornado warning.

"Three thousand it is," the man said.

He studied my lips so I studied the adapters.

"Super," I finally replied.

He checked his watch. "Get a ticket to Limoges for noon tomorrow. Just add the cost to your invoice. We'll have a car waiting for you at the station. You'll spend the night."

iii.

At the table, I was digesting uneasily. Maybe it was the alcohol, maybe the rabbits (who smelled), or maybe the eaten meat (I was a bad vegetarian, always eager for a chance to relapse). Most likely, though, my subconscious was conspiring with my stomach to tell me something was amiss. Some call the gastrointestinal system your second brain, and say your gut knows you better than you do, so I cross-examined mine. Found a lot of dread, but that was chronic and therefore inconclusive. I thought about how vultures projectile-vomit in self-defense. How lucky it was that I didn't.

In the dessert room, the fire snapped. I gazed at a herd of porcelain caribou in a distant cabinet, dreaming little apocalypses into it, as the therapists told me not to do, and if I lost my focus, I could see halos radiating from the guests, who were so gorgeous and afraid of death it made me believe in God a little.

I sneezed back into the night to find an espresso set before me, paired with the subject of jawless fish.

"Jawless fish," said the Host, cracking his knuckles, "are a laughingstock. What's the *point* of them? And how did they *make it* all these years without being cast off on the side of the road by a better mutation?"

I was no expert, but I happened to write social media copy for a few natural history museums, so I felt compelled and entitled to correct him. "Actually," I said, clearing the introversion from my throat. "Agnatha can be terrible."

"She speaks," said the Host. "Agnatha?"

"A superclass of jawless fish. About a hundred species total. And in fact," I continued, gaining velocity, "a group of jawless fish *was* cast off on a road this past July—a coastal highway in Oregon. Not on the side of it, but smack dab middle. It was a Thursday. A flatbed truckful of live hagfish overturned. Chain collision, five cars, thousands of prehistoric creatures—like three and a half tons of them—spilled onto the asphalt, each producing buckets of anti-predator slime, as they do when stressed."

The party observed me as though I had just walked out of the tapestry.

"Buckets *per minute*," I added.

"I heard about this!" contributed the Senator. She wore blue shoulder pads—the armor of her sport. "Slime eels, no?"

"Yes!" I said, delighted. "Some call them slime eels, but that's actually a misnomer. Hagfish aren't eels. Neither are 'electric eels,' by the way." But I was losing the crowd, so I rushed like the Startup Guy. "Anyway no human injuries but a very bad day for the hagfish, who mostly died. Or perhaps you haven't been following the doomsday news?" I eyed the Host.

"Why were they traveling on a highway?" asked a Finnish composer, his mustard wool buttoned to the neck.

"They were being shipped to Korea," I said.

"For holiday?" he asked.

"For consumption," murmured the Activist darkly.

"So yes," said the composer's husband. "Somebody's holiday."

"I've had hagfish in Seoul, actually," said the Filmmaker. "Tasty, once you stop thinking."

"Most things are," said the Senator.

"Skinned alive and tossed onto the grill, body writhing," whispered the Activist. "I've read the recipes."

"Like a cruise," said the Husband. He and the Composer exchanged smirks in a private, spousal language.

"Good Lord," coughed the Tennis Player, who looked like Florida. "Skinned alive?"

"Well I see what's terrible about *us*," said the Host. "But not the hagfish."

"I mean terrible as in the Greek *deinos*," I said. "As in *deinos-sauros*. Terrible as in *fearfully great*."

"Alright," volleyed the Host. "So tell us what's so *deinos* about them."

"Where to begin!" I was getting going now, bemusing the socks off the Astronaut, who did not fear combustion. "I remain with the hagfish: a prime example of jawless horror, basically the ambassador of Agnatha. The hagfish is the only known creature to possess a cartilage skull but no vertebral column. Boneless as pudding. Blindish. Hasn't changed for three hundred million years. Living fossil. Can go months without food, but when it does eat, eats carcasses. And yes. So do we. But the hagfish finds its food *dead* or *dying*, right there on the seafloor."

"Sounds like a supermarket meat department to me," said the Host.

This was a good point. "That is a good point," I conceded, and forgot the origin of my animus.

"Supermarket meat department," incanted the composer. "Supermarket meat department supermarket meat department supermarket meat department super—"

"Hagfish," saved the Astronaut. "They're just like us!"

"Go on," the Host instructed me, not meaning it. "What else?"

"Well, the hagfish eats its food from the inside out," I obeyed disobediently, "burrowing deep into the flesh of the corpse to gnaw. And let's talk about the slime. What spectacular biomaterial!"

The Senator said, "Maybe not over dessert?"

"We were having a pleasant time," frowned the Actress.

"Who *are* you?" asked the Startup Guy. Most startup guys enjoy me—my runty measurements—but this one preferred women to be tall and silent, according to the wife on his Instagram.

"She's my interpreter," chuckled the Host. "My *backup* interpreter."

"Hagfish slime," I glared, "clogs the gills of predators. When threatened, hagfish glands release mucous cells and thread cells, which swell and burst in seawater. The thread cells produce this tightly coiled material—arranged in skeins, like yarn—which measures only twelve nanometers in width, but up to fifteen centimeters in length, and seawater dissolves the protein glue that—"

"Snore," said the Tennis Player. "Also, vom."

"I'm so tired of *information*," sighed the Actress.

"I hear—" began the Startup Guy.

"And *hagfish mouths*!" I exclaimed. "Stuff of nightmares!"

"What do you mean?" asked the Journalist hesitantly. Against his will, he cared about the details.

"Picture a vagina with teeth!" I cried.

And I could tell I had disturbed everyone, but people still didn't *get it*, so I did what I had to do. I conjured a hagfish video. "Watch it!" I yelled, although my spotlight had long expired. "See for yourselves!" I tried not to knock anything down. The Man in the smoky eyeliner pinched my arm, as a good friend does when you're egging your own front door, and yes I had outgrown my cute, but the Astronaut took my screen and took my side and ogled my evidence like a horror flick, concluding, "I'll be damned," which dilated the pupils and raised the temperature and objects in motion stay in motion so I passed the screen to every hand until every eye watched the clip, until everyone got it for real.

I will forever associate that peculiar blend of fire smoke and live rabbit with humiliation; the odor was my only companion as the party squinted at me through its own exclusive perfume, which I threatened to pollute, each body important and shifting, each face radiant as a doughnut, all the hair charged with static, no mind free to turn inside out and dream, because of me, because of my rotten deposits—and I felt it loping toward me, my shame, set to a different time zone but dogged and windy and catching up, as it always managed to do, and the Archduke snapped a photo of me but forgot to silence first, and if you're not a ginger then you don't know the first thing about blush.

"To bed, I think," said the Host, smirking in his trapper hat. "Before she amuses us all to death."

"I like a little education in my nightcap," said the Astronaut.

The Man in the eyeliner laughed.

iv.

Sometime after midnight, I kicked off the blankets and pushed through the ghosts—of which there were far more than three, a whole soggy penumbra of them—my weight clinking a suit of armor, creaking doors, trial and error, until I found the Astronaut's room.

The sex was sunbathish despite the fortress chill. Sleepy and shy. Feline. Once our bodies had spent their electricity, we breathed spinedown, belly-up, and let the blood tides ebb. On a mattress stuffed with history, I learned his elbows as he learned my knees. Like all casual sex, ours was scalene, but we weren't trying to equilateral anything, which is to say he held my body, but not my gaze.

We did not discuss dinner.

"Indian pythons are great at foreplay," I said, to break the silence and stave off the fear that I was just telomerase to him. He was at least fifteen years older than I.

He shifted in the bed. "Oh?"

"The male is smaller than the female, so he knows he has to be suave, even though he has two penises, because she has the physical advantage. First he licks her scales, then he massages her with his vestigial legs. Once their cloacae are aligned, that is."

"Vestigial legs?"

"Little bones buried in the hind muscles. 'Spurs.' They're evolutionary hangovers."

"Huh," said the Astronaut. "I imagine it feels like one of those massage chairs in the mall."

It was such an accurate analogy, it made my eyes water. "Yes," I whispered. "The females can measure up to twenty-one feet, and weigh as much as two hundred pounds."

Another silence.

"I'm from Kansas," he offered.

I tried not to appear too thrilled to hear this, but it was tricky. There's nothing more thrilling than information. "And where do you live now?"

"D.C."

"Do you . . . grow tomatoes?"

He paused. "How did you know that?"

"How did you get here?"

"What do you mean?"

Then we both said "existentially" at the same time, and as we laughed, I felt a spark of hope. Maybe his neuronal pathways shared some urban form with mine. Maybe he could help. I mean make this tragicomedy more confetti than beached whale—I mean, we're all just trying to look forward to old age, right? "I mean did you come here just for this?"

298

"Oh," he said. "I was in Bonn for the climate summit."

"Everything's a metaphor for the environmental crisis."

"No." He sighed. "We're beyond metaphor, now." He turned, and I could feel his eyes on me in the dark. "And you? You arrived on Noah's Ark, I presume? You were in charge of the bookkeeping?"

Which made me feel so legible I could have just gone blind. "Did you know," I began, "that only five species are known to recognize their reflections in the mirror?"

"Is that so?"

"Guess which."

"Oh, I don't know. Tell me."

"Just guess."

He paused for a moment. "Great apes, bottlenose dolphins, Asian elephants, orca whales, Eurasian magpies, and . . . ants?"

So I gave him a blowjob, because—wow!

"I've looked that up before," he gasped afterward. "Your voice. Are you a soprano?"

I'm just trying to understand economics, I wanted to confess. I'm just trying to understand the natural world before it's natural history. "Alto."

"Good." He bit my shoulder. "Sopranos always die young."

But I was a soprano and I would die young, if my choir teacher and dermatologist were to be trusted.

"Do you feel like there's something very American about this?" I blurted.

"About what?"

"About all this stuff," I said, looking around. The room was heavy with European antiques, clotted with shadow. "Not the stuff itself, but the *fact* of the stuff. About how somebody has to pay for it, and it's not the Host, and it's not the Hostess, and it's not us—it's a girl across the globe with a head wound caused by a bomb, caused by a war, caused by a drought, caused by emissions, caused by Americans and all their American stuff. And yes, there's more to it than that, but do you see what I mean? I know we're in France—that's the point: we take ourselves everywhere we go. I just think there's something very American about how we're interfacing, with all of our highways and burgers and guns and jeans and stuff, with the stuff?"

He paused for a long time. "I'm not sure I follow," he said. "But yeah. I think I agree."

No more Pyrenean ibexes. No more Formosan clouded leopards. No more Pinta giant tortoises. No more Maui 'akepas. No more Baiji river dolphins. All of these animals were alive when I was born, and now they weren't. I never got to see them. I didn't even Google them before it was too late.

"Sorry?" asked the Astronaut. "I can't hear you."

Through a gale of embarrassment, I realized that I had been muttering the species under my breath. Abruptly, it occurred to me that I was lying heat-to-heat with atoms that had been to the moon. But no, that wasn't right—every year, nearly all of your atoms are replaced. You lose a few grams of them each day. Maybe his bones were the same? But no, I'd read that human bones regenerate every decade. Was there anything permanent about the body? Tooth enamel, maybe. Lenses of your eyes. Brain cells? My pulse quickened.

"I wish I knew more about biology," I muttered, crestfallen. "I wish I knew more about everything."

"You're weirder than you look," the Astronaut said affectionately, pulling me closer. And then: "When I get sad about the extraction economy, I think about how great life will be for the nonhumans once we kill ourselves off."

We were silent for so long, I thought he fell asleep. But when I looked over, his eyes were open, studying the ceiling.

"What's it like in outer space?" I asked.

"Cramped," he replied. I laughed, then he laughed, and pretty soon we had laughed the possibility of sleep from our bodies.

"It's the coffee," I said, still catching my breath.

"It's the wine," he said. And then: "What else keeps you up at night?" Like he really wanted to know.

"Harpy eagles."

"What?"

"They live in the Amazon. Once you see a photo of one, you'll never forget it. It's like a man in a bird costume. Or a bird in a man costume. They eat monkeys."

"Yikes."

I envisioned my toy soldiers. "You?"

He thought. "This Book of Revelation that we call the news, I suppose."

"Best-case scenario, we sprout gills."

"Oh sure, just backpedal natural selection a few millennia," he collaborated.

I wanted to excavate him further but refrained because he was quiet and maybe even a dad.

Still we couldn't sleep so we paced to the bathroom; we had both read the same studies on insomnia and knew that you weren't supposed to stay in the bed. He pledged my hand to his chest, inside which his heart drummed fast as my late chinchilla's. The Astronaut lit a candle, transferred the iPad from the porcelain tub to a windowsill, poured the salts, and drew water from the faucet. The fortress offered running water but limited electricity, so we bathed in the warm blue predawn, deep in a primordial humidity that made us both feel dumb and good. Like our only job was to have a good time, and forget about the bad time it caused everyone else. He washed and rinsed my hair. I found the scar from his appendicitis. He helped me out, toweled

me off, pressed his last pair of boxers into my hands and shuffled
toward the bed.

"I'm finally tired," I said.

"I'm married," he said.

v.

I wandered out of our shared phantasmagoria to my room, wearing tears and his boxers as proof.

But got lost due to fucking environmental agnosia, which I
define as the opposite of synesthesia, which I also happen to have,
because the sensory pathways of my brain resemble summertime
subway construction in New York City—all lines either mixed up
or shut down. Everything delayed. Space and time have never
been easy for me, is what I'm trying to say, so you can imagine
my psychic bedlam in the fortress. Bedlam comes from Bethlehem
Hospital, an asylum for the mentally ill in England, rebuilt in 1676
to resemble a castle. It was opulent on the outside, but abusive on
the inside—the staff did things to the patients that made me trem-
ble and vomit when I first read about them. You have to be careful
with facts; if they find you in the wrong state, they can make you
puke. Where was I? Whenever you start to feel like you're not the
sharpest knife in the drawer, my mother would say, just think:
maybe you're a *spoon*. No screen to save me now, so I had three
options: Return to Astronaut. Wait for dawn. Search at own risk.

One and two repelled me so I chose to roam. Moonlight
beamed through window slits, enough to catch the white of my
breath and reveal the swords and animal heads mounted on the
walls. Mostly hogs, bears, and wolves. I tried to imagine the life
of each one—the food, families, orgasms, injuries, and fears. The
snow under paws. The hagfish on the highway. The Astronaut's
wife. The NRA. Tragedies accumulated and gained momentum

down the slope of my bad night. I had a tendency to spiral. I had a tendency to favor interesting situations over healthy ones. I had a tendency to over-purchase floss. I gripped the tusks of a boar and cried the breath from my lungs, because the Amazon was burning, and the harpy eagles were starving, and we had No Real Future. Mostly I cried because I was twenty-four. After a few minutes, I pulled myself together and marched onward. Castles make me dramatic.

Socks on carpet, socks on stone, socks on stairs; my socks delivered the terrain to me, loyal as a pair of therapy dogs. I focused on my socks to cope—socks, the oldest type of clothing to endure into contemporary fashion. Haven't changed much. The hagfish of garments. When I considered all the gifts I received in childhood, I could recall nothing but the socks. In the fortress, I studied my warm, innocent socks, my sweet, American socks— made in China—and felt like I had some company. When you get lost, my mother once advised, it's best to give up finding the right *place* and try to find the right *people*.

She meant "you" in the particular, not the general; you as in me. But what to do when there were no right people, just acute angles and the smell of rabbits.

The smell of rabbits.

I stopped walking and peered down the hall: yellow light spilled from a door. When I reached it, I pressed my ear to its wood. I could hear motion beyond it but whose weight, what mass, what end—I didn't know. In gothic novels, there are always keyholes to spy through. Not here. Disappointed, I leaned against the stone wall. Heard a masculine grunt. Silence. Then, abruptly, the door swung open, parting a curtain of light, nearly flattening me, and a man stalked out, holding a basket.

The man was the Host. The basket contained rabbits. Nobody noticed me.

Through the unlit corridor, I followed him without choosing to do so, furring my steps and keeping my distance. It made me itchy, of course, to follow a man, especially this one, considering the circumstances. The math between us was crooked, hard to replicate, and the calculations yielded repeating decimals that knotted my gut. Also, he wasn't wearing pants. Just briefs. You've got power as long as they want something from you, is another thing my mother would say, her nose pink and peeling, her hands stained from a day in the blueberry patches. This axiom proved most relevant in August—she made it harvest's epigraph. The briefs were red, and as he walked, he adjusted his cock with the flare of a man who has recently ejaculated. Panic stampeded through me; for a moment I thought I had copulated with the Host instead of the Astronaut. Reality a wet bar of soap in my hands.

He kicked a shadow, which dawn—rosy and confused in fog— revealed to be a door. I watched him step outside, onto a balcony, holding the basket of rabbits. The door was slow to shut, so I dashed toward it and observed while I could.

Due to the advance of the end, it was already hard not to think about mortality but even harder when the Host removed a rabbit from the basket by the fat of its orange neck and dropped it off the balcony, into the moat below. He lifted another and dropped it. Another. They fell quiet as snow.

The heavy door shut.

Host Hurls Rabbits Off Fortress Balcony. Wealthy American Has Too Many Animals, Executes Them. Energy Man Drowns Rabbits at Dawn. Stranger in Fur Hat Murders Own Pets. AMERICAN ABROAD.

Heart thudding a techno beat, I repeated permutations of this headline until it fact-checked itself true.

Microscopic crowds rallied inside me, wielding tiny pitchforks and ordering me to stop him, to save them. Go out there! they cried. Take the rabbits and let them shit in your bed! Take the heads of the hogs and the bears and the wolves, take the Man in the eyeliner, the Senator, Filmmaker, Activist, Composer, Husband, Hostess, Astronaut—oh, take the bad ones too! Why not! Redemption! Take the Archduke and Actress and Host himself—huddle them onto an ark, feed them blueberries, braid their hair! Start a revolution! Do something worthwhile with your mis-wired consciousness or you might as well be dead!

But instead, I ran for an exit. Ran as fast as I could, powered by some ancient programming, my vision neon, the tissues of my body searing with a mandate to escape this place, to find the main road, find a car, find a bike, find the Right People. People kill each other all the time, I reminded myself. You're no exception.

But in the stone maze I took a wrong turn, found myself breathless in a goddamned kitchen. It was a large and creamy kitchen, built for a cook and many assistants, an architectural Frankenstein of blinking tech and medieval design. I squinted at the mounds all over the counters and gasped: here were the carcasses, here was the blood, here was the mess of our feast. Why had nobody cleaned up the kitchen? I tried not to see the decapitated ox head but it was there. Green stems, skins of flesh and carrot flung around the kitchen like wedding rice. Duck feathers. The shells of pheasant eggs cracked in half. Thirteen doves emptied of themselves, their invaded bodies so fragile, stunning, and flightless it made me want to die.

Someone cleared her throat and I jumped. That's when I noticed a small table in the corner. In a cone of skylight, the Hostess was sipping tea with a calculator. Rue petals bobbed in her mug, yellow and crimped. I recognized the smell. Rue petals—repellent to dogs, cats, and Japanese beetles—were once crushed into holy water for exorcisms. For a moment, my terror cleared and the soothing infinity of a search engine pixelated, overtook me like a sauna; I wondered if the phrase *rue the day* had its origin in those flowers, wondered if it was all about doom, in the end.

"May I help you?" asked the Hostess. Her voice was like campside embers, dying and prohibited. She had a Dublin accent.

"Oh." I was shocked by my own visibility. I was afraid I would vomit on my poor socks, like a vulture. I was an interpreter who couldn't interpret a thing. "Oh."

The Hostess looked like a mother, gutted and gone and a little clairvoyant. She looked like *my* mother, so despite my escape plan, I gave her a frantic, malfunctioning pep talk. Choice! Cottage! Power! "You don't have to do this!" I cried. "I don't care how overpopulated we are—your husband is coldblooded!" I spun around frantically, gesturing to the animal parts. "And what the hell is this!"

She paused, as if there were a live-news lag between my deliverance and her reception. The clock ticked and ticked. Finally, she rolled her eyes and stood. Her unusual height fit the reality of her but not my impression of her. Unscarfed and unjeweled, her neck of annual rings was beautiful, showcasing all the time it had spent holding up her brain.

"Don't act like some kind of saint," she said in a low voice. "You ate every course, didn't you?" Then she approached me with slow, exact steps, stopping inches from me. "Dan will give you a ride to the train station."

I turned to the doorway and saw the Man with the eyeliner standing there, a ring of keys clenched in his fist. He nodded. A fuzzy yellow bird stood at his heel.

The Hostess sighed. "Dan, what in God's name?"

He shrugged, and the duckling mimicked. "I went for a walk by the lake this morning," he said. "Wrong place, wrong time, I guess. A case of mistaken identity."

I was too sick to be surprised by his voice, which was fleecy and perfect. Perhaps two silent people could only speak when they found themselves alone together, I thought. Then I remembered myself.

The Hostess looked at him like he'd stolen her wallet. "You're not saying that it—it *imprinted* on you?"

Dan nodded somberly. The duckling inspected his boots.

"Well!" The Hostess cried like an exasperated parent. "What are you going to do about it?"

Dan lowered his head.

"It needs to learn to fly and swim. To be a *duck*," said the Hostess. "What's it going to become under *your* watch? A software engineer?"

Dan turned and began to walk out. His duckling followed.

"All of you make me carsick," spat the Hostess, looking at me, but not quite addressing me. "Don't you have enough?"

When she exited, she orphaned the tea, but took the calculator.

vi.

Dan drove a pickup truck that smelled like Christmas, one wide seat in the front. The duckling sat between us, nervously studying its mother.

"So," I said. "Where are you from?"

"All over."

"Oh?"

"Desert, mostly."

"Did you . . . enjoy it?"

"No." He glared at the windshield, and I didn't press. But about five minutes later, his face softened. "Military dad. Angry guy. Bad time."

At a roundabout, the duckling lost its balance, spilling into me. "And what do you do now?" I asked, correcting the bird, whose body was so light it seemed to have negative weight.

Evidently, my question disappointed Dan, and he made no reply. He fiddled with the radio, settling on static, then turned it up, externalizing the volume of my fear.

When we arrived at the train station, he looked at me sadly. "Groundskeeper. Left home to get away from myself." He paused. The duckling inched closer to him, pushing its pink beak in his shirt and chirping twice. He touched it tenderly, a touch of real love, and the duckling closed its eyes. "Truth is, I've never felt more American." His left hand tapped the steering wheel while his other petted the duckling. We stared at a bee on the windshield, letting the static swell between us. His fingernails were clean.

vii.

A week later, I received a piece of mail without a return address, my first name in ruby ink on the front. I opened the envelope, tossing it at the toy soldiers on my desk, toppling them. Inside, a check for 3,450 euros was folded around a note in narrow handwriting.

> *Train fare and gratuity included.*
> *You're a deinos interpreter.*
>
> *P.S.*
> *You of all people should understand*
> *that eels must also eat.*

I spent it all.

Contributor Notes

Linnea Axelsson is from Porjus in northern Sweden, but now lives in Stockholm. She studied humanities at Umeå University and received her PhD in Art History in 2009. Her debut novel *Tvillingssmycket* was published in 2010 and in 2018 the acclaimed epic *Ædnan* won the August Prize, Sweden's highest literary award. Her next novel *Magnificat* will be published in March 2022.

Diego Báez is a writer, educator, and abolitionist. He is the recipient of fellowships from the Surge Institute, the National Book Critics Circle, and CantoMundo. His poems and book reviews have appeared online and in print. He lives in Chicago and teaches at the City Colleges.

Chiara Barzini is an Italian screen and fiction writer. She is the author of the story collection *Sister Stop Breathing* (Calamari Press) and the novel *Things That Happened Before the Earthquake* (Doubleday).

Samiya Bashir is a writer, performer, librettist, and multimedia poetry maker. Author of three poetry collections, most recently the

Oregon Book Award–winning *Field Theories,* her honors include the Rome Prize in Literature, Pushcart Prize, Oregon's Arts & Culture Council Individual Artist Fellowship, and two Hopwood Poetry Awards. Sometimes she makes poems of dirt. Sometimes zeros and ones. Sometimes variously rendered text. Sometimes light. Called a "dynamic, shape-shifting machine of perpetual motion," by Diego Báez, writing for *Booklist,* Bashir's work has been widely published, performed, installed, printed, screened, experienced, and Oxford comma'd from Berlin to Düsseldorf, Amsterdam to Accra, Florence to Rome, and across the United States. Bashir's poem "Here's the Thing:" erupted through a collaborative choral process with composer Julian Wachner for The Washington Chorus. Its debut performance is forthcoming. An Associate Professor at Reed College in Portland, Oregon, Bashir lives in Harlem.

Rick Bass, the author of thirty books, won the Story Prize for his collection *For a Little While* and was a finalist for the National Book Critics Circle Award for his memoir *Why I Came West.* His most recent book is *Fortunate Son: Selected Essays from the Lone Star State.* His work, which has appeared in the *New Yorker, The Atlantic, Esquire,* and the *Paris Review,* among many other publications, and has been anthologized numerous times in *The Best American Short Stories,* has also won multiple O. Henry Awards and Pushcart Prizes, as well as NEA and Guggenheim fellowships. Bass lives in Montana's Yaak Valley, where he is a founding board member of the Yaak Valley Forest Council.

Stuart Dybek is the author of two collections of poetry, most recently *Streets in Their Own Ink,* and six books of fiction. His work has received a Guggenheim Fellowship and awards from the Lannan and the MacArthur foundations.

Martín Espada has published more than twenty books as a poet, editor, essayist, and translator. His last book of poems, called *Floaters* (2021), won the National Book Award. He has received the Ruth Lilly Prize, and teaches at the University of Massachusetts Amherst.

Kali Fajardo-Anstine is the author of the novel *Woman of Light* and the short story collection *Sabrina & Corina*, a finalist for the National Book Award, the PEN/Bingham Prize, and winner of an American Book Award. She is the 2022/23 Endowed Chair in Creative Writing at Texas State University.

Camonghne Felix, poet and essayist, is the author of *Build Yourself a Boat* (Haymarket Books, 2019), which was longlisted for the 2019 National Book Award in Poetry, shortlisted for the PEN/Open Book Awards, and shortlisted for the Lambda Literary Award. Her poetry has appeared in *Academy of American Poets*, *Harvard Review*, *Literary Hub*, *PEN America*, *Poetry Magazine*, and elsewhere. Her essays have been featured in *Vanity Fair*, *New York Magazine*, *Teen Vogue*, and other places. Felix's next book, *Dyscalculia: A Love Story of Epic Miscalculation*, is forthcoming in February 2023 from One World, an imprint of Penguin Random House.

Matthew Gavin Frank's latest nonfiction book, *Flight of the Diamond Smugglers*, was selected as one of NPR's Best Books of 2021, and as a finalist for the 2021 Heartland Booksellers Award in Nonfiction. He is also the author of the nonfiction books *The Mad Feast, Preparing the Ghost, Pot Farm*, and *Barolo*, and three books of poetry.

A. Kendra Greene is the author and illustrator of *The Museum of Whales You Will Never See*. When she was eighteen, the keepers at the Zoológico Nacional de Chile put her to work vaccinating jabalís and taught her the "right way" to reach into the mouth of a hippo. She's been captivated by collecting institutions ever since. A guest artist at the Nasher Sculpture Center and fellow of Harvard's Library Innovation Lab, her essays have appeared in *Zyzzyva*, *The Guardian*, and *Atlas Obscura*. She's working on a bestiary. Her familiar is a giraffe.

Tess Gunty is the author of *The Rabbit Hutch*. She holds an MFA in Creative Writing from New York University, where she was a Lillian Vernon fellow. She lives in Los Angeles.

Debra Gwartney is the author of two book-length memoirs, *Live Through This* and *I Am a Stranger Here Myself*. Her recent essays have appeared in *Granta*, *The Sun*, and *Virginia Quarterly Review*. She was awarded a 2020 Pushcart Prize. Gwartney lives in Western Oregon.

Ameer Hamad was born in Jerusalem in 1992. He holds a degree in computer science from Birzeit University. In 2019, he was awarded the Al-Qattan prize in two categories for his first two books: *Gigi and Ali's Rabbit*, a collection of short stories, and *I Searched for Their Keys in the Locks*, a collection of poetry.

Janet Hong is a writer and translator based in Vancouver, Canada. She received the 2018 TA First Translation Prize and the 2018 LTI Korea Translation Award for her translation of Han Yujoo's *The Impossible Fairy Tale*, which was also a finalist for the 2018 PEN Translation Prize and the 2018 National Translation Award. Recent translations include Kwon Yeo-sun's *Lemon*, Ha

Seong-nan's *Bluebeard's First Wife*, and Keum Suk Gendry-Kim's *Grass*, which won the 2020 Harvey Award for Best International Book and the 2020 Krause Essay Prize.

Cynan Jones is an acclaimed fiction writer from Wales. His work has appeared in over twenty countries, and in journals and magazines including *Granta* and the *New Yorker*.

Mieko Kawakami is the author of the internationally bestselling novel *Breasts and Eggs*, a *New York Times* Notable Book of the Year and one of *TIME*'s 10 Best Fiction Books of 2020. *Heaven* has been shortlisted for the International Booker Prize in 2022. Her latest work translated into English is *All the Lovers in the Night*.

Sasha taqʷšəblu LaPointe is a Coast Salish author from the Nooksack and Upper Skagit Indian tribes. Her memoir *Red Paint* is available through Counterpoint Press and her collection of poetry *Rose Quartz* is forthcoming from Milkweed. She lives in the Pacific Northwest.

Antonia Lloyd-Jones has translated works by several of Poland's leading contemporary novelists and reportage authors, as well as crime fiction, poetry, and children's books. She is a mentor for the Emerging Translators' Mentorship Programme, and former co-chair of the UK Translators Association.

Anuradha Roy is a writer and potter based in the Indian Himalaya. Her books have been widely translated and won various awards, including the DSC Prize for Fiction. She has been longlisted for the Man Booker Prize and shortlisted for the International Dublin Literary Award. Her fifth novel is *The Earthspinner* (2021).

Yasmine Seale is a writer and translator living in Paris. Her work has received a PEN America Literary Grant and the Wasafiri New Writing Prize for Poetry. Her books include *Aladdin: A New Translation* (Liveright, 2018), *The Annotated Arabian Nights* (Liveright, 2021), and *Agitated Air: Poems after Ibn Arabi*, co-written with Robin Moger (Tenement Press, 2022).

Shanteka Sigers is a graduate of Northwestern University and New York University's MFA Writers Workshop in Paris. Her work has appeared in the *Paris Review*, *Best American Short Stories*, and the *Chicago Reader*'s Pure Fiction issue. She lives in Austin, Texas.

Son Bo-mi is a writer based in Seoul, South Korea. Since making her debut in 2009, Son has written numerous novels and short story collections, including *Dear Ralph Lauren*, *Little Village*, *Bringing Them the Lindy Hop*, and *The Fireflies of Manhattan*. She has won a number of prestigious literary prizes, such as the Hankook Ilbo Literary Award, Dong Ilbo Short Story Award, the Munhakdongne New Author Award, and the Daesan Literary Award.

Arthur Sze's eleventh book of poetry is *The Glass Constellation: New and Collected Poems* (Copper Canyon Press, 2021). He lives in Santa Fe, New Mexico.

Olga Tokarczuk is the recipient of the 2018 Nobel Prize in Literature. She is the author of nine novels and three short story collections and has twice won the most prestigious Polish literary prize, the Nike Award, for *Flights* in 2008 and for *The Books of Jacob* in 2015. Her most famous novels include *Primeval and Other Times* published in 1996, *House of Day, House of Night* published in

1998, *Flights* published in 2007, which, in a translation by Jennifer Croft, also won the 2018 Man Booker International Prize and was shortlisted for the National Book Awards in Translated Literature 2018, and *Drive Your Plow over the Bones of the Dead*, which was published in 2009 and, in a translation by Antonia Lloyd-Jones, was shortlisted for the 2019 Man Booker International Prize and several other awards. *The Books of Jacob* was published in English by Fitzcarraldo, Riverhead, and Text Publishing in 2021 in a translation by Jennifer Croft. Her work is translated into more than fifty languages. Tokarczuk lives in Wrocław, Poland, where she is establishing a foundation offering scholarships for writers and translators and educational programs on literature.

Lily Tuck is the author of seven novels, three story collections, and a biography of the Italian writer Elsa Morante. Her novel *The News from Paraguay* won the National Book Award and she is the recipient of a Guggenheim Fellowship.

Saskia Vogel is a writer and translator from Los Angeles, now living in Berlin. Her debut novel *Permission* (2019) was published in five languages and was awarded the 2021 Berlin Senate Grant for Non-German-language Literature. *Ædnan*, forthcoming with Knopf, is the focus of her work as Princeton University's Fall 2022 Translator in Residence.

Hitomi Yoshio, associate professor of Japanese literature at Waseda University, has authored articles and book chapters on women's writings and literary communities in modern Japan. Her translations of Mieko Kawakami's works have appeared in various literary journals and *The Penguin Book of Japanese Short Stories*. During 2022–2023, she will be a visiting scholar at the Harvard-Yenching Institute.

About the Editor

John Freeman was the editor of *Granta* until 2013. His books include *Dictionary of the Undoing, How to Read a Novelist, Tales of Two Americas,* and *Tales of Two Planets*. His poetry includes the collections *Maps, The Park,* and the forthcoming *Wind, Trees*. In 2021, he edited the anthologies *There's a Revolution Outside, My Love* with Tracy K. Smith, and *The Penguin Book of the Modern American Short Story*. An Executive Editor at Knopf, he teaches writing and literature classes at New York University. His work has appeared in the *New Yorker* and the *Paris Review* and has been translated into twenty-two languages.